Narratives Online

Stories are shared by millions of people online every day. They post and re-post interactions as they retell and respond to large-scale mediated events. These stories are important, as they can bring people together, or polarise them in opposing groups. *Narratives Online: Shared Stories in Social Media* explores this new genre – the shared story – and uses carefully chosen case studies to illustrate the complex processes of sharing as they are shaped by four international social media contexts: Wikipedia, Facebook, Twitter and YouTube. Building on discourse analytic research, Ruth Page develops a new framework – 'mediated narrative analysis' – to address the large-scale, multimodal nature of online narratives, helping researchers interpret the micro- and macro-level politics that are played out in computer-mediated communication.

RUTH PAGE is Senior Lecturer in the Department of English Language and Applied Linguistics at the University of Birmingham. Her research interests lie in sociolinguistic approaches to narrative, language and gender, and new media. She has published extensively in all three fields, and is the author of *Stories in Social Media* (2012) and *Literary and Linguistic Approaches to Feminist Narratology* (2006). She is editor of *New Perspectives on Narrative and Multimodality* (2010) and co-editor of *New Narratives, Theory and Practice* (2011).

Narratives Online

Shared Stories in Social Media

Ruth Page

University of Birmingham

CAMBRIDGE
UNIVERSITY PRESS

CAMBRIDGE
UNIVERSITY PRESS

University Printing House, Cambridge CB2 8BS, United Kingdom

One Liberty Plaza, 20th Floor, New York, NY 10006, USA

477 Williamstown Road, Port Melbourne, VIC 3207, Australia

314–321, 3rd Floor, Plot 3, Splendor Forum, Jasola District Centre,
New Delhi - 110025, India

79 Anson Road, #06-04/06, Singapore 079906

Cambridge University Press is part of the University of Cambridge.

It furthers the University's mission by disseminating knowledge in the pursuit of education, learning, and research at the highest international levels of excellence.

www.cambridge.org
Information on this title: www.cambridge.org/9781107139916
DOI: 10.1017/9781316492390

First published 2018

Printed in the United Kingdom by Clays, St Ives plc

A catalogue record for this publication is available from the British Library.

Library of Congress Cataloging-in-Publication data
Names: Page, Ruth E., 1972– author.
Title: Narratives online : shared stories in social media / Ruth Elizabeth Page.
Description: New York : Cambridge University Press, 2018. | Includes bibliographical references and index.
Identifiers: LCCN 2017035388 | ISBN 9781107139916 (hardback)
Subjects: LCSH: Social media. | Online authorship. | Narration (Rhetoric) – Social aspects. | Storytelling – Social aspects. | Online social networks. | Discourse analysis, Narrative. | BISAC: LANGUAGE ARTS & DISCIPLINES / Linguistics / General.
Classification: LCC P96.N35 P33 2018 | DDC 302.23/1 – dc23
LC record available at https://lccn.loc.gov/2017035388

ISBN 978-1-107-13991-6 Hardback

For my mother, who taught me to read and shares with me the love of a good story.

Contents

Figures

Tables

Preface

This is a book about the shared story as a distinctive narrative genre that flourishes in online contexts. There are two reasons to write a book about shared stories:

1 Stories remain a pervasive genre that people use to make sense of the world around them.
2 'Sharing' has become a dominant keyword in online contexts, particularly associated with the ability to distribute and redistribute content within large networks of connections.

Shared stories that are told in online contexts are interesting for a number of reasons. This book focuses on the language and the mediated contexts in which shared stories are produced and consumed. The first chapter introduces shared stories and traces their analogous conversational, artistic and journalistic antecedents. Later chapters explore shared stories as they are told in four online sites that have become well established over the last decade, and which have international reach: Wikipedia, Facebook, Twitter and YouTube. Many of the examples of online interactions discussed in this book are available at the time of writing, but their longevity cannot be guaranteed. In the quoted excerpts from the stories, I have retained the exact spelling and punctuation that was used in the original, not always using *sic* to indicate unconventional spelling or usage. Sometimes – although not always – that unconventionality is part of the narrator's style.

Shared stories involve many tellers as they unfold over time and draw together many different kinds of texts. Although this book is not a shared story, it has unfolded over the process of several years, and there are many people who have helped along the way and to whom I owe a debt of thanks. Paul Thompson helped me clean up the data from the Wikipedia talk pages and provided the reference corpus of Wikipedia talk pages. Taha Yasseri created the revert graph of the Wikipedia editors' interactions with the 'Murder of Meredith Kercher' article and allowed me to reproduce it in this book. Maria Bortoluzzi and Lorenzo Mastropierro helped me translate the extracts from the Italian Wikipedia 'Omicidio di Meredith Kercher' article and pages. Earlier versions of some chapters were presented as work in progress at various conferences and seminars over the last three years. I am grateful for the comments and conversations that followed. I am especially grateful to Alexandra Georgakopoulou and Anna De Fina, who helped me see the connections between shared stories and small story research. Some of the analysis in Chapter 3 is drawn from Page (2014): an article which is available via the doi 10.1177/0963947013510648, and parts of which are printed here with permission of SAGE Publications.

I began work on this book whilst I was a member of the School of English at the University of Leicester, and completed it as a member of the Department of English Language and Applied Linguistics at the University of Birmingham. I have been fortunate to find truly collegial scholars in both academic contexts, whom I count as friends, and who have helped my work in numerous ways. Thanks go to Julie Coleman, who read early versions of several chapters, and to Jeannette Littlemore and Susan Hunston, who read the later versions of those chapters and helped me frame the opening and closing of the book. Thanks go also to the Discourse and Stylistics Reading Group at the University of Birmingham (Michael Toolan, Joe Bennett, Johan de Joode, Jai MacKenzie, Nick Groom) for reading Chapter 4 and helping me see at least some of the trees I needed to cut down from the metaphorical wood. Extra special thanks go to Clare Anderson, who read the entire typescript and helped me spot the corrections that were needed. It goes without saying that this book is better for my colleagues' contributions and any remaining errors are my own.

On a more personal note, there are also a number of people who have shared the story of this book and without whose encouragement it simply would not have got finished. Thanks go to Kate Coleman, whose timely mentorship meant that redrafting the chapters became a process of re-vision that extended beyond this book. Thanks also to Natalia Bateson, Libby Proctor and Becky Lucas for our early-morning meetings and to all my friends in the Northside Community who have kept cheering me on. As always, the final words of thanks go to my family, who have lived through yet another book-length project. Gavin, Isi and Toby: thank you for patience, love and understanding. I am so glad we get to share our lives and stories together.

Acknowledgements

Chapter 3 contains extracts from: Ruth Page (2014) 'Counter narratives and controversial crimes: The Wikipedia article for the "Murder of Meredith Kercher"', *Language and Literature*, 23 (1), pp. 61–76, http://dx.doi.org/10.1177/0963947013510648.

1 Introducing Shared Stories

Introduction

'Sharing' and 'stories': these two terms dominate our contemporary communicative landscape. Stories remain a pervasive genre that people use to make sense of themselves and the surrounding world. Sharing has become ubiquitous as an iconic action – for example, clicking a 'share' button – which reproduces content across networks of online connections. Sharing and stories can bring people together. At the same time, because they are so powerful, sharing and stories can become a site of struggle between the people who engage with them.

Let me begin with an example of a story that was shared in online contexts. On 16 June 2016, British Member of Parliament, Jo Cox, was murdered whilst on her way to a meeting with her local constituents. Her death prompted a deep affective response, not least because of the brutal nature of the attack, but also because it took place a week prior to the controversial referendum which determined the United Kingdom's position within the European Union. The news of the attack, and of her death shortly afterwards, was reported by local and national news outlets, including reports on social media sites like Twitter. The Twitter-based broadcasts of the breaking news unfolded rapidly as the real-time events took place. For example, the Twitter account @NewsExecutive posted eight tweets in one hour, successively reporting the details of the attack, the response from the police, the arrest of the killer and the decision of some politicians to suspend their referendum campaigns. Tributes to Jo Cox began to be posted in their thousands. Some contained people's reactions to the murder, whilst others circulated links to other stories and documents about Cox's life and campaigns, such as her first speech in parliament and the last document she posted on Twitter. I, like many others, responded by reposting some of these stories on Twitter and via other social media sites. At a time when the United Kingdom was politically divided, the collective responses on Twitter to Jo Cox's death united around hashtags which expressed solidarity, such as #ThankyourMP, #lovelikeJo (launched on what would have been her birthday, 22 June 2016) and #moreincommon (a phrase quoted from her maiden speech, and used by those who shared her political commitment to remain within the European Union). On Twitter alone, it is estimated that over 340 000 tweets containing the phrase 'Jo Cox' or '#JoCox' were posted in June and July 2016 (Goodson and Kwasny, 2016). Collections of social media tributes, rallies and vigils that followed in the weeks afterwards are, at the time of writing, still curated on social media sites like Storify. The story of Jo Cox's death brought together many tellers, who produced and reproduced many texts as they reported and responded to the events in social media contexts, and together promoted a shared attitude towards her death.

As we move further into the twenty-first century, the scale on which stories are shared in online contexts should not be underestimated. The major social media sites, platforms and apps attract millions of members, who engage actively with content available online. Shared stories can include reported events which are retold many thousands of times. For example, on 3 November 2016, the Twitter account @POTUS (the account maintained for the President of the United States of America, who at that point was Barack Obama) posted an update as part of a shared story that celebrated the success of the American baseball team, the Chicago Cubs:

> It happened: @Cubs win World Series. That's change even this South Sider can believe in. Want to come to the White House before I leave?

The tweet was reposted again at least 75 000 times, received over 4500 replies and was marked as a 'favourite' by over a quarter of a million users. The scale of these audiences is not limited to Twitter, but is typical of other social media sites and platforms. At the time of writing, it is estimated that over 300 hours of video are uploaded to the video-sharing site YouTube every minute (Smith, 2017). The scale of use is similar for content-sharing sites like Instagram, Pinterest and Tumblr, and for messaging apps like WeChat and Whatsapp. The powerful combination of sharing and stories has not gone unnoticed, and is embedded in the formats that online sites use to encourage participation. For example, at present, the BBC website publishes news reports which conclude with the invitation to 'share this story'. In 2016, the social network site Instagram introduced a 'stories' feature to boost interaction with the site as a form of 'sharing' (Newton, 2016). Likewise, the Snapchat app created 'stories' as a way in which its members could share content more publicly (Moreau, 2016). As these examples suggest, sharing and stories come together in many ways. In this book, I focus on how they are combined in a distinctive narrative genre: the shared story.

The shared story is important for several reasons. First, it is a type of narrative that has not yet been documented or defined in relation to its contemporary use. Second, there is the scale of its impact: shared stories can involve many thousands of people as they are collectively produced, consumed and reproduced.

Third, it is influential, for it appears to promote a particular way of representing events, people and places: one that emphasises common ground. Because of their scale and influence, shared stories are often complex, and they may be resisted, reshaped and negotiated by the many tellers involved in their co-production. Shared stories can focus on any kind of topic and can be found in many kinds of online contexts. In this book, I concentrate on examples of large-scale shared stories about events that were reported in the mainstream and social media. I focus on shared stories as they were (re)produced and consumed in four international social media contexts: Wikipedia, Facebook, Twitter and YouTube. These four sites have been established for over a decade, and their use and format have evolved in ways that are embedded in the contemporary history of social media. Focusing on these sites allows us to examine shared stories in relation to well-recognised, mediated forms and contexts. It also contributes to the wider debates about the socio-cultural politics and purposes that the use and design of these sites might serve. A central tenet of this book is that shared stories are never neutral or straightforward. The choice to examine shared stories on these four sites thus opens up questions about their different ideological implications. The questions that I tackle in this book are:

- What is a shared story?
- How can we analyse shared stories?
- How are shared stories shaped by the mediated contexts in which they occur?
- Whose interests do shared stories serve?

Mediated Narrative Analysis

The focus of this book on sharing and stories pushes forward the frontiers of what I call 'mediated narrative analysis'. This takes its name as an echo of Scollon's (2002) seminal work on mediated discourse, later developed as mediated discourse analysis (most notably by Norris and Jones, 2005). As Jones and Hafner (2012, p. 2) point out, a medium is something that stands between people and facilitates their interaction. Similarly, I am interested in three ways in which stories, as a form of interaction, mediate and are mediated. First, stories mediate between the people who produce, consume and reproduce them. Second, shared stories are mediated by various technological resources used in the contexts of production and reception. Third, mediated discourse as a form of analysis moves from examining concrete interactions to considering the constitutive role that these interactions might have in their social and cultural context. Similarly, my approach to shared stories moves from the detailed analysis of the particular textual, mediated forms of shared stories to question what these stories do and how they are mediated by their various socio-cultural contexts. By emphasising the three aspects of the mediated discourse (first, the ways in which shared stories mediate their tellers; second, how they are mediated by their online contexts; third, their mediated position between the tellers and their social contexts), I want to draw attention from the outset to the human agency and social implications of the shared story, rather than necessarily foregrounding the technological nature of the shared story as the sole object of study for this book.

That said, this book is distinctive in its focus on the online contexts in which shared stories are produced, consumed and reproduced. In this sense, mediated narrative analysis as a theoretical enterprise can be thought of as emerging from the steady body of work that has examined the narratives produced through mediated discourse such as the print and television news (Bell, 1991; Montgomery, 2007; Van Dijk, 1991). More recently, in my own work (Page, 2010, 2012a; Page and Thomas, 2011), alongside other scholars in computer-mediated discourse analysis, I have begun to explore the narratives found in online contexts. This includes studies of blogs (Hoffmann, 2010; Walker Rettberg, 2014), consumer reviews (Vasquez, 2014), health websites (Thompson, 2012), employee testimonials (Maagaard, 2014), SMS messages, YouTube videos (Georgakopoulou, 2008, 2015) and social network sites such as Twitter (Dayter, 2015) and Facebook (Giaxoglou, 2015a, 2015b; West, 2013, 2015). For the most part, the studies thus far have tackled relatively small-scale examples of storytelling in specific, online contexts. Shared stories differ from the storytelling observed in this earlier research in terms of the shared story's potential to proliferate into very large numbers of interactions involving thousands of tellers. As large, multifaceted objects of study, shared stories present a new challenge for the methods of mediated narrative analysis. My approach to shared stories moves mediated narrative analysis forward, first by developing our understanding of a new genre – shared stories – and second by drawing together an innovative combination of the methods used to analyse it.

In so doing, mediated narrative analysis echoes a second, important aspect of mediated discourse. Like Scollon, I position mediated narrative analysis as a nexus of interconnected theoretical frameworks. Scollon drew on interactional sociolinguistics, linguistic anthropology, conversation analysis and Critical Discourse Analysis. His work was taken up more widely to incorporate other frameworks – such as social semiotics and multimodality – in recognition that the relationship between interactions and social meanings was not achieved by verbal communication alone. Likewise, mediated narrative analysis is an inevitably and deliberately interconnected project that draws on insights from a number of frameworks within discourse analysis, including Critical Discourse Analysis, interactional sociolinguistics, social semiotics and narrative analysis, and combines them with other methods and models in order to deal with the scale and nature of the shared stories told in online contexts. This combination of methods is necessary in order to explore shared stories in their observable forms (for example, the visual and verbal content and context) as a type of social practice, and as such it questions their function within wider socio-cultural contexts.

The interconnected approach of mediated discourse lends itself well to narrative analysis, which over the last five decades has developed extensively within the humanities and social sciences. As a transdisciplinary project, narrative analysis has opened up many avenues of inquiry, but these have for the most part evolved as distinct research traditions. There have been clear separations between literary-critical narrative theory (taking artistic examples of storytelling as its object of study), discourse analytic approaches to narrative (which focus on 'everyday', often conversational examples of storytelling practice) and the study of narrative in discursive psychology (where the interest lies in narrative as a mode of thought). The analysis of shared stories in this book is most strongly centred in the discourse analytic approach to narrative. However, in line with the nexus of practice at the heart of mediated narrative analysis, I also draw on concepts from these other fields, as they help elucidate the forms and functions of the shared story. In this chapter, I begin with an overview of the definitions of narrative that are found in the different traditions of scholarship, and explain how they are important for understanding shared stories.

What Is a Story?

The first challenge when analysing shared stories is to establish the object of study. In order to do this, we need to understand what a story is. A shared story is a type of narrative. However, the term 'narrative' is used in broad and narrow senses in both everyday and academic contexts. For researchers working in the various research traditions, the different uses of the term can be important. In discursive psychology, for example (as in the work of Bruner, 1986, 1991), 'narrative' is taken to refer to cultural patterns or scripts. As such, it is used quite loosely and does not refer to a specific textual artefact, but rather to a shared set of assumptions. The story-like nature of cultural patterns is perhaps best summarised in Lyotard's (1979) use of the term 'grand narratives'. This broad sense of the term 'narrative' appears in day-to-day contexts, too, such as news headlines and institutional reports. For example, Greg Jericho uses the phrase 'economic narrative' in a *Guardian* article:

> Good debt? Hopefully this means the end of the dumbest economic narrative of our times. (*Guardian*, 14 December 2016)

These 'narratives' are not specific, verbal accounts of a particular set of events, but rather a general way of describing events or patterns of social-cultural behaviour. For shared stories, this macro-social meaning of 'narrative' is useful as a way of describing some of the social patterns of belief that stories help to constitute (for example, that certain people will behave in a particular way, or that certain outcomes are to be expected).

However, the broad use of 'narrative' does not stand up to the rigour of linguistic inquiry. The analysis of shared stories is rooted in the empirical analysis of concrete examples of interaction. To understand shared stories, we need a narrower definition that allows researchers to identify the textual objects that count as a 'narrative'. In academic contexts, the narrowest definitions of 'narrative' were proposed within narrative theory. Narrative theory emerged as a distinct field within structuralist approaches to literary criticism in the 1960s. In this theoretical paradigm, it was important to separate 'narrative' as the underpinning event structure from the various ways in which said underpinning events might be told. Porter Abbott (2002, p. 16) puts it like this: 'story is an event or sequence of events (the action), and narrative discourse is those events as represented'. However, later critics contested the rigid separation of these levels (Herman and Vervaeck, 2005) and the pre-existence of a recoverable 'original' story (Hutcheon, 2006). Similarly, in this book, I avoid the narrowness of the structuralist definition and will use 'narrative' and 'story' interchangeably.

In discourse analytic approaches to narrative, there are also narrow definitions of a narrative as a particular kind of text. Whilst the scholars working in literary-critical narrative theory attempted to set out a universal model that would account for all narratives, the texts from which they generated their models were rather more modest in range, focusing primarily on examples from literature and folklore. Reacting to this, the sociolinguist William Labov claimed that we would know more about such complex narratives once 'the simplest and most fundamental narrative structures' were taken into account: oral narratives of personal experience (Labov and Waletzky, 1966, p. 12). Labov and his colleagues analysed stories told by African American adolescents, elicited through sociolinguistic interviews about what he claimed were 'universal centers of interest' (Labov, 2013, p. 4), such as matters of life and death. Based on these examples, he defined narrative as 'one method of recapitulating past experience by matching a verbal sequence of clauses to the sequence of events which (it is inferred) actually happened' (Labov, 1972, pp. 359–360). Like the structuralist narratologists, Labov's definition of narrative emphasised events (as opposed to description), which are reported in a sequence. But his definition was more narrow still, suggesting that the reported events are sequenced so as to match iconically the order in which the 'real-world' events occurred. Whilst eventhood and temporal sequence remain key characteristics which set narratives apart from other kinds of texts, the limits of these minimal, narrow definitions soon became apparent.

In both the literary-critical and sociolinguistic traditions of narrative research that developed in the decades following the work of the structuralists and of Labov, there was a broad move away from 'all-or-nothing' attempts to classify narratives (where a text is either classified as a narrative or it is not) and towards a more flexible recognition of the diverse forms and functions of narrative. This is framed within debates about narrativity, as a scalar concept where a text can be perceived as more or less like prototypical examples of narrative. From a literary-critical perspective, perceptions of narrativity are associated with a number of factors which are part of an open-ended, 'fuzzy' list (Ryan, 2007). These include:

- textual features such as tense and aspect (Herman, 1997);
- structural elements such as the logical connections evoked between reported events, where there is a preference for causality above temporality alone (Onega and Landa, 1996);
- the extent to which events are combined in a 'plot' with a clearly marked beginning, middle and end (Ryan, 2007); and
- the subject matter of the story, which centres on trouble but is resolved later (Polanyi, 1985).

These factors allow us to make contrasts between texts which appear more or less like a prototypical narrative. The greater the presence of the features in the list, the more prototypical the narrative. Some texts would not count as narratives at all. Not all posts that are published on social media sites are story-like. For example, the following tweet posted by the Chicago Cubs' Twitter account on 20 March 2017 is a greeting:

> Wishing a happy 40th birthday to everyone's favourite Grandpa, David Ross!

Without any reported events, the greeting does not meet even the minimal forms of narrativity. Where posts do contain reported events, the events can be reported in different ways. For example, comparing @POTUS' tweet with the account of the Chicago Cubs' success as reported in the English Wikipedia article for the club, we can observe a number of differences.

Tweet:

> It happened: @Cubs win World Series. That's change even this South Sider can believe in. Want to come to the White House before I leave?

Extract from Wikipedia:

> The Cubs won back-to-back World Series championships in 1907 and 1908, becoming the first major league team to play in three consecutive World Series, and the first to win it twice. Most recently, the Cubs won the 2016 National League Championship Series and 2016 World Series, which ended a 71-year National League pennant drought and a 108-year World Series championship drought, both of which are record droughts in Major League Baseball.

The Wikipedia report appears more like a prototypical narrative, using past-tense verbs, and includes a longer sequence of events that has a

Table 1.1 *Narrative dimensions and possibilities*

Dimension	Possibilities
Tellership	Whether a story is told by a single teller or multiple tellers
Tellability	The value of a story as highly worth telling or seemingly irrelevant
Embeddedness	The extent to which a story can be detached from or embedded in its context
Linearity	The structural qualities of a story as closed, temporal sequence or open-ended and multilinear
Moral Stance	The narrator's attitude towards reported events, which may be certain or fluctuating

Adapted from Ochs and Capps (2001), p. 20.

beginning, a middle and an end. The 'trouble' of the Cubs' former lack of success in the World Series Championship is more clearly stated and resolved in the Wikipedia article. In comparison, the tweet is much less like a prototypical narrative. Although the tweet includes a reported event, it is partly narrated in the past tense ('it happened') and partly in the present ('Cubs win'), as if reported in real time. These examples show us that in social media contexts, some texts may not be narratives at all (like the greeting from the Chicago Cubs), some may resemble prototypical narratives (like the Wikipedia article), and some may have only weak narrativity but still include events reported in time, and so may still be classed as narratives (like @POTUS' tweet).

The shift to a more flexible approach to narrative allows the shared story to incorporate examples that are not just plot-like, past-tense reports of troublesome events. Indeed, the shared stories in this book are quite different to the literary examples examined in narrative criticism and the narratives of personal experience scrutinised by Labov. They are not what would be considered a 'prototypical narrative'. The mediated narrative analysis of shared stories thus builds on a key trend in discourse analytic approaches to narrative which sought to position prototypical examples within a broader spectrum of storytelling practices. There are two turning points in the development of discourse analytic narrative research that inform my approach to shared stories. The first is the move towards a dimensional approach to narrative, as set out in Ochs and Capps' (2001) work. Ochs and Capps recognised that there are many forms in which a story might be told. In broadening the foci for narrative analysis, they did not just focus on the various patterns that could structure the narrative text, as did literary-critical theorists interested in narrativity. Instead, they considered the sequential organisation of events as one of five dimensions which can be used to compare the qualities of different narrative examples. These dimensions are tellership, tellability, embeddedness, linearity and moral stance (summarised in Table 1.1). Because they are taken up in the discussion of the different shared stories in the later chapters of this book, I will briefly introduce each here (fuller discussion can be found in Page, 2012a).

Ochs and Capps' (2001) schematic outline projects the differences in the various narrative dimensions as series of a scalar contrasts between binary alternatives. As the glosses in Table 1.1 indicate, tellership contrasts the degree of involvement from the narrative interlocutors, tellability is a relative judgement of value (the story is more or less worth telling) and embeddedness compares the extent to which the narrative text is detachable from its context. Linearity contrasts the structural aspects of the narrative. Moral stance is constant or variable. Ochs and Capps (2001) argued that Labov and his successors tended to privilege narrative examples which combined factors from the same end of the spectrum for each dimension. This resulted in a focus on single-teller narratives about highly tellable topics (usually dangerous events or conflicts), which are relatively decontextualised, have a clear moral stance and have a defined macro-level linear structure. Without question, these kinds of narratives continue to be important (Labov, 2013). However, as De Fina and Georgakopoulou (2012, p. 9) point out, the focus on more prototypical examples has influenced the choice of subject matter in narrative research to the neglect of atypical examples. The analysis of shared stories in this book is a further attempt to redress the neglect of narrative examples that fall beyond the early Labovian paradigm.

In turning my attention to shared stories as an 'atypical' form of narrative, I also build on a second, key turning point in discourse analytic narrative research: the small stories paradigm. Small story research positions itself as a strategic shift, an 'antidote to canonical research' (Bamberg and Georgakopoulou, 2008, p. 377) in which the analytic focus is turned towards 'a gamut of underrepresented narrative activities' (2008, p. 381). It is thanks to the work of those scholars within this paradigm that we have begun to know much more about the range of storytelling practices that fall outside the canonical end of the narrative spectrum, examples of which include breaking news, hypothetical stories and projections of future events (Georgakopoulou, 2007), refusals to tell (Bamberg and Georgakopoulou, 2008), narrative stance-taking (Georgakopoulou, 2013a) and conversational shared stories (Georgakopoulou, 2005, 2007). These small stories are highly embedded in their interactional contexts, often falling on the periphery or margins of the main topic of the talk. In line with the emphasis on their emergent, interactional contexts, small stories are often co-constructed rather than the accomplishment of a single narrator. They are typically fleeting rather than fully developed with a 'completed' linear structure, and like other kinds of 'small talk' (Coupland, 2000), they often report events which are mundane and everyday in nature rather than landmark examples of tellable topics. The description of these examples as 'small' thus operates on two levels. As Bamberg and Georgakopoulou (2008, p. 381) put it:

> These tellings are typically small when compared to the pages and pages of transcript of interview narratives. On a metaphorical level, though, the term locates a level and even an aesthetic for the identification and analysis of narrative: the smallness of talk, where fleeting moments of narrative orientation to the world can be easily missed out by an analytical lens that only takes fully fledged ('big') stories as the prototype from where the analytic vocabulary is supposed to emerge.

The bold juxtaposition of 'small' and 'big' in this description is rhetorically useful for giving impetus towards the exploration of atypical narrative examples. However, atypical narrative examples can vary considerably and may not all be 'small' in the same way, either in size or in subject matter. As I have suggested from the outset, shared stories can be very large in size and can, as a form of social practice, be the means by which tellers engage with large concerns beyond mundane and everyday matters. On one hand, the small story paradigm serves as an important point of reference for the analysis of shared stories, for even very large datasets may contain a myriad of small moments of narrative interaction. However, the large scale and highly tellable nature of shared stories suggests that a small story approach needs to be complemented with other methods when integrated within mediated narrative analysis.

My study of shared stories is in line with a dimensional approach to narrative and the small stories paradigm as a contextual approach that analyses the narrative as a form of social practice. I propose that any account of shared stories must take into consideration the co-tellers and the local and socio-cultural contexts in which the storytelling takes place. In keeping with Ochs and Capps' (2001) work and the small story paradigm, I take a flexible approach to defining the shared story as a narrative which retains eventhood as a core component but does not anticipate that the reports of the events need form a past-tense, complete sequence that reaches a point of resolution. In line with mediated narrative analysis, I am specifically concerned with examining how the contexts of interaction, as forms of co-tellership and embeddedness, mediate and mediatise (Agha, 2011) the shared story. However, unlike the small stories that are concerned with the more fleeting, ephemeral and aesthetically small moments of narration, shared stories open up the possibility of examining the wider variety of a-typical interactions that are now emerging in online contexts alongside their 'small' counterparts. In a culture of connectivity where 'small stories', like the tweet from @POTUS, can be shared many thousands of times and become part of larger, public interactions, the principles of small story research now need to be brought into conversation with other narrative approaches. This is all the more important given that the socio-cultural hierarchies between the tellers of stories and the mediated forms of narration blur a sharp contrast between the 'everyday' lay person, who can interact with stories online, and the use of social media to document large-scale matters of public concern.

What Does It Mean to Share?

The mediated narrative analysis of shared stories brings the discourse analytic study of narratives into dialogue with concepts that have been developed most fully in media and communication studies. The critical debates in media studies help us understand the complexity of what it means to 'share' and the socio-cultural values in which sharing practices are implicated. As a keyword associated with online interactions, 'share' has recently begun to be theorised, most extensively in a paper by John (2013). In his overview, John argues that 'share' has two distinct meanings: a communicative meaning (where 'share' is synonymous with 'tell') and a distributive meaning (where 'share' refers to the exchange of tangible items, as in sharing food or resources). Both communicative and distributive functions are brought together in the use of the verb in online contexts, which began to become prevalent between the years 2005 and 2007 (John 2013, p. 168), a period which immediately followed the rise of social network sites. The two meanings of 'share' are important, for they point to the interrelated but separable communicative aspects of the shared story. First, shared stories are told. They are textual artefacts that consist of words, images and other multimodal resources that narrate events. Second, shared stories are mediated in forms that can be produced and disseminated in an iterative fashion. They are repeatedly shared, for example, by clicking on icons like the 'share button' to recontextualise content without changing it. It is also possible for the content of these stories to develop creatively through successive interactions, for example, as new tellers add more content or remix the earlier content with fresh material.

The two functions of sharing found in online contexts bring into question the relationship between language and its mediated forms. In computer-mediated communication, one way of interpreting this relationship draws on the concept of affordances. Gibson (1977) coined the term 'affordances' to explain the ways in which the characteristics of a particular environment both constrain and enable particular kinds of activity. From this perspective, an affordance is a design feature that enables certain kinds of actions to ensue. For example, the organisation of social network sites which include a timeline that presents content in a linear sequence might increase the potential for that content to be interpreted as part of a narrative. However, others do not see affordances as solely the product of a medium. Instead, affordances can become part of social actions, which are 'not determined by what the resources naturally offer but are shaped by how people perceive what various representational resources can or cannot do for them' (Lee, 2007, p. 227). In line with the view of affordances as part of a social action, the mediated forms of sharing that are explored in this book – such as linking, reproducing, ranking and remixing online content – do not alone determine how the shared stories are told. Instead, a mediated view of these affordances is interested in how people use them for creative ends. The purposes that the mediated forms of sharing serve often exploit the wider affordances of networked publics, as described by Boyd (2014). Boyd points out that networked publics are characterised by material that is both persistent and replicable. These are important qualities of the media in which shared stories are produced and consumed, for the replicable quality of the stories means that they are readily reproduced, often on a vast scale. Her term, 'persistence', reminds us that unlike stories that are told in face-to-face contexts, which are ephemeral and must be recorded and transcribed, shared stories leave traces of their presence online. Importantly, persistence applies to the content that is shared (such as the visual and verbal stories published online) *and* the interactions that redistribute that content (such as the metadata that is left in the archives of online sites, allowing those with access to it to trace who has interacted with the material, and when and where these interactions took place).

The scale of these replicable stories and their persistent format are powerful resources that are valued within online sites for what they might suggest about the people who have 'shared' their content. The socio-cultural politics of sharing are widely debated within media and communication studies. The mediated affordances of sharing as a form of distributing content have attracted considerable discussion within media studies in relation to the agency that is involved in the various aspects of the sharing process. Early studies framed the potential for content to be shared, remixed and redistributed in optimistic terms as enabling a participatory culture that blurred the distinction between content producers who held socio-economic power (such as the mainstream media) and those lay persons now able to contribute to the online (re)creation of content in various ways. Jenkins (2006) famously described the socio-political shift as a form of 'convergence'. Similarly, Bruns (2008) blended the nouns 'producer' and 'user' to coin the term 'produsage' in recognition that the boundaries of production and reception in social media sites were no longer as straightforward as they once might have seemed. More recently, there has been a more critical view of the socio-economic and political potential of sharing. Most notably, Van Dijck's (2013) critique of the design and use of many of the contemporary social media sites rightly draws attention to the varying forms of creative labour and privilege that are involved in the different aspects of sharing. Telling a story and redistributing that story are interrelated but different practices that may be carried out by different people and valued in different ways. In this book, I draw on this critical perspective to question what purposes the shared stories serve, how the different aspects of sharing are valued and how this mediates the relationship between the co-tellers involved therein.

The need to look beyond a surface meaning of sharing is at the heart of John's (2013) paper. He argues that the choice of 'share' as a keyword within the rhetoric of social network sites evokes positive connotations, where sharing helps form social bonds that will make 'the world a better place'

(p. 178). Indeed, the meaning of 'sharing' as an indication of common ground (as in a 'shared belief') echoes the widespread assumption that the use of social media supports the activities of people who seek out those who are similar to themselves. The notion of homophily is echoed in other similar concepts developed in media studies, such as affinity spaces (Gee, 2004), and in social semiotics, such as ambient affiliation (Zappavigna, 2011) and bonding (Tann, 2010). Sharing as an intersubjective process does not just connect digital texts; it is also a process by which people position themselves relative to the content which they (re)produce, and relative to one another. This meaning of sharing is important, for the analysis of shared stories explores the ways tellers construct, contest or negotiate common ground through the stories that they tell and through the ways in which they interact with one another. Within media studies, the rhetoric of sharing as a means of social connection is seen as strategic on the part of social network site creators. As Van Dijck and Nieborg (2009, p. 866) put it, 'Facebook does not want to link friends to friends, it is in the business of linking people to advertisers and products. Not content, but connections and profiled actions are the new commodities.' In line with this, I take a contextualised approach to shared stories, which considers the localised, mediated interactions in which narratives are (re)produced and consumed and interprets them within this wider critical context of the socio-economic politics of online interaction. The intersubjective nature of sharing does not happen in isolation, but is part of a wider process, where the mediated nature of the sharing can be co-opted for other purposes, be they socio-economic, political or cultural.

The Antecedents of the Shared Story

The shared stories which I examine in this book are all produced and consumed in online contexts. However, the shared story has antecedents in stories told in conversational, literary and journalistic modes of narration. The characteristics of the shared story found online are shaped by these three predecessors. Typically, each has been studied in relation to a different tradition of narrative research, where conversational narratives have been explored within discourse analytic research, literary narratives within narrative criticism and news narratives within Critical Discourse Analysis. As a nexus approach, mediated narrative analysis brings these three trajectories together. In this section, I outline how each tradition brings to light the characteristics of the shared story found online.

Shared Stories in Conversational Contexts

The term 'shared stories' originated within the small stories paradigm, when Georgakopoulou (2005, 2007) used it to define a particular type of small story.

She used 'shared story' as the 'umbrella term for stories that are oriented to as familiar in interactions, either because they have been told in the past or because the events reported in them are known to all or some of the participants' (Georgakopoulou, 2007, p. 50). Georgakopoulou's definition points to two central characteristics of the shared story. First, it is a retelling of, or a reference to, a previous story. Second, it involves more than one teller. Within discourse analytic traditions of narrative research, the exploration of retold stories has a rich history (see, for example, Georgakopoulou, 2005; Günther, 2005; Lambrou, 2014; Norrick, 2000, 2005; Polanyi, 1985). In these studies, the notions of entextualisation, contextualisation and recontextualisation are crucial and, in turn, illuminate how the processes of sharing operate within the shared story. Bauman and Briggs (1990, p. 71) define entextualisation as 'the process of rendering discourse extractable, or making a stretch of linguistic production into a unit – a text – that can be lifted out of its interactional setting'. Sharing, as a form of telling, is a form of entextualisation, whereby the narrator entextualises an aspect of lived experience, for example, by narrating events in verbal form as words or in visual form as images. Contextualisation involves the participants making sense of the story and its significance within its interaction (Gumperz, 1982). Most importantly, for the shared story, recontextualisation is the process by which a text – here, the story – is 'lifted out of its interactional setting' (Bauman and Briggs, 1990, p. 71) and reinserted into a new context, and thereby opened up to new meanings, interactions and interpretations. As stories are redistributed – 'shared', in its interactional sense – they are recontextualised.

In discourse analytic studies of retold conversational stories, earlier research has investigated how certain parts of a narrative are recontextualised whilst other parts either remain the same or are not included in subsequent retellings. Given the face-to-face nature of the stories told in conversational and interview settings, the differences in retellings have been explained as tellers tailoring the retelling to the specific needs of audience. A story might need to be retold in its entirety to someone unfamiliar with the events, but it might be understood by the briefest allusion if all members of the audience are very familiar with the events or with the story itself (Georgakopoulou, 2005). In her work on life stories, Linde (1993, p. 31) suggests that these changes to narration can also be attributed to the teller's values over time, which may alter as they gain access to new information or resolve traumatic life experiences. In their studies, both Norrick (2005) and Georgakopoulou (2005, 2007) point out that the familiarity of the retold stories of collective experience seems particularly to be understood as an invitation to co-tellership. In these cases, the co-tellership of shared stories can be bound up with the shared experience of events; the right to retell the story may depend on the teller's presence at the time of the events (Georgakopoulou, 2005, p. 207). The resulting social relationship between the co-tellers is one that echoes the intersubjective characteristic of sharing by affirming relationships between the narrative participants. Shared stories are said to 'enhance feelings of group identity' (Norrick, 2000, p. 84), and can become part of the interpersonal history for the group (Georgakopoulou, 2005, p. 230).

Retellings in Literary Contexts: Adaptation Studies

For the most part, the discourse analytic narrative research about retold stories mostly focused on stories of personal experience that were narrated in face-to-face settings. The transmedial expansion of literary-critical narrative criticism also explored retold stories, but was more interested in the ways that the stories were adapted from one mediated form to another (for example, comparing a printed novel to a film adaptation). Within the field of adaptation studies, the versatile term 'share' finds its way into discussions of the intertextuality that characterises literary examples of retold stories. For example, Hutcheon (2006, p. 4) described literary adaptations as stories which 'openly announce their relationship to prior texts' in a process of 'Western culture's long and happy history of borrowing and stealing, or more accurately, *sharing* stories' (my emphasis).

The intertextual nature of sharing is a key focus in adaptation studies. In contrast to fidelity studies, which place value on preserving the original text as it is recontextualised in later forms, adaptation does not prize replication. Instead, it emphasises the creative reworking and transformation of material as it is recontextualised; the attractive quality of adaptation is its ability to combine familiar (shared) stories with new variations. Like other media scholars, Hutcheon sees the intertextual adaption of one story in another form as a positive move, one which opens up fresh possibilities for interpretation. One way in which adaptations open up new interpretations is by changing the media in which the narrative is produced and consumed. Early work in adaptation studies was dominated by comparisons of literary source texts and their relationship to filmic or televised versions (see Leitch, 2008 for an overview). More recently, the questions of medium specificity and its role in facilitating different narrative interpretations have been taken up more broadly (Grishakova and Ryan, 2010; Page, 2010; Ryan, 2004). The analysis of these transmedial adaptations brings the multimodal affordances of sharing into focus. For example, Hutcheon (2006) approaches this by making a bold distinction between the kinds of engagement that are offered by different media, where visual resources foreground showing (positioning the audience as a viewer), verbal resources (where the author is a reader or listener) and interactive resources (where the audience is a game-player who directs the outcome of the narrative). As the shared stories told online incorporate a range of multimodal resources when they are (re)produced, the interpretive potential of words, images and interactions to engage the tellers in the process of sharing comes to the fore as a key aspect of the analysis in this book.

Shared Stories in Reporting the News

The ideological positioning of one telling relative to another has been a central concern in the Critical Discourse Analysis of stories told in the news. As in discourse analytic narrative research, Critical Discourse Analysis understands narratives as subjective tools for ordering events, but it focuses more prominently on the ways in which power (in a Foucauldian sense) is practised. The selective nature of the stories retold in the news is seen not as neutral, but rather as a tool for persuasion which exploits the expectations that narratives will hold the attention of the audience, create affective responses and render an experience 'authentic' and hence more credible (De Fina and Georgakopoulou, 2012, pp. 137–141). The potency of narrative as a mode of representation and of the mainstream news as an influential broadcast medium means that news narratives are important for understanding the ways in which shared knowledge is constructed in the form of 'master narratives' or tacit patterns of belief about society. Journalists project the authority of their role as 'gatekeepers who manage the flow of information' (Bogaerts and Carpentier, 2012, p. 63) as a form of public service. The ethical responsibilities involved in managing this broadcast process have been framed in relation to notions of objectivity and truth. However, there have been many studies of the ways in which news discourse can naturalise the stereotypes and presuppositions that promote social inequalities and serve the interests of those with social and economic power (who often also control the dissemination of mainstream news). A comprehensive review of the manifold forms of inequality perpetrated through news media discourse is beyond the scope of this chapter, but Van Dijk (1991) and van Leeuwen (1996, 2008) explore racist discourse in the press, Baker et al. (2013) examine the representation of Islam in the British press, and Clark (1992), Caldas-Coulthard (1992) and Page (2003) point to the gendered asymmetries that occur in the tabloid and broadsheet press. In these and the many other studies of retold stories in newspapers, the comparisons between one telling and another focus less on what stays the same and more on the ways in which the lexico-grammatical resources and textual organisation are used to legitimate one version of events above another. More recently, Critical Discourse Analysis has begun to take a more multimodal approach (Machin and Mayr, 2012), with a focus on the social semiotic interpretation of images (van Leeuwen, 2008), especially as these relate to the development of photojournalism (Caple, 2013). The comparison between retellings in the news is most concerned with the ideological contexts which shape each version of events and thus interpret reports in relation to the newspapers' political affiliations, their statuses as broadsheet or tabloid, the national context of the news and, for long-running news stories, the changes in reported events over time.

The narrative analysis of news reports has shown that their textual organisation is quite different from the temporal order suggested by the Labovian definition of narrative and the closed structures associated with prototypical narrative examples in Ochs and Capps' (2001) dimension of linearity. Instead, news reports are inherently open-ended: there is always new news to report. In print news, the structure of reports does not follow temporal sequence, but is shaped by the ideological salience of the headline and lead (Bell, 1991). White (1997) describes reports as organised in 'satellites', which variously contextualise, elaborate or appraise the main event summarised in the headline. News reports are themselves often replete with retellings, and are characterised by high levels of redundancy (Hoey, 2001) generated by the repetition of events in quotations from eyewitnesses and experts, whose stories and evaluations are recontextualised by reporters. The selection of these recontextualised stories, the structure of the news report (its linearity, in Ochs and Capps' terms) and the selection of the report as tellable material in the first place are all driven by news values.

The socially constructed nature of news values in shaping news media has long been recognised in journalism (Conboy, 2006) and in Critical Discourse Analysis (Bell, 1991; Fowler, 1991; Richardson, 2006). More recently, news values have begun to be understood as socially constrained and discursively constructed, rather than existing as intangible qualities 'outside' the text itself. They are entextualised in verbal and visual choices, such as the lexicogrammatical patterns, images and layout of the report (Bednarek and Caple 2012, 2014, 2017). News values are of particular interest in the analysis of shared stories, for, as an interpretive framework, many of the news values identified thus far (at least in the mainstream, Western press) are similar to the factors that prompt interpretations of narrativity and are found at the more 'typical' end of Ochs and Capps' (2001) set of narrative dimensions. The news value of negativity is similar to the assumption that narratives must entail some kind of trouble, whilst the value of novelty (the unexpected aspects of events) reinforces the narrativity which requires events to be seen as a departure from the norm. The news value of eliteness and personalisation are akin to the requirement that a narrative be told about particular participants, with a preference for human experience. Other news values reflect a particular kind of evaluative stance. For example, the values of superlativeness (which suggests the intensity of events) and impact (which assesses the significance of events) emphasise the relevance of the reported events and their exceptional nature. The tellability of news events is also governed by ideological values which uphold the dominant belief systems, as suggested by the news value of consonance (which refers to the reinforcement of expected or stereotypical behaviour, usually of particular marginalised or discredited groups). The news values of timeliness and proximity emphasise events which are close to the geographical, cultural and temporal location of the audience assumed to consume the news.

The study of the production of news narratives is also important for understanding the co-tellership of the shared story. News production has always been a collaborative project between journalists, editors and production teams (Cotter, 2010). The transition of newspaper journalism into online and convergent cultures means that the possibilities for sharing the production and reception of news stories have become more complex. Within journalism studies, the agency of the people involved in (re)producing and consuming the news has been a matter of ongoing debate as a political concern. This is brought most forcefully into focus in the developments of citizen journalism, which Goode (2009, p. 1288) describes as the 'range of web-based practices whereby "ordinary" users engage in journalistic practices'. He observes that some of these activities involve the creation of content – emphasising what we might call 'sharing as telling' – where people blog or upload videos or photos relating to current news (for example, as eyewitness accounts or as commentary on events which may or may not have been included in mainstream news broadcasts). Other forms of citizen journalism include what Goode (2009, p. 1290) calls 'meta-journalism', which encompasses commentary, tagging, ranking and reposting of news items: activities which emphasise more strongly the distributive meanings of 'sharing'. Goode argues that whilst there are obvious differences in these types of activities, the meta-journalistic functions of citizen journalism are not meaningless, but are important interpretive acts which remediate and recontextualise the news content, opening it up to new interpretation and to being repurposed within other social media activities. More broadly, debates about citizen journalism and mainstream news production echo similar themes to those found in media studies which focus on the ideological implications of sharing and the purposes to which sharing is put.

The Characteristics of Shared Stories

The shared stories that occur in conversational contexts, literary adaptations and the news media have four distinctive characteristics. They are characterised by:

- narration shared between multiple tellers;
- intertextual references which connect shared texts;
- distributed linearity, whereby narrative content is produced and reproduced across multiple units; and
- an assumption of commonly held beliefs.

Based on these characteristics, I define the shared story as *a retelling, produced by many tellers, across iterative textual segments, which promotes shared attitudes between its tellers*. In the closing sections of this chapter, I flesh out the

Table 1.2 *Spectrum of co-tellership activities as types of sharing*

Meaning of 'share'	Sharing as telling	⟵	⟶	Sharing as dissemination
	Creates content	Remixes existing content with new material	Comments on existing content	Reproduces content
Co-tellership involvement	High	⟵	⟶	Low

importance of these characteristics for the study of shared stories in online contexts.

Co-tellership

Shared stories always involve more than one teller; they are co-constructed narratives. As with its offline antecedents, the co-tellership of the shared story in online contexts is interested in the relative agency, rights and relationship between the co-tellers. This extends the research from discourse analytic traditions, which traced the interactional roles found in each telling (Bamberg and Georgakopoulou, 2008) and the teller's entitlement to tell the story (Shuman, 2005). Building on adaptation studies, in online contexts, the tellers of a shared story can be contrasted according to whether they created the source or a subsequent version of a story. The Critical Discourse Analysis of retellings in the news brings focus to co-tellers as producers who have a particular ideological affiliation, and whose words may be recontextualised through quotation or redistribution of online content.

The mediated nature of shared stories in online contexts extends these concerns by exploring the kinds of narrative practices in which co-tellers might participate. The meanings of 'sharing' as they are shaped within a critical view of participatory culture differentiate between the co-tellers' role in creating, curating, commenting on and remixing content. The mediated types of co-tellership activities vary in terms of how their roles emphasise creating or disseminating the content of the shared story. The relationship between the co-tellership activities and types of sharing is summarised in Table 1.2.

A mediated approach to the co-tellership of shared stories considers how these activities are afforded or constrained by the social media contexts in which the narration is embedded. This has been an ongoing area of interest in earlier work in mediated narrative analysis. For example, as with online storytelling more generally, the design of social media sites means that the co-tellers can have varying degrees of control over different parts of the shared story, where some have the right to author posts, whilst others can only add comments (see Page, 2012a, p. 197). The mediated contexts of narration can open up opportunities to observe distinctive forms of narrative practice, such as the ways in which tellers remove or edit the written contributions made by others on wiki pages (see Page, 2013). In other cases, the mediated resources may be important as a way of showing who has interacted with a text; for example, by taking a stance towards a post by clicking on a 'like' or reaction button on Facebook. More generally, a mediated perspective on co-tellership considers the site-specific roles which are open to co-tellers as administrators, page owners, commenters or viewers. These site-specific roles also afford and constrain different kinds of representation, rights and responsibilities that co-tellers can take up within the processes of sharing stories online.

More than any other narrative dimension, co-tellership foregrounds the intersubjective nature of sharing and the ways in which the interactions of storytelling contribute to the identities that are co-constructed for the tellers. The relationship between identity and interaction has a long-established history in narrative research more generally (see Page, 2012a, pp. 16–19 for an overview). Co-tellership of shared stories focuses in particular on how collective identities are constructed, negotiated and brought into play as positioning resources (Davies and Harré, 1990) within these mediated contexts. The types of collective identity extend beyond the digital realm, and may include the ways in which tellers make reference to national, political and regional aspects of identity. Other kinds of collective identities that are relevant to the shared story are based around particular interests or activities of producing and consuming narrative content as fans, audiences or performers. More generally still, these collective identities can be more or less explicitly signalled through such interactions, creating in-groups and out-groups. The collective identities can also carry different kinds of ideological value; for example, as a group which might support or oppose a particular national, political or celebrity figure.

Distributed Linearity

The co-construction of shared stories means that they are distributed between the multiple contributions of different tellers, such as a post and its successive comments or the iterative versions of a Wikipedia page. In line with this, shared stories are open-ended and typically lack a single end point. The distributed linearity of the shared story is important for narrative research, as it opens up further exploration of a-typical and as yet underscrutinised patterns of narrative structure. Although Ochs and Capps (2001) posed a binary polarisation between types of linearity as open or closed, there are many, varied forms in which 'open-endedness' might occur. These mediated forms of open-endedness are often multimodal and therefore test how far existing models of narrative structure might need to be adapted in the light of the shared stories found online.

Examining the distributed linearity of shared stories is also an important counter-balance to the assumption that all social media interactions are dominated by a temporal shift towards recency. In my earlier work (Page, 2010, 2012a, pp. 190–192), I noted how certain forms of social media, such as social network sites, were characterised by stories that promoted recency in present-tense or prospective accounts of events. This is in line with certain types of small story, such as breaking news and projections, which have begun to flourish in these online contexts where the affordances of the site constrain the interactions to fleeting, literally small posts (such as the 140-character restriction on a tweet). This tendency remains part of the contemporary online landscape, typified by apps like Snapchat which limit the time for which a post is publicly available and limit the format to video clips of no more than 10 seconds in length. However, given that the four social media sites considered in this book (Wikipedia, Facebook, Twitter and YouTube) have now been in mainstream use for over a decade, these sites hold sizeable archives of interactions that extend over years. Both Facebook and YouTube have lifted restrictions on the size of the content that can be uploaded to their sites (such as the length of a post on Facebook or a video on YouTube). In all four cases, we might also expect that a variety of subject matter could be reported. This expansion of the social media contexts means that as we similarly expand our analytical perspective beyond the small stories of breaking news and projections, other forms of open-ended narration that incorporate retrospection alongside recency will be found.

The distributed linearity of shared stories offers a mediated perspective on two aspects of storytelling: the patterns which relate to the reported events and the patterns which relate to the narrative reporting. The difference between the two aspects has been described in earlier research, where the reported events are ordered within a 'tale world' (Bamberg and Georgakopoulou, 2008) – or what Herman (2002) described as a 'story world' – whilst the reporting of those events takes place in the 'telling world', in which interactions unfold over time, including sharing as a form of distribution. The mediated forms and contexts of the shared story allow us to explore the dimensions of these interactions in ways that shed new light on their temporal unfolding. In particular, the contextual metadata in the form of time-stamps provides semi-automated forms of evidence that can help us better understand the relationship between the ways that reported events are represented and when people report and reproduce them. This can be important, as shared stories can have different kinds of temporal durability (Blommaert et al., 2016). For example, as retellings change over time, certain parts may be redistributed more often and for a longer time period than others, or else may shift in line with changes to the socially mediated contexts in which they are produced and consumed.

Intertextual Embeddedness

As retold stories, shared stories are inherently intertextual; one text refers back to another. However, the intertextuality of shared stories extends beyond this, as the stories typically are connected to other texts over and above the preceding 'telling'. Within the research that explored the antecedents of the online shared stories, intertextuality has been widely studied, not only in literary-critical narratology and adaptation studies (see Genette, 1980; Hogan, 2014; Hutcheon, 2006) but also in relation to discourse analysis, as a communicative function of all language (de Beaugrande and Dressler, 1981), which emphasises the dialogic nature of all texts as echoes of those that have come previously (Bakhtin, 1984). Within the analysis of conversation stories, the use of quotation to recontextualise the words of another has been analysed using Goffman's (1981) framework of footing. In each of these fields, intertextuality can be more or less explicitly signalled in the verbal content of the stories, ranging from a brief allusion through to a fully announced adaptation. These forms of intertextuality continue to be important in shared stories told online. However, the mediated forms of sharing and the replicable qualities of digital textuality more generally bring this aspect of the shared story to the fore. In particular, the potential for mediated forms of intertextuality – for example, hyperlinks and site-specific resources such as hashtags and reposting – opens up new avenues for understanding the forms and functions of intertextuality within these narratives. Similarly, the multimodal forms of intertextuality (for example, in macros and memes that combine images and captions, mashup videos and parody songs) require us to evaluate the ways in which these semiotic resources contribute to the narrative meanings in different ways.

The intertextuality of the shared story considers not just the meaning of the text, but also its exchange value, or what Blommaert et al. (2016) describe as the transpositional implications of the shared story as a type of interaction. This refers to the interpretive implications of the intertextuality. For example, as an intertextual referent is recontextualised, it can open up many different kinds of new interpretations for the tellers and their audiences. The recontextualisation can involve greater or lesser creative input from the co-tellers, who may leave the referent relatively unchanged or may alter it significantly. The intertextual referent may seem highly similar to its new context of use, or it may be very different in genre, tone or style. The transpositional implications of the intertextuality also point to the varied ways in which shared stories co-construct shared attitudes between their tellers. Tellers can express a stance towards the intertextual referent, and in so doing, may choose to align with or differ from other tellers (Du Bois, 2007). The ability to recognise an intertextual reference in the first place may also unite or differentiate the tellers involved therein. There is no guarantee that an intertextual reference will always be recognised, or interpreted in line with other tellers' intentions. The shared knowledge that is presupposed, implicitly or explicitly, by the intertextuality of the shared story points once again to the intersubjective and ideological nature of sharing that is explored in this book.

Why Do We Need to Understand Shared Stories?

Shared stories are important because, as an object of study, they are so prevalent in our contemporary communicative landscape. Understanding the workings of shared stories is important because of the ways in which it advances narrative scholarship. First, it develops our understanding of a narrative genre that has thus far remained relatively underscrutinised. In turn, this offers new ways of thinking about narrative structure, the tellers of stories and the multilayered contexts in which stories are produced, reproduced and consumed.

The analysis of distributed linearity brings fresh impetus to the study of the most central of narrative theory's concerns: the structure of stories. The types of 'open-ended' narrativity, especially as they are emerging in online contexts, still require explication and categorisation. The shared stories analysed in this book provide examples of distributed linearity that show how open-ended narrative patterns can be more or less innovative in the forms that they take. The contextualised approach of mediated narrative analysis does not just observe these forms but also examines how the resources and contexts for telling promote some aspects of narrative structure rather than others. The analysis of the shared story's distributed linearity treats structure not as an abstract factor, but as a resource that can be put to various ideologically informed ends.

A second aspect of mediated narrative analysis focuses on the production, reception and reproduction of shared stories by particular tellers. This builds on the trajectory of narrative analysis that sees identity as inextricably bound up with interaction. The case studies in this book will explore the various mediated ways in which shared stories represent their tellers, what roles the tellers take up, how the right to retell a shared story is constructed and what kinds of relational work emerge from the tellers' interactions with the shared story.

Mediated narrative analysis considers shared stories in their multilayered contexts. The factors that contribute to the mediated forms of interaction require careful examination and expand on those found in earlier narrative research to include metadata, templates and the formats in which shared stories are told online. The mediated forms of retelling that are used in the shared story draw particular attention to interdiscursive contexts, where stories are connected not only to their predecessors but also to other intertextual resources via the networked publics of social network sites and the Internet more broadly. Intertextual connections are understood as a crucial aspect of the shared story which allows tellers to interact with one another through their interpretation of these resources.

The exploration of shared stories is important, for it advocates a nexus approach to narrative analysis. The methodological principles of this book explicitly value complementary models of analysis which provide a multidimensional account of the data in question. Mediated narrative analysis promotes the building of methodological bridges that allow researchers from different disciplines to benefit from the combined exchange of ideas. The analysis of shared stories is therefore of benefit to narrative scholars who might wish to tackle large-scale verbal datasets (and so employ corpus approaches to selecting and analysing the data), to those who might benefit from social semiotic insights into multimodal and mediated forms of communication, and to those who have an interest in identity and interaction in both small story research and the pragmatic analysis of (im)politeness. Mediated narrative analysis has much to offer scholars of applied linguistics, in part by providing challenging data that require researchers to refine their existing methods and models and in part by opening up questions about the ongoing forms through which people tell stories to make sense of themselves and the world around them.

The empirical analysis of shared stories also draws on the current debates in media studies about the meanings of online interactions (such as sharing) and the various social and political uses to which such interactions are put. The linguistic characteristics of the shared story (distributed linearity, co-tellership, intertextuality) allow researchers in the wider social sciences to frame their critical evaluation of social media with more precision, and with more empirical evidence of the forms and functions that sharing can take in a range of contexts. In so doing, this book contributes to the ongoing discussion about the relationship between mainstream and social media as forms of communication and the socio-economic and political outcomes that can emerge from sharing stories in online contexts.

Conclusion

In this chapter, I have introduced the shared story as a distinctive narrative genre that flourishes in online contexts. I have defined the shared story and described its key characteristics: namely, co-tellership, distributed linearity and intertextuality, all of which contribute to its intersubjective and ideological impact as a means of producing shared attitudes between its tellers and audiences. I have examined how these characteristics of the shared story emerged from its antecedents in conversational, literary and journalistic contexts.

As an object of study, shared stories need to be understood in relation to the key trends in narrative research and current debates in media and communication studies. Following the dimensional turn in discourse analytic narrative research, I am interested in the shared story as a narrative genre which differs from the traditional accounts of narrative found in structuralist and Labovian models. I take a flexible approach that retains eventhood as a central property of the stories that are shared, but I do not confine the shared story to past-tense, plot-like sequences told by a single teller. Following the critical turn in media studies that has questioned the agency, values and ideological meaning of 'sharing' within a so-called 'participatory culture', I question how the co-tellership, linearity and intertextuality of the shared story can serve different socio-cultural purposes and be embedded in complicated economic and political contexts.

The analysis of shared stories is part of the field of mediated narrative analysis. This field began to emerge via the study of narratives in various broadcast media, and has expanded in relation to the stories produced and consumed in digitally mediated contexts. As such, the analysis of shared studies brings a particular, mediated focus to the contextual turn in narrative research that has occurred across many disciplines. Like the mediated discourse from which mediated narrative analysis takes its name, the study of shared stories requires an interconnected approach which draws on multiple frameworks of analysis from across discourse analysis and media studies in order to move beyond the relatively small scale of the analysis of online storytelling that has taken place to date. As this nexus approach is an important methodological contribution led by the study of shared stories in particular, I set out in the next chapter the multifaceted toolkit of mediated narrative analysis.

2 Mediated Narrative Analysis: The Toolkit for Analysing Shared Stories

Introduction

In Chapter 1, I positioned shared stories within the field of mediated narrative analysis, which as a theoretical approach, deliberately and explicitly draws together multiple methods of analysis. In this chapter, I set out the methods that are combined in the mediated narrative analysis used in this book. The nexus approach is typical of mediated discourse analysis (Norris and Jones, 2005; Scollon, 2002), and is in keeping with the use of mixed methods in applied linguistics (Tashakkori and Creswell, 2007). Similarly, Markham (2013) uses a 'remix' metaphor to characterise how media scholars have moved freely between methods of analysis from sometimes strikingly different disciplinary origins in order to investigate the layers of meaning that occur in examples of online interaction. However, a nexus approach is relatively less common within narrative research, where despite efforts to bring different fields together in the spirit of a transmedial narratology (Grishakova and Ryan, 2010; Herman 2004; Mildorf and Thomas, 2017; Page, 2010), disciplinary boundaries have remained a persistent factor that separates rather than integrates the narrative traditions that have studied the offline antecedents of the shared story. The mediated nature of shared stories told in online contexts means that a nexus approach to narrative analysis is now more necessary than ever. Shared stories are inescapably multimodal and cannot be analysed solely in the light of the verbal content they include. The scope of the data which are available for analysis is large and multifaceted. Lastly, the contexts in which shared stories occur are multilayered and require more than one approach to make sense of the social and cultural purposes that these stories serve.

Mediated narrative analysis develops the multidimensional approach to narrative interaction that has been emerging in recent years, one that takes a contextual perspective and so views stories as interactional accomplishments. Mediated narrative analysis develops this contextual approach in two important ways. First, it examines the multimodal aspects of the narrative text and its context. Second, it opens up new avenues of inquiry by bringing frameworks together that have for the most part developed separately thus far, either in distinct traditions of narrative inquiry or in other subdisciplines from applied linguistics and media studies. This benefits narrative scholars by extending the analytic range of the tools used to explore the forms and functions of storytelling that occur, not only in the ever-increasing range of online contexts, but also in the other forms of mediated interaction (such as those found in broadcast talk). In this chapter, I begin by explaining how the contextualised approach to shared stories can be applied at three levels of analysis. I move on to the preliminary methodological matters that are raised by the mediated nature of the data studied in this book, the ethical decisions that I made in collecting the data and the tools that I used to collect them. I then introduce the three analytical frameworks that are combined in the mediated narrative analysis I propose for shared stories, which include corpus approaches, social semiotics and interactional pragmatics. I conclude with an outline of the data that will be explored in the four case studies.

The Three Levels of Analysis for Shared Stories

In Chapter 1, I defined the shared story as *a retelling, produced by many tellers, across iterative textual segments, which promotes shared attitudes between its tellers*. Shared stories have four key characteristics: multiple tellers, distributed linearity, intertextuality and an emphasis on common ground. The characteristics of the shared story shape the way that the content is told (echoing the meaning of 'sharing as a form of telling'), the contextual ways in which the story can be reproduced in online interactions (echoing the meaning of 'sharing as a form of dissemination') and the social meanings and effects that emerge. These aspects of 'sharing' operate at three levels, each with a different analytic focus:

Level 1: Sharing is analysed as a form of telling a story.

Level 2: Sharing is analysed in relation to its online interactions of (re)production and consumption.

Level 3: Sharing is analysed as the 'familiar' values and socio-cultural myths that are indexed or presupposed through the unfolding story.

This tripartite model of sharing is akin to the analytical distinctions made in other contextual paradigms that inform mediated narrative analysis and which have been used to study the conversational, literary and journalistic predecessors of the shared stories that are told in online contexts. For example, in discourse-centred approaches to narrative analysis, scholars have drawn on positioning theory, as developed in Davies and Harré's work (1990, p. 48). Bamberg and Georgakopoulou (2008, p. 385) set out a heuristic framework which distinguishes between the analysis of positioning at three levels. In this framework, the analyst considers the identities of participants in terms of:

Level 1: How the characters are positioned within the reported events of the story.
Level 2: How the tellers are positioned within the interactive situation.
Level 3: How the tellers position their identities in relation to master narratives.

Within narrative research, the key contribution of this tripartite model has been to point towards the importance of the meso-level factors in the production and reception of narratives as discursive processes embedded within localised interactions (level 2 analysis), rather than relying on interpretation of the narrative text alone as the means of analysing the identities of the narrative participants. However, Bamberg was by no means the first to point to the interrelationship between text, interaction and social context. Similar distinctions were made in other fields of applied linguistics. For example, within Critical Discourse Analysis, Fairclough's (1989) three-dimensional approach included micro-analysis of the text and meso-level analysis of the text's production and reception in the light of macro-social meanings which shape particular socio-political contexts. This has been adopted and expanded particularly within the Discourse-Historical approach within Critical Discourse Analysis (see Reisigl and Wodak, 2001). In social semiotic approaches to discourse, Halliday (1994) described the different ways in which a text could be embedded as the 'context of situation' (the localised interactional context emerging between the participants in a specific exchange) and the 'context of culture' (the shared beliefs, knowledge and norms in which a specific exchange can be situated, but which are also available to other members of a wider community of participants). A nexus approach, which brings together these frameworks, broadens the range of factors and methods that might be included within contextual analysis of the narrative interaction, beyond those scrutinised thus far in face-to-face examples of storytelling.

In this book, I analyse the four characteristics of the shared story in relation to each of the three levels of analysis: the text, its context and its social meanings. The central assumption is that all three levels of analysis are important, and that the interpretation of sharing as a social practice cannot be approached without recourse to the first two: the narrative representation and its multilayered, mediated, interactional contexts. In subsequent chapters, I address the following areas of interest. First, through analysing the content of the shared story as a form of narrative representation, I ask:

Distributed linearity: What story content (events, participants, setting or evaluation) is entextualised? How is story content distributed between different textual segments?

Co-tellership: How are characters from the 'tale world' represented? Whose voices are heard, and how are their words quoted?

Intertextuality: What are the resources used to connect one text to another? What element of the story content has been recontextualised?

Shared meanings: What stereotypes are stated or invoked? What shared knowledge is presumed or presupposed?

At level 2, the analysis of the narrative interaction may address contextual questions about the characteristics of the shared story, such as:

Distributed linearity: How are the textual units of the story arranged within larger interactional exchanges?

Co-tellership: What positions do the shared story's co-tellers take up within the interaction?

Intertextuality: What is the provenance of the intertextual material? Where has it been used previously or re-used subsequently? What resemioticisation has occurred in the transformation of the recontextualised material?

Shared meanings: What are the community norms and rights associated with the narrative interactions? How are these evidenced through the interactions?

The third level of analysis explores the socio-cultural contexts and ideological implications of the shared story. From this perspective, the content of the story and its interactional context are not neutral, but are part of wider socio-cultural structures that privilege certain tellings and tellers whilst marginalising others. The four characteristics of the shared story may each relate to these broader concerns. This raises questions about the use of the shared story, such as:

Distributed linearity: How does the distribution of content privilege one version of events rather than another? What master narratives shape and are shaped by the selection and evaluation of content?

Co-tellership: What macro-social categories and stereotypes are invoked for tellers? How are in-groups and out-groups created between participants?

Intertextuality: What are the social meanings indexed through combining intertextual material? What shared knowledge is required to interpret the intertextuality? How far is this knowledge context-spanning or contextually specific?

Shared meanings: Whose interests does the shared story serve?

The multidimensional nature of the shared story also poses challenges for the ways in which the data are collected and prepared for analysis. As Bolander and Locher (2014) point out, there are four methodological issues that are brought to the fore in the study of computer-mediated communication: ethics, multimodal complexity, mixed methods and the development of Web-based corpora. These are all relevant to the research methods that I will use to examine shared stories.

I begin by explaining how I negotiated these concerns in relation to the methods of gathering data from social media sites (ethics and tools) and then explain the methods of analysis that help develop the model of shared stories from its qualitative roots in conversation analysis and move it towards a mixed-methods approach that can tackle the large-scale bodies of data that constitute the shared stories that emerge online.

Methods for Gathering Social Media Data: Ethics

The methods of gathering data for the study of shared stories told in online contexts must begin with considering the ethical implications of accessing, analysing and reproducing content from social media sources. Currently, there are no internationally agreed systems that govern the ethical decision-making for the linguistic analysis of online interactions. Different countries, institutions and disciplines operate a variety of guidelines and protocols that ensure that research is carried out without the risk of harm to those involved. Because of the diverse complexity of online materials and the research used to explore them, ethical decisions are often negotiated on a case-by-case basis, as overseen by particular authorities (such as an institution, funding body or research organisation). Given that mediated narrative analysis brings together methods that bridge different disciplines, it may be necessary to consult multiple guidelines to inform the process of gathering data. The ethical decisions that I made in determining how the data discussed in later chapters could be gathered, analysed and presented were guided by reports published by the Association of Internet Researchers (Markham and Buchanen, 2012) and by the British Association for Applied Linguistics (2016). One of the preliminary ethical issues raised in both reports concerns the researcher's access to the materials that they hope to analyse. Accessing such data includes deciding whether consent should be given (or not) by each person whose online materials have been observed, so as to respect their right to autonomy. There are a number of questions that a researcher might ask; for example, whether or not the data come from a site that is publicly available. If the data are publicly available, the participants may or may not orient to that site as a public context for interaction, and the subject matter may be 'sensitive' in some way. The focus of the research and the methods of analysis also influence the extent to which individual informed consent might be negotiated. In some cases, where very large numbers of participants are involved and where the research focus is not on the individual participants, but rather a collective perspective on the text (as in building a corpus of Web-based materials), the practicalities of gaining individual informed consent can be problematic.

The datasets in this book were selected from publicly available sites, where the interactions were clearly oriented to a public audience rather than a semi-private or private audience of known intimates. The subject matter deals with stories that gained high levels of public scrutiny across mainstream media (broadcast in news reports, documentaries, films), as well as social media sites and platforms. The content that was shared within social media was often recontextualised from other sources that were broadcast to the general public. The size of the data samples was very large. Thousands of participants contributed as co-tellers in the various case studies covered in the later chapters of this book. My analysis is concerned with the collective effects of co-tellership, not the close scrutiny of particular tellers and their personal identity. Indeed, in many of the cases, the participants' online identity carefully preserved their anonymity in ways that made it difficult to contact them. On these grounds, I did not seek informant consent from every individual whose words were part of the datasets compiled for the analysis. In order to offset the potential risks of exposing participants' identities, where the posts are not attributed to an individual or company with an established public identity, the user names were anonymised (along with other potentially identifying information), and images have not been reproduced, but are instead described. Where illustrative examples are included, wherever possible, I chose examples that were no longer 'searchable' via online search engines (that is, the post or comment could no longer be traced back to its original context of publication) or from accounts that were not maintained by individuals.

Gathering Data: Tools

The online contexts of shared stories offer the researcher opportunities to gather narrative content and context on an unprecedented scale. There are many automated tools and services that can be used to gather textual content and contextual metadata from online sites. These tools are constantly under development, and so although I list the examples I use here, I fully anticipate that in later years they will be superseded by others. In the future, there will no doubt be alternative tools and services which allow researchers to elicit or scrape online data in many different kinds of ways. The terms and conditions of individual sites that allow tools and services to work with their API (application program interface: the interface that allows developers to interact with the Web content of a particular site) also change. This means that the opportunities for researchers to gather data can fluctuate, as sites may open up or restrict their access over time. For example, in 2012, Twitter imposed restrictions on the ways that 'third parties' (including researchers) could work with its API, making it much more difficult at that time to build datasets of Twitter materials retrospectively. The extent to which data can be gathered retrospectively from a site also varies according to the timescales of that site's archives, for some sites make their archived material available for longer than others.

Further complexities arise from the fact that the tools that work for gathering data from one site may not work for another. The way data are presented once they are archived for analysis also can decontextualise certain aspects of the text and metadata from the original formats and contexts of interaction. In order to analyse the shared story from a mediated perspective, there is often considerable further preparatory work that must be undertaken before the researcher can begin analysis. For example, additional information about the interactional context may need to be sought out and appended to the dataset, or stored in a series of separate files (such as screenshots). It is possible to develop bespoke scraping tools that gather this multimodal content and archive it over time, but these are as yet in their infancy.

The dynamic nature of the online contexts in which shared stories are told poses further challenges for the researchers who gather these materials. Sites change their design and templates, or remove content from public view. Shared stories, as retellings, can be reproduced iteratively over long periods of time, meaning that the data collection may need to take place repeatedly in order to keep pace with changes. As with all research, the data collection of shared stories is inevitably partial. The shared stories in this book are no exception, and my discussion of them is best regarded as a chronologically limited snapshot, located at particular moments in which these stories emerged. Given the site-specific tools, archives and datasets that form the basis of my analysis of shared stories in Wikipedia, Facebook, Twitter and YouTube, the individual methods used for each case study are explained in relation to the chapters in which these datasets are discussed. However, for each dataset, the same combination of analytical tools was drawn together to interpret the data, which included corpus-assisted discourse analysis, social semiotics and interactional pragmatics. In the next three sections, I introduce each in turn.

Corpus Approaches: From Small Stories to Bigger Data

The shared stories that emerge in online contexts can become very large in scale, consisting of many thousands of interactions contributed by many thousands of tellers. This poses challenges for qualitative methods of narrative research, such as those found in discourse analytic traditions. For example, qualitative methods are well suited to the relatively small text-based interactions that small story research took as its primary object of scrutiny. The virtues of paying close attention to the content of the narratives needs to be retained when we turn to the stories told in social media contexts. However, in the data that I consider in this book, a purely qualitative approach based on manual scrutiny of the textual content is untenable. Instead, the mediated narrative analysis I propose combines qualitative examination of the shared story's dimensions with quantitative approaches as established in corpus approaches.

On first sight, the combination of small story research and corpus approaches might seem surprising, if not antithetical. Small story research set itself out as an analytic shift away from examining 'big' stretches of narrative data, with a commitment to paying attention to the less frequently occurring and often overlooked stories and their tellers. Corpus approaches seem to emphasise the opposite aspects of analysis. The composition of a corpus (as representative examples of a language variety available in electronic form: Sinclair, 2004) values large bodies of data, for the principles of corpus linguistics are quantitative: they count and then organise the lexical patterns in a given corpus according to frequency. As such, lexical patterns which occur with high frequency (rather than outliers) can be emphasised, and the items that occur less frequently might be easy to overlook. However, as I suggested in Chapter 1, not all stories that fall outside the prototypical patterns of narrative need be 'small' or 'small' in the same way. Given that shared stories emphasise commonly repeated elements, corpus approaches might be well suited to identifying lexical patterns that are 'shared' across different parts of the storytelling text.

Mediated narrative analysis contributes to the triangulation which combines corpus approaches with qualitative techniques of discourse analysis as a form of 'methodological synergy' (Baker et al., 2008; see also McEnery and Baker, 2015). Within this growing field, there has been particular interest in the use of corpus approaches and Critical Discourse Analysis which have examined news media (see, for example, Baker et al., 2013), although this has not yet considered the narrative nature of reports that are included with the studies. Instead, corpus approaches as applied to narrative texts are most well known in within literary-critical research traditions, particularly within corpus stylistics (see Mahlberg, 2016 for an introduction, and Toolan 2009, 2016 for extended examples of narrative analysis). Within sociolinguistic research, corpus-assisted approaches have also begun to emerge (Norrick, 2008) as tools for examining conversational narrative or archives of oral history (Salway and Herman, 2011). Given the relative ease with which online interactions can be compiled as large-scale principled data collections, there is an increasing recognition that corpus approaches have much to offer the discourse analytic study of the stories that are produced and consumed online.

Corpus linguistic techniques use concordancing software to automate analysis of the lexical content of electronic texts, and thus are well suited to the analysis of the narrative content (as opposed to its context). There are a range of concordancing tools available, which continue to be developed. Some are proprietary (such as Sketch Engine), whilst others are freely available. In this book, I use Antconc, the concordancing tool developed by Laurence Anthony (2014). My reasons for this are twofold. First, Antconc provided the range of functions that allowed me to examine the data in ways that were needed. Second, as a freeware tool, it allows the methods I use in this book to be replicated by scholars who may not have access to the concordancing tools that require payment of a licensing fee. My use of corpus approaches is in line with the 'corpus-driven' paradigm (Tognini-Bonelli, 2001), which starts with the examination of the relative frequencies of the lexical patterns in the data and moves from there to a close examination of the concordance lines and interactional context in which the lexical pattern occurs. I use the theoretical concept of 'keyness' most often to identify the lexical patterns that are of interest in the shared stories in this book. In corpus linguistics, keywords are identified quantitatively as the lexical items that occur with statistically greater frequency (or infrequency) in one corpus as compared with another (Bondi and Scott, 2010, p. 3). The keywords are often more interesting than the raw frequency of a given lexical pattern in relation to a single text, for keyword analysis allows the lexical signals of a particular topic or style to emerge in that text as compared to others in ways that may suggest the existence of a particular type of discourse or ideology (Baker, 2004). The keyword list and its concordance lines can provide a way of downscaling the data to those parts which can be given the close reading more typical of small story research. Whilst the use of quantitative criteria such as keyness might appear to provide an objective measure by which the downscaling of the data is selected, there are limitations to this kind of approach. The statistical measures by which keyness is calculated (which, in this case, used the Log Likelihood tests within Antconc) may exaggerate points of difference. The narrative nature of the shared story can also skew the types of lexical repetition that occur, for example, by over-emphasising the names of participants (Toolan 2016), in which case additional thresholds may need to be applied in order to offset the kind of lexical prominence. Following Baker (2004), I also applied other thresholds when selecting a cut-off point for the items on a keyword list that were used to select data for further analysis. This included comparison of the number of texts in which the keyword occurred (where the 'texts' consisted of tweets, comment threads and so on) and of the absolute frequency of the lexical items, along with their keyness. This is discussed in more detail in the chapters where these keywords are presented.

These decisions reflect the subjectivity with which corpus approaches are inflected. Using a corpus approach as part of mediated narrative analysis requires the researcher to consider a number of factors as they select and prepare the data for analysis. First, as with any corpus, if the analysis is required to be representative of a particular genre, the design needs to be principled. The researcher may choose to balance the size of the corpus in order to reflect wider patterns of production related to a particular genre. Thus, in the corpus-assisted analysis of the comments appended to YouTube videos about the former Paralympian, Oscar Pistorius in Chapter 11, I balanced the composition of the comments so that they reflected the relative proportion of the types of videos that were found about Oscar Pistorius in YouTube (which included news reports, sports coverage, comedies and music). Second, if the researcher wants to make use of a keyword search, they compare one corpus (called a specialised corpus) with another, larger corpus (the reference corpus). Because corpora derived from online data such as those found on social network sites are often highly specialised in subject matter (for example, as determined by the timeliness of public debate or events), they can be skewed in their lexical focus. Deciding on a suitable reference corpus can therefore sometimes be difficult. There are precedents for using reference corpora derived from offline materials. Examples include the British National Corpus, a 100 million-word corpus, comprising a range of spoken and written genres in British English, and the Corpus of Contemporary American English, comprising 520 million words of spoken and written genres. Generalised corpora of particular Web genres are beginning to emerge (a recent example being the Corpus of Online Registers of English: Biber et al., 2015), and no doubt will continue to do so long after this book is published. The basic principle when choosing a reference corpus is that there should be an appropriate comparison with the specialised corpus. Factors that may need to be considered include the language variety, the period of time over which the data was collected and the genre in which the narrative is embedded.

There are further complexities relating to the online form in which shared stories are told. As with any kind of digital material, the researcher needs to make decisions about how to 'clean' the data; for example, by removing metadata such as time-stamps or links, and by making other kinds of metadata (for example, hashtags) fully searchable by the concordancing tool that is used. Moreover, the characteristics of the shared story as a retelling make it likely that the corpora created to explore such stories will contain high levels of repetition. Corpus-based searches that place emphases on high-frequency lexical items are not always useful, especially where datasets contain high numbers of posts that have been reduplicated in some way (and so redound with frequency that is not meaningful). For example, extracting all the versions of a Wikipedia article from a page history and searching them using a concordancing tool is not the most helpful way to proceed: the reduplicated text that is produced when only small changes are made iteratively to the article can render the procedures of corpus linguistics somewhat limited. With other kinds of data in which reduplication occurs (such as retweets within a Twitter corpus), other choices need to be made about how to treat this (see Chapter 8).

Corpus approaches also decontextualise the content under analysis, and can strip out the interactional context – including the multimodal aspects, such as the images, video, interactive icons or linked content, that might be embedded within the co-text, templates or site design of a particular story. Whilst corpus approaches have much to offer as a principled way of moving into the qualitative analysis of the verbal aspects of the narration, they cannot account in full for other levels of the shared story, especially those which relate to its mediated contexts of production and reception. Corpus approaches need to be combined with other analytical frameworks, including those which are better suited to account for multimodal communication (such as social semiotics) and which take account of the implied meanings that underpin the construction of common ground (interactional pragmatics). It is to the first of these that I now turn.

Social Semiotics: Multimodal Approaches to Narrative Content and Context

The analysis of shared stories draws on frameworks from social semiotics in order to explore the multimodal range of resources that are involved in sharing as an act of telling and as an interactive process. A social semiotic approach, as its name suggests, sees language not as a decontextualised or abstract object, but rather as part of a larger semiotic system which is inextricably connected to its wider social contexts. The shared stories found in online contexts incorporate a range of semiotic resources, including verbal and visual elements which are used to tell the story and which shape the contexts in which tellers interact with the stories as they are (re)produced and consumed. The visual resources of the shared story can include a wide variety of materials, such as the following nonpictorial visual content:

- icons, such as the 'buttons' on social media sites,
- graphicons (Herring and Dainas, 2017), such as emojis,
- the template design and the images uploaded to social media sites, which can range from photographs to macros or other visual genres.

The extent to which these various visual resources contribute to the shared story can vary. In this introductory section, I explain how images as a form of visual resource are particularly important for the three aspects of 'sharing' as (re)telling in online contexts.

A central question for the semiotic analysis of shared stories is how far the images found in these stories can convey narrative content. The possibility that images might tell a story has been much debated in earlier literary-critical narrative research. The more flexible approach to narrative (see Chapter 1) allows us to move beyond past-tense narrative events reported in temporal sequence as a definition that would preclude many single images. However, as Ryan (2004, p. 15) points out, there is arguably no medium better than language for conveying narrative. This claim rests on the assumption that whilst verbal content can convey explicit narrative meaning effectively, visual representations tend to imply or infer the narrative meanings of action and reaction, or eventhood in time. The extent to which narrative meaning can be inferred from any given image rests on a number of factors, including those associated with narrativity more generally (see Chapter 1). This includes the type of content that is represented, such as whether the image is 'pregnant' with content that is 'easily connectable and narratively significant' (Ryan 2004, p. 141). Images with high narrativity might represent the participants involved in some kind of action, especially where the action implies some kind of 'trouble'. The narrativity of an image does not relate just to what is shown, but to also how it is shown, as indicated through the composition of the image. In social semiotics, the composition of images and their narrative potential was taken up by Kress and van Leeuwen (1996) in their work on visual grammar. They suggested that the 'vectors' created through the relative composition of participants could encode the kind of information often conveyed by verbal 'action verbs' (1996, p. 46), for example, by implying a trajectory along which a particular movement would occur. Whilst a helpful start point, the composition of single images can only take the analyst so far, especially given that in shared stories, images can appear in a sequence across the multiple textual elements of the story. Other visual aspects of the shared story may be important here, such as the ways in which the arrangement of the images within an archive encourages the interpretation of temporal order. As with comic books (McCloud, 1993), the reading patterns associated with particular social media sites can prompt interpretations of time frames and hence narrativity for the informed audience. For example, even a sequence of Facebook profile photographs can be 'read' with some degree of narrativity by an audience which recognises that the collection of images are organised by the time of upload and so represent a change over time. In these cases, the distributed linearity of the shared story across its multiple textual segments allows the images to 'share' the narrative content which is conveyed, either in successive images, or through images combined with verbal content, such as a caption.

The varying extent to which images represent narrative content may mean that the use of images and icons to 'tell a story' is ambiguous or open to interpretation. However, this affordance lends itself well to the flexible ways in which images can be recontextualised and so contribute to the intertextuality of the shared story. If an image is less tied to a specific narrative report of events, it can be more readily re-used in future tellings that recontextualise the event over time. Like the generic quality of many contemporary photographs (Machin, 2004), whilst images may not contain the linguistic specificity required to prompt higher perceptions of narrativity, they can carry symbolic meaning that is transferred, even when the image is recontextualised. The use of redistributed images in the shared story points to the intersubjective ways in which they create narrative meaning. The ability of the audience to recognise the image as an intertextual reference that is shared with its original context relies on factors that lie outside the image itself, some of which may be highly likely to be shared between members of the audience, others of which are not. The inherent plurality of interpretation means that images can be ambiguous (prompting many different interpretations of a story) or iconic (standing as a referent point to a recognised, familiar master narrative), depending on their context.

The images that are found in the shared story contribute to the narration that is shared between its multiple tellers. The multiple tellership of the visual content can include taking into account the persons involved in producing, reproducing and responding to the images. The images are not just resources for representation, but are also a resource for the co-tellers to use to position themselves relative to the image and to one another. In social semiotics, this reflects a difference between the ideational meaning of the images (the content which they represent) and the interpersonal meanings that can be conveyed. Social semiotic analyses consider the interpersonal meaning of images in a number of ways. In Kress and van Leeuwen's (1996) visual grammar, this includes the construction of social distance, where a close-up shot is interpreted as implying social meanings of intimacy, whilst a longer range shot might imply the opposite (1996, pp. 124–129). A separate interpersonal dimension of an image concerns how involvement is projected between the audience and the person represented. In this system, Kress and van Leeuwen (1996) make a distinction between images where the gaze of the represented person appears to directly address the viewing audience and those where it is directed elsewhere. In these cases, the assumption is that the more directly the gaze addresses the assumed viewer, the greater the involvement that is constructed. Third, the audience can be positioned relative to the person or object in the image with respect to the angle with which the camera represents them. A person or object can be viewed from the front, at the same level, from the side, from above or from below. Within this system, the perspective constructed in the image can be meaningful: for example, by suggesting social hierarchies, where the viewer is made to look down on or up to the represented object or person in question. More recently, Zappavigna (2016) and colleagues (Zappavigna and Zhao, 2017) have extended these systems of meaning by adding choices for interpersonal meaning that relate to subjectivity. The affordances of the cameras built into smartphones allow those producing photographic images choices about how to infer or imply their presence, so that the viewing audience is more or less positioned with the producer of the image.

These interpretations are, of course, highly subjective and are not the only options for interpreting the social positioning of the tellers. The multiplicity of the interpersonal meanings that can be construed from a given image can vary as much as the ideational interpretation of the narrative content. Perhaps because of this inherently open-ended affordance of the image to construct meanings that can be more or less shared, they are also important resources that prompt co-tellers to respond to one another. In this respect, they are similar to stance objects (Du Bois, 2007) where the tellers can use their evaluation and interpretation of the image to position their responses relative to others within the same interactive context (such as a comment thread responding to a Facebook post).

Social semiotics offers a second important contribution to the nexus of mediated narrative analysis. Its analytic perspective can be applied not only to the content of the shared story, but also to the contexts in which shared stories are (re)produced and consumed. As such, this marks an important point of departure from discourse analytic traditions of narrative research, where for the most part the narrative interaction is rather less easy to observe, or focused on a particular mode of communication (such as speech or gesture, which is then transcribed in the analysis of interviews or conversational data). The shared stories found in online contexts offer researchers the opportunity to observe narrative interaction in mediated contexts that are open to scrutiny and are more permanent than offline forms of audience observation, and which involve multimodal factors that have been relatively less well discussed in relation to narrative theory, such as the design of templates, layout and archives.

A social semiotic approach to shared stories takes into account the multi-layered nature of context. This builds on the contextual analysis of the offline antecedents of shared stories, such as the close attention paid to the localised co-texts which shape conversational contexts (Duranti and Goodwin, 1992), or the priority that Critical Discourse Analysis places on the meso-level factors of textual production and reception (Reisigl and Wodak, 2001) and on work in mediated discourse (Jones, 2005), which recognises the ways in which online practices are embedded in physical situations that in turn create imagined interactional contexts in which the participants are positioned. In my earlier work on stories in social media (Page, 2012a, pp. 14–15), I argued that these aspects of context were part of the narrative dimension of embeddedness that reshaped the possibilities for online storytelling. The social semiotic analysis of the online contexts of the shared story in particular takes this contextualised approach further, in two ways. First, the multimodal nature of the contextual layers is explored more fully. Second, the social semiotic approach foregrounds the question of how multimodal context helps construct ideological meaning. The layers of context which are important for the shared story expand those given in my earlier work to include:

The co-text: the localised contexts in which the narrative is embedded, including the structural organisation of the text into larger discourse units (such as turns in an exchange, speech acts or episodes within a longer narrative sequence).

The formats for interaction: the layout, templates, threads, architectures and algorithms that organise the content posted to a particular site or platform and the relative permanence of the content.

The contextual metadata: the information appended to the uploaded content, which may be more or less visible, but is often accessible within the archives of social media data.

The generic context: the purpose of the site or platform, its status as public or private, its terms and conditions, its rules for conduct and stated purpose.

The behavioural context: the physical setting in which a person accesses and interacts with the social media materials, such as the time, place and technological devices involved.

The interdiscursive context: the relationship between the text and its intertextual predecessors.

The socio-cultural context: the broader social, cultural and political contexts in which the interaction takes place.

Multimodality is important for understanding each of the different layers of context. For example, analysis of the co-text does not just include verbal content, but also considers how the different semiotic resources (such as images, emojis and other kinds of visual resources) within the co-text relate to one another. The site format is itself a multimodal composition, where the layout and architecture use particular visual and spatial resources that present some content as the default view, whilst organising other material so that it requires a person to make further interaction in order to view or change it. For example, the timelines of Twitter and Facebook present updates in a reverse chronological sequence. The site format can also shape the options for co-textual combinations of multimodal content. In some instances, images and video can be embedded directly within a post or comment, but in others, the multimodal content may be hosted on an external site to which the post is linked (such as an image on Instagram which is shared via Twitter). Templates may integrate words, icons and resources which participants can use to respond to a story, including the ubiquitous 'sharing' button, or icons such as Twitter's 'favourite' button and Facebook's and YouTube's 'like' options.

The generic context may also influence the choice of multimodal content by setting terms and conditions for the use of resources like images, music and sound. For example, copyright restrictions which govern particular countries influence which audio-visual material can be uploaded legally to YouTube, and Wikipedia's image use policy sets out what kinds of visual content can be used and how it should be incorporated within an article. The purpose of the site may also shape the ways in which multimodal content is recontextualised. For example, proprietary sites like iTunes may require a person to pay for the content they download. Beyond the contexts observed on the screen, the behavioural context includes the factors in the offline world that may shape the ways in which participants interact with different kinds of multimodal content. For example, social television practices typically draw together viewers, who watch the same broadcast content in geographically remote locations, but at the same time. These behavioural contexts can then be entextualised in forms such as the metadata that marks the tweet as being posted at a particular time or as an image which displays the viewer's location and activity whilst watching the television programme. Similarly, the interdiscursive context, as 'the intertextual . . . relationship of the respective speech event to other relevant events' (Wodak, 2007, p. 211), can be realised in many multimodal forms that resemioticise one text into another, and which may be mediated in more or less tractable ways.

Most importantly, a social semiotic approach does not interpret any of these contextual resources as abstract, but rather sees them as socially meaningful and as the means by which broader socio-political meanings can be construed. The relationship between the observable forms of the semiotic content and context and their social meanings is never straightforward. It would be naïve to assume that particular patterns of use carry unequivocal social meanings that can give rise to particular ideological interpretations, such that one group of tellers might be more 'powerful' than others. An ongoing challenge for social semiotics is how to move between the analysis of the text and the discussion of the socio-cultural processes in which the text is produced. A remaining element in the analytical toolkit for mediated narrative analysis is required: one which examines the connection between the interactional context and its wider social meaning.

Interactional Pragmatics: The Relational Work of Sharing

Interactional pragmatics is the last of the analytical frameworks combined in the nexus of mediated narrative analysis used within this book. Like social semiotics, interactional pragmatics also takes a contextualised approach to language in use, but rather than focusing on broad, ideological aspects of the context, it considers how the social norms for narrative interaction might operate, and what these might suggest about the relationship between the tellers of shared stories. Despite the extensive body of scholarship emerging from interactional pragmatics in the field of politeness, there has been little cross-over of this work with narrative research. This is perhaps all the more surprising given that there are parallels in the analysis of (im)politeness and narrative vis-à-vis their shared interest in the interactional construction of identity (Georgakopoulou, 2013b, p. 56). Interactional pragmatics, and the study of politeness in particular, makes an important contribution to the analysis of shared stories by providing a bridge between the second and third levels of analysis of the shared story: the interactions between the tellers and the social outcomes of sharing at an individual and cultural level. 'Sharing' as a form of narrative interaction is not simply a matter of clicking an icon on a screen, such as the 'share' button; it is a social practice, which implies a certain set of relational outcomes, such as options to align more or less closely with other tellers, and to create, maintain or threaten rapport. These topics have been developed extensively in the field of politeness research.

The field of politeness emerged from Brown and Levinson's (1987) landmark study in which they set out a series of linguistic strategies that speakers might use in order to smooth communication and avoid conflict (see Eelen, 2001, p. 21 for a summary of work that shares this emphasis). Although Brown and Levinson's work was field-shaping, it has also been subject to critique, for example, for imposing a universalised set of categories that are used to minimise conflict, and for emphasising the resources that speakers use to avoid offence rather than taking into account the range of strategies that they might use for the opposite effect (Locher and Watts, 2005, p. 11). In order to avoid the connotations that 'politeness' as a field of study is limited only to the range of interpersonal strategies that avoid conflict, Locher and Watts (2008, p. 96) propose the term 'relational work' instead, to encompass '*all* aspects of the work invested by individuals in the construction, maintenance, reproduction and transformation of interpersonal relationships among those engaged in social practice' (my emphasis). Similarly, in this book, I recognise the full range of relational work that is achieved through shared stories. The frameworks from interactional pragmatics bring to light the ways in which sharing may or may not be harmonious, and result in many kinds of relational work.

In order to account for the variation in relational work, other scholars have proposed different labels in place of the term 'politeness'. For example, Spencer-Oatey (2002, 2005, 2007) uses the term 'rapport' to cover 'the (dis)harmony or smoothness-turbulence in relationships' (2007, p. 647). However, relational work and rapport are not synonymous. Relational work concerns the interpersonal actions and practices in which individuals engage, whilst rapport is one of the social outcomes which emerge from it. The evaluation of the interactions as smooth or turbulent, inappropriate or impolite is highly subjective. As such, scholars have begun to avoid assuming that any linguistic feature can always be interpreted as resulting in a particular rapport outcome, such as the offence which results from impoliteness. Instead, evidence of the relational disharmony is interpreted from the participants' own judgements, as found in the surrounding co-text and comments, which can include explicit meta-language, such as evaluations that language is 'rude' or 'disrespectful', or other nonverbal responses (such as gestures, facial expressions and so on that might indicate a negative evaluation).

This close attention to the relational work as evidenced from the interactional context helps bring to light a second important aspect of shared stories: the social norms that shape the interaction. In this way, politeness research provides us with an analytical lens through which to think about the third meaning of 'sharing' as a macro-social notion of 'familiar, common ground'. Eelen (2001) describes this as 'sharedness', or the contextual knowledge about the norms for communication that are accepted by a particular group or culture. One of the reasons that sharing can be more or less harmonious is that the shared norms for interaction are implied, rather than explicitly codified. Eelen (2001, p. 243) goes on to argue that whilst sharedness is regarded as a fundamental requirement for politeness, it is extraordinarily difficult to pin down, where 'in the end, sharedness remains an a-priori assumption rather than observed fact'. Like the third level of 'shared stories' and its macro-social meanings, the contextual assumptions of 'sharedness' in pragmatics often are extra-textual in nature, and can only be recovered by a process of interpreting the 'observed' evidence of the interactions in which the participants are involved.

It is not only the norms for communication that can make shared stories difficult to interpret. The stories that are shared can also convey their content more or less explicitly. This principle is explained by a central concept within pragmatics and politeness, namely that speakers are not limited to construing literal meanings as they interpret utterances (which, in this book, can be taken to include the full multimodal range of resources used to convey narrative content). The philosopher Grice (1975) developed this concept in his theory of implicatures, where he made a distinction between the content which is expressed literally and the meanings which are hinted at or suggested. Grice suggested that implicatures could be interpreted in a principled way, relative to shared norms of interaction (Haugh, 2015, p. 58), which he called the 'co-operative principle'. Grice's (1975, pp. 45–47) co-operative principles include those of quantity (saying too much or not enough), quality (trying to make your contribution one that is true: 1975, p. 46), manner (aiming for clarity rather than ambiguity) and relation (being relevant). A full overview of the ways in which his ideas have been developed in pragmatics is beyond the scope of this book (see Haugh, 2015 for a recent introduction). However, the extent to which these principles function as norms for narrating shared stories is a matter that is explored in the later chapters.

Implicatures are particularly important for the analysis of shared stories, for several reasons. First, they allow us to analyse the many, often indirect ways in which meanings can be conveyed through narrative interactions. Second, the indirectness of the implicatures points to the vulnerability of 'sharing' and the possibility that shared meanings can be misunderstood or disrupted. Third, the indirectness of implicatures means that the analysis of the story cannot consider the surface meaning of the content in isolation. The interpretation of the story content has to be understood in context, and where the shared knowledge implied by the implicatures can give rise to a range of relational work between the tellers. The risky potential for implicatures to give rise to competing interpretations of a text has been particularly important in the developing frameworks of (im)politeness. Scholars such as Culpeper (2011) and Haugh (2015) use the concept of implicatures to explain how content that does not appear on the surface to be offensive might result in evaluations of offence. Conversely, content that appears highly offensive may be treated by the participants as appropriate and rapport-enhancing. Given the indirectness of implicatures and the contextually determined but usually unstated norms used to interpret the relational work of the utterance, it is possible for the same interaction to generate multiple relational outcomes, which are shared by some tellers and not by others. Sharing is clearly a complicated process, with interpersonal outcomes that do not straightforwardly result in the homophily that the surface meaning of 'sharing' might presuppose. Instead, it requires careful scrutiny of the stories that are told, the interactive context and the resulting relational work between the tellers.

The Shared Stories Analysed in This Book

The nexus approach of mediated narrative analysis is brought to bear on four case studies which illustrate sharing practices in different social media sites and platforms: an analysis of the 'Murder of Meredith Kercher' article in the English and Italian Wikipedias, the online mourning on Facebook community pages in response to the deaths of the landmark political leaders Nelson Mandela and Margaret Thatcher, social television practices on Twitter that responded to the international franchise *The X Factor* and the YouTube coverage of Oscar Pistorius from his time as a Paralympian athlete who represented South Africa to his controversial trial for the murder of Reeva Steenkamp. These case studies were selected so as to incorporate a varying semiotic range of the resources used in story telling and its contexts of production. At one end of the spectrum, Wikipedia articles tend to emphasise written contributions, with images and sound files playing a subordinate role. At the other, YouTube is a video-sharing site and so necessarily revolves around the audio-visual content uploaded to its archive. In between these two end points, the social network sites Facebook and Twitter allow their members to create posts and comments which contain verbal content alongside images and links to other websites.

The sites also differ in terms of their policies that regulate the social norms for sharing. Wikipedia has extensive guidelines for the contributions and conduct that take place within the site. The norms for interaction are heavily ratified, and enforced by a sizeable community of volunteers. In Facebook and Twitter, the norms for interaction are managed locally by the owners of particular pages or accounts, and are overseen by the commercial organisations which own each site. Although YouTube similarly is governed by site-specific terms and conditions, the interactions which take place in the comment threads are notoriously 'noisy', playful and strongly affective. These social media sites were chosen for their contrasting ethoses. Wikipedia is a not-for-profit project, which maintains an open, democratic support for consensus. YouTube is owned by Google and offers its participants the opportunity to generate economic benefit from sharing content and generating interaction with the site. Once again, Facebook and Twitter occupy mid-points on this scale, where the use of the sites can be harnessed for the political or socio-economic gain of particular groups or individuals who become members.

The case studies emphasise the different ways in which sharing is a collective endeavour, but one which can be used for different purposes that result in complex outcomes. The analysis of the Wikipedia articles shows how selective the narration of shared stories can become, so that even in the most democratic of online contexts, the representation of certain participants can be favoured to the detriment of others. The analysis of the Facebook community pages shows how sharing can be used to polarise tellers into competing groups. The social television practices on Twitter suggest that sharing is implicated in a double logic which simultaneously empowers and exploits the tellers who participate. The responses to the YouTube coverage of Oscar Pistorius suggest that, on the one hand, the site design can be used to promote the interests of mainstream media producers, whilst on the other, commenters can subvert the affordances of the site so as to make the interactions meaningless. Together, the four case studies provide contrasting datasets which illustrate the forms that sharing takes, showing how the interactions are contextually shaped by these online sites and the complex social meanings that sharing can create in our contemporary communicative landscape.

Conclusion

In this chapter, I have set out the model and methods that are used to analyse shared stories. As a form of mediated narrative analysis, I take a nexus approach which draws together a combination of methods that have not yet been brought to bear on narrative data, but which are essential for the study of shared stories. Corpus-assisted discourse analysis allows the researcher to tackle large datasets that can be compiled using semi-automated tools to extract interactions from online contexts. Social semiotics provides a multimodal perspective on the resources used for sharing as a form of narration and on the mediated contexts in which the shared stories are (re)produced and consumed. Interactional pragmatics brings analytical focus to the relational work that is negotiated between tellers and opens up the possibility that sharing can be ambiguous, misunderstood or disrupted. These methods confirm the importance of a contextualised, multidimensional approach to narrative analysis that has been nascent in discourse analytic research, extending this contextualisation with reference to the multifaceted – and in many cases, tractable – forms of narrative interaction that are observable in online contexts.

Although this combination of tools was selected for its capacity to provide analytic lines of inquiry through the online forms of the shared story that are the focus of this book, it is also highly appropriate for mediated narrative analysis of other kinds of storytelling, such as those produced in the news, television or other forms of broadcast talk. As multimodal archives containing stories of many kinds continue to be developed, the importance of a nexus approach to narrative analysis should not be underestimated. Nor is mediated narrative analysis limited to the combination of corpus-assisted and social semiotic methods used in this book. A nexus approach is in its very nature flexible and open-ended, and can be adapted according to the various contexts in which storytelling of many kinds may be mediated.

3 Stories in Wikipedia Articles: Is Sharing Ever Neutral?

Introduction

In this chapter, I examine Wikipedia as a site for shared stories. Wikipedia is not usually thought of in terms of its narrative potential, yet stories abound in the articles and discussion pages that constitute the site. The analysis presented in this chapter is the first to identify how the narrative dimensions of Wikipedia's stories are shaped by the mediated contexts of the site; how stories in Wikipedia change over time and across cultural contexts. In line with the nexus approach of mediated narrative analysis, I use a combination of Critical Discourse Analysis and corpus-assisted discourse analysis to explore the patterns of representation in the reported events (the tale world of the shared story) in selected Wikipedia articles. The analysis focuses on a particular article as a case study, the 'Murder of Meredith Kercher'. I focus on two aspects of the shared story: its linearity and intertextuality. The analysis of these aspects is important, for they point to the ideological influences that shape the content in this article, and in Wikipedia more generally. Despite the core content policies of Wikipedia, which promote the notion of neutrality, the stories told in the articles may privilege one version of events rather than another and are shaped within wider socio-cultural patterns that reinforce difference along the lines of gender and national identity. The chapter contributes to a critical re-evaluation of Wikipedia, which shows that sharing is never neutral but is shaped by the mediated contexts in which stories are told.

Wikipedia as a Site for Shared Stories

The online encyclopaedia, Wikipedia, was launched by Jimmy Wales in 2001. In its first decade, Wikipedia expanded into a large-scale, multilingual project. Currently, there are nearly 300 language versions of Wikipedia, containing many millions of articles (Wikipedia Contributors, 2014a). In the last decade, Wikipedia has consistently ranked within the top ten most visited websites globally (Alexa.com), and has become one of the main resources for those searching for information on the Internet. Of all the social media contexts considered in this book, Wikipedia most closely characterises the aspirational aspects of 'sharing' in its participatory culture. As Stein (2013) points out, in contrast to other social media sites like YouTube and Facebook, the openness and participation of Wikipedia are reflected in the terms and conditions which frame the site and in the processes of democratic consensus which characterise the practices and philosophy of the project (Firer-Blaess and Fuchs, 2014). Anyone with access to Wikipedia via the Internet can become a volunteer and participate in creating the content of articles and in the governance of Wikipedia. This openness is reflected in the medium factors which characterise Wikipedia as a site for shared stories.

Wikipedia is an asynchronous environment, where the contributors who create and discuss articles are remote from one another in time and geographical space. Unlike a print encyclopaedia, where this process takes place in semi-private spaces and is not directly observable in the finished product, Wikipedia is a transparent environment, where the articles and the process by which those articles are created are publicly available in the archives of the site. These archives are sizeable: there is no technological limit on the length of a Wikipedia article or on the size of the discussion forums on the site. The archives are persistent and replicable, beginning with material in 2002 and continuing to accrue on an ongoing basis at the present time of writing. Although wiki technology was 'designed for manipulating text' in its verbal form (Viégas, 2007, p. 2), the Wikipedia archives are multimodal. Written text can be accompanied by illustrative images (held in a central repository known as the Wikimedia Commons) and sound files. The affordances of wiki technology are important for understanding the content contained within Wikipedia's archives, for every time a page is updated, its previous version is saved in the page history.

The archives of Wikipedia are structured as distinct multimodal areas with templates and layout according to their purpose: the articles, the user pages, the talk pages and community resources. These archives provide different contexts in which shared stories can be embedded. I make a broad distinction between the pages of Wikipedia, where editors can work together to create the content of particular shared stories (as they are constructed within a given article), and the areas within the site where they discuss the process of creating that text (the article talk pages, user talk pages and dispute forums). The distinction between the narrative content depicted in the tale world of the article and the interactive context of the narration in the telling world is represented in Table 3.1. As Van Dijck (2013, pp. 151–152) points out, these two 'layers' of Wikipedia are positioned within its archive strategically, so that the article front page as a 'visible layer of consensus' is promoted relative to the 'invisible yet accessible layer of discussion and a heterogeneous interpretation of the history and edit pages'. My analysis of the shared story interrogates both the visible and the 'invisible but accessible' areas within Wikipedia's archives. I begin with the

Table 3.1 *The Wikipedia archive as a context for shared stories*

Archive space	Article front page	Article page history	Article talk pages	User talk pages and their history	Dispute fora
Narrative level	Tale world (which contains reported events relevant to the article's topic)		Telling world of the narration (which reports the process of the article's creation)		

reported events as narrated in an article, and its comparative retellings available in the article's page history.

In order to understand how shared stories are told in Wikipedia, it is necessary to understand not only the architecture but also the norms for interaction that shape Wikipedia as a community. Co-ordinating the co-creation of an article in Wikipedia is complex. Deciding what material should be shared and negotiating how sharing might take place is fraught with the potential for disagreement and dispute. In order to manage this complexity, Wikipedia's community has developed many collective practices guided by core content policies, which include Neutral Point of View (NPOV), No Original Research (NOR) and Verifiability. These principles are important points of reference for interpreting the selection of content, intertextuality and co-tellership within Wikipedia, and so will be described in detail. In Wikipedia, editors cannot simply add their personal knowledge or opinions to an article. Wikipedia's editors do not see themselves as directly producing knowledge, but rather as reflecting the current views or representations of events (Bruns, 2008, p. 114). The principle of NOR states that content can only be added if it is substantiated by a reliable source. Wikipedia articles thus cannot take the form of a personal narrative of experience, nor a single authored biography or account of events. Instead, the content developed in Wikipedia articles relies on the synthesis of information from other sources. Intertextuality is a crucial aspect of the shared stories in Wikipedian articles, for, as the policy for Verifiability says,

> [Wikipedian] content is determined by previously published information rather than the beliefs or experiences of its editors. Even if you're sure something is true, it must be verifiable before you can add it. (Wikipedia Contributors (2017b))

Wikipedia's editors are responsible for the selection and use (rather than the authorship) of these reliable sources. However, not all sources will agree. Where there are conflicting versions of events that might be included in an article, Wikipedia's principle of NPOV is invoked. NPOV governs the selection, representation and balance of cited material, and states that,

> Editing from a **neutral point of view** (**NPOV**) means representing fairly, proportionately, and, as far as possible, without bias, all of the significant views that have been published by reliable sources on a topic. (Wikipedia Contributors, 2015a, emphasis in the original)

Of course, as Myers (2010, p. 147) points out, 'neutrality' is impossible to achieve in terms of freedom from bias. All knowledge is produced within particular social, cultural and historical contexts. The extent to which Wikipedia's editors comply with the three core content policies is open to variation. The articles which emerge can be vulnerable to selective representation, favouring one point of view rather than another. This selective representation may occur in any Wikipedia article and can be traced through comparative analysis of the content within a given article and its previous versions, but it is perhaps most evident in articles that deal with controversial topics.

Data and Methods: The 'Murder of Meredith Kercher' Article

Wikipedia contains many articles which are considered controversial (Yasseri et al., 2012). This includes crimes which remain unresolved, or where convictions have been later overturned. The following analysis focuses on one recent crime which has been highly controversial and has drawn international media attention on a significant scale. Meredith Kercher was a British student who was murdered in Perugia, Italy on 1 November 2007. The suspects accused of the crime were Amanda Knox (an American student who shared a flat with the victim), Raffaele Sollecito (Knox's Italian boyfriend at the time of the crime) and Rudy Guede (from Côte d'Ivoire, but resident in Italy from childhood). The crime became sensationalised in the media from the outset, with a suggested backdrop of sex games, drugs and even occult practices (Liddle, 2011). However, the key controversy centred on the guilt or innocence of the suspects, in particular Knox and Sollecito. All three suspects were convicted of murder and sexual violence in 2009. However, Knox and Sollecito always maintained their innocence, and in 2011, both were acquitted and released from prison. In 2013, the Italian Supreme Court granted the prosecution the right to appeal the acquittals. Knox and Sollecito were re-tried, and in January 2014 were found guilty of murder and sentenced once again. Finally, in March 2015, Knox and Sollecito were exonerated by the Supreme Court. Despite the definitive judgement, the highly mediatised nature of the case means that debates about the perceived guilt of the key protagonists are likely to remain unresolved (Clifford 2014, p. 506).

As a high-profile shared story that has evolved over many years, there is no single account of the crime and its aftermath. The multiple narratives that surround the 'Murder of Meredith Kercher' are complex. At one level, there are accounts of the murder narrated by the suspects. Each suspect's narrative differed from that given by the others, and Knox made allegations against a fourth suspect (Patrick Lumumba), which were later dismissed as slander. Knox and Sollecito also gave multiple, contradictory accounts of the night of the murder (later explained in the light of memory loss caused by taking drugs), and withdrew material which had initially been submitted to the police. Guede also changed his account once imprisoned. Beyond this, the media reports of the crime and later convictions varied considerably. The media's controversy focused most prominently on the guilt or innocence of Knox, with opposing sides differentiated according to national context (Annunziato, 2011). In Europe, the media frequently demonised Knox as the guilty party, painting her as a femme fatale whose alleged behaviour after the murder and under interrogation appeared out of keeping with that expected from an innocent witness. In North America, the media coverage tended instead to be sympathetic to Knox, argued for her innocence and presented her as a victim of the negative coverage she had suffered in the Italian media and the treatment she had received from the Italian police and legal system.

The contrasting narratives of Knox as guilty villain or innocent victim drew on powerful master narratives of race and gender. The negative treatment of Knox made much of her alleged sexual activity. In this schema, female sexual behaviour was treated as the subject of surveillance and suspicion. In contrast, and at least in part as response, the European media representation of Knox was considered by some an example of anti-Americanism. Over the years, the dominant narratives told by media reports (in the United Kingdom, at least) have shifted as new evidence has come to light, and the stance towards Knox has changed accordingly. The media narratives told about the Kercher case neatly exemplify the relative and dynamic positioning of shared stories. The national context (American, British or Italian) determines which version of events was positioned as dominant, and the positioning was subject to change over time.

There was considerable social media discussion of the Kercher case, and of the trials which have followed. There are websites, forums and Facebook pages where the pro-innocence and pro-guilt supporters of Knox and Sollecito gathered over the years to argue their points of view. Amongst these social media sites, the Wikipedia article about the 'Murder of Meredith Kercher' was from the outset a battleground between opposing groups who attempted to co-construct the story of the crime and its aftermath. The struggle to construct a coherent article which balanced the multiple versions of the stories surrounding the Kercher case is particularly marked in the English Wikipedia, but there are also versions in the German, Persian, Finnish, French, Italian, Japanese, Polish, Russian and Simple English versions of the site. The discussion in this chapter compares two of these: the versions in the English Wikipedia and the Italian Wikipedia.

The article in the English Wikipedia was first authored on 13 November 2007, and between that point and the final exoneration was edited over 9000 times by over 1000 distinct editors. The content of the article and the behaviour of the editors were the subject of considerable controversy. The arguments reached such proportions that, in 2010, the page was completely deleted and rewritten after a petition claimed that European editors were suppressing the inclusion of material which supported Knox's innocence. The article for the 'Omicidio di Meredith Kercher', available in the Italian Wikipedia, was first authored on 29 October 2008. Between that date and the final exoneration of Knox and Sollecito, it was edited over 1000 times by over 300 distinct editors. Unlike the version in the English Wikipedia, the Italian article was not subject to complete deletion, although it might be considered contentious in other ways.

To analyse the content of every revision made to the English and Italian 'Murder of Meredith Kercher' articles to date is beyond the scope of this chapter; the content of the page history for the English Wikipedia version of the article alone exceeds the length of this book. Instead, in the analysis of the article and its page history, I provide a selective overview of the article over time, based on five versions from the English Wikipedia and five from the Italian. The versions selected come from one month after each of the key events in the unfolding case: the crime itself (November 2007), the first convictions of Knox and Sollecito (December 2009), their acquittal (October 2011), their second conviction (January 2014) and their final exoneration (March 2015). As the Italian version of the article was not created until 2008, the first version sampled for analysis was taken from one month after the article was first authored. In the following sections, these selected versions of the article are analysed in relation to level 1 of the shared story, focusing on the content that was included in the article in terms of its linearity and intertextuality. Drawing on Critical Discourse Analysis, I concentrate on the selective representation of the events and the participants, particularly using the analysis of transitivity and reported speech to explore the relative blame that was associated with the different suspects involved in the case.

Linearity

Wikipedia articles are inherently open-ended, insofar as they are always open to revision. In terms of content, individual versions can also selectively arrange events in such a way as to imply a single, unified plot or to represent alternative storylines. The versions archived in the page history for the 'Murder of Meredith Kercher' within the English and Italian Wikipedias varied in terms of the material that was included in each version and the ways in which that material was arranged to imply a final outcome for the reported events. A comparison of

Table 3.2 *A summary of the Table of Contents from selected versions of the 'Murder of Meredith Kercher' article in the English and Italian Wikipedias*

	English Wikipedia article			Italian Wikipedia article		
Date	Number of sections	Closing subsection	Biography for suspects	Number of sections	Closing subsection	Biography for suspects
December 2007 (crime)	8	'Tributes'	None	6	'Suspects'	None
January 2010 (first conviction)	23	'Media Coverage'	Guede, Knox, Sollecito	6	'Suspects'	None
November 2011 (first acquittal)	45	'Support for Knox and Sollecito'	Knox, Sollecito, Guede	13	'Movies'	None
February 2014 (second conviction)	32	'New Trial'	Guede	18	'Books'	None
27 April 2015 (exoneration)	33	'Exoneration'	Guede	40	'Influence in Mass Culture'	Sollecito, Knox, Guede

the narratives and their sequential arrangement indicates how little the articles shared in terms of a common narrative. An overview of the articles is indicated by the Table of Contents for each version in question, which are summarised in Table 3.2.

At a first glance, the differences between these versions seem to result from the articles' expansion to include subsequent events as reported in additional subsections. However, in these versions of the 'Murder of Meredith Kercher' article, the selection of the additional events varied, and differed in stance towards the figures in the English and the Italian articles over time.

In the Italian Wikipedia, sections added to the article presented Knox in a negative light, such as the 'Secondo processo ad Amanda Knox per calunnia' (Second Trial of Amanda Knox for Slander), in which Knox's claims of maltreatment by the Italian police were thrown into question, and in which she was convicted for slander against Lumumba. From 2011, the closing sections of the Italian article did not focus on the final outcome of the trials, but instead listed the media coverage of the crime, so that the conclusion to the article did not emphasise the legal ruling but rather the case's ongoing media legacy. In the English Wikipedia, the content added in each version varied more widely in its stance towards the suspects, especially in the content that closed the article. In 2010 and 2011, the versions of the article closed by emphasising reactions to the legal outcomes rather than events of the crime or trial. In both cases, the evaluation of Knox was polarised. In the version from 2010 (after Knox and Sollecito's initial convictions), the final section, 'Media Coverage', recontextualised the sexualised news representation of Knox. However, after Knox and Sollecito's first acquittal in 2011, this content was replaced with a section entitled 'Support for Knox and Sollecito', emphasising instead their innocence and documenting criticism of the original trial.

By 2014, after the second reconviction, the information about support for Knox and Sollecito was removed and the article ended with a section that focused on the most recent outcome of the legal proceedings. Within the main body of the article, other subheadings returned to events which presented Knox in a controversial light, such as her self-incrimination and her role in the wrongful involvement of Lumumba. These subsections remained in place until after the final exoneration in March 2015, when the article also closed with the most recent legal event, which by that point in time was the final ruling that cleared Sollecito and Knox of murder charges. The difference in the linearity of the articles shows how the events were selected to emphasise different aspects of the crime and its aftermath. These choices bring into question how far the Wikipedia policy of NPOV was sustained in the article. In order to explore the variation in narrative representation further, a specific subset of the articles' content is considered more closely: the biographical stories that were told about each of the suspects.

Biographical Stories of the Suspects

The biographical stories about the suspects found in the Wikipedia articles are optional content, which contextualises the persons involved in the main events and functions as a form of personalisation. Like the personalisation found in news media reports, these stories foreground the identity of particular people at the expense of reporting events or political issues (Machin and Mayr, 2013). Where the events have moral implications, the selective nature of the biographical narratives is particularly important in constructing social narratives of appropriate or inappropriate conduct. The relative presence or absence of a suspect's biography within the article is therefore an indication of the extent to which they were implicated within moral narratives of judgement. The biographical narratives for the three suspects are not present evenly throughout the history of the articles. In the English Wikipedia article, biographical accounts appeared for the three main suspects in the versions from 2010 and 2011, but after 2014 only the biographical account of Guede remained. Conversely, in the Italian Wikipedia article, biographical accounts were only added after the exoneration of Knox and Sollecito in 2015. The content of the stories varied according to the suspect whose biography was given, the version of Wikipedia

Table 3.3 *Biographical stories, by word length, in selected versions of the 'Murder of Meredith Kercher' article*

	Year	'Guede'	'Knox'	'Sollecito'
English Wikipedia	2007	0	0	0
	2010	130	69	61
	2011	513	230	82
	2014	286	0	0
	2015	311	0	0
Italian Wikipedia	2015	343	82	98

being looked at (English or Italian) and the date of the article. A summary of the word length for the biographical stories is given in Table 3.3.

A comparison of the lengths of the biographical narratives suggests some initial differences between the representations of the figures, where the biography of some suspects was given greater space than the biography of others. Guede's story is the longest: more or less twice the length of the other suspects' stories in all versions of the article. In contrast, in the English Wikipedia, when Sollecito's biography is narrated, it is always the shortest of the three, and is always presented last, whilst in the Italian Wikipedia, it appears first in the sequence of biographical accounts. The representation of Knox also varied, particularly between the English Wikipedia versions in 2010 and 2011. The representation of the suspect whose guilt was not legally contested (Guede) remained the most consistent across all versions of the article. The personalisation of the suspects through the inclusion of their biography thus varies in line with the moral judgements afforded to them, where the suspect whose guilt was uncontested (at least in the legal rulings) was presented at the greatest length in the Wikipedia articles.

The ways in which the suspects are represented as social actors (van Leeuwen, 2008) suggests further differences in how these biographical accounts implied moral positioning. In the English Wikipedia article, the stories about each suspect represented them using classification categories such as their age at the time of the crime and their nationality. Additional characteristics, such as their relational identity (their status within personal networks) and how they were functionalised (represented in terms of their actions or occupation), varied in ways that constructed differing narratives of class and gender. In 2010, after the first conviction of Knox and Sollecito, the background stories of all three suspects made reference to their parents. Guede's personal history includes his immigration to Italy and provides details of 'his father, Pacome Roger Guédé, who worked as a labourer in the 1990s' and his later adoption by 'wealthy local businessman, Paolo Caparali'. The description of Sollecito as 'from an affluent family... the son of a urologist from Bari' similarly includes the occupation of his parents, and hence his family's implied economic status. However, when Knox's parents are mentioned, there is no indication of their occupation (which might position her family within a particular socio-economic group), but instead they are described in relation to their marital status: a couple 'who divorced when she was two'. In contrast, whilst Knox's personal history is the most truncated in this English version of the article (at only sixty-nine words long), her evaluation by third parties is the longest. In the biographical background stories, Guede and Knox were appraised in quotations from external sources. In the 2010 version of the article, Guede was characterised as a 'tremendous liar' in a two-word quotation attributed to his adoptive father. The appraisal of Knox appears in two longer quotations which repeat her demonisation current in the mainstream media at the time: she is described as having 'the face of an angel but the eyes of a killer' and as 'that most-loved of villains – the middle-class monster whose appearance hides a diabolical soul'.

In the version of the article current one month after the first acquittal of Knox and Sollecito (2011), the details included in these biographical narratives changed. In the subsequent, longer account of Guede's personal history, more detail was given of his criminal history in order to report events which paralleled notable features of the crime and so reinforced an interpretation of the verdict where he alone was responsible for Kercher's death. In contrast, the changes to Knox's biographical background no longer cast her in a negative light and instead emphasised a narrative of her innocence. More details of her family were given, including her sisters' names and her parents' occupations, which were functionalised as a 'teacher' and 'vice-president of finance'. Her education in a 'Jesuit-run school' and achievements of 'making the Dean's list' positioned her within a framework of educated, middle-class success and normality. In line with this change in stance, the quotations used to evaluate Knox following her acquittal contrasted sharply with the sensationalised interpretations at the time of her first conviction. Instead of media quotes demonising her, her friends were quoted, describing her as engaged in healthy, domestic pursuits, 'as energetic, athletic, and kind, a pacifist hippie who loved making cakes and jam, doing yoga, playing soccer and guitar, rock climbing and cycling'. Unlike the preceding versions of the article in 2007 and 2009, this wholesome representation of Knox's early life was given greater precedence in the textual organisation of the version current after her acquittal, being positioned first in the sequence of biographical stories, before the accounts of Sollecito and Guede. The optimistic narration of Knox's personal history was not to remain in the article, however. Shortly after the second conviction of Knox and Sollecito in 2014, the structure was changed. The largely unmodified version of Guede's incriminating history was returned to its more prominent position of first in the introductions to the suspects, with Knox's and Sollecito's accounts of the events merged together. The biographies of Knox and Sollecito were removed and remained absent from the article after their exoneration.

The addition of the biographical narratives to the Italian article after the exoneration of Knox and Sollecito in 2015 adds further complexity to this picture. Until the exoneration, the selected content of the Italian article suggested a negative stance towards Knox. It is perhaps surprising, then, that there are no biographical narratives in the earlier versions of the article, as these are a resource for implying moral judgement, as is evident in the English version. However, the relative absence of the personalisation in the Italian versions is perhaps explained by an examination of the source material which the contributors used in the service of complying with Wikipedia's principle of Verifiability. This is analysed in the next section, which considers the intertextuality of the articles as a resource for ideological positioning.

Intertextuality

The stories included in a Wikipedia article must be negotiated carefully between contributors, who use Wikipedia's policy of Verifiability in order to justify their editorial choices. The story content of a Wikipedia article is determined by its intertextuality in the form of cited sources. The kinds of materials that can be cited as source material must be carefully negotiated in line with Wikipedia's purpose as an encyclopaedia. Wikipedia's guidelines for Identifying Reliable Sources advise the use of source material produced with editorial oversight, such as 'university level text books, books published by respected publishing houses, magazines, journals and mainstream newspapers'. However, as this list indicates, these sources can be more or less overtly positioned in terms of their ideological stance. The definition of what counts as 'reliable' from a Wikipedian point of view acknowledges the inevitable partiality of material, saying, 'reliable sources are not required to be neutral, unbiased or objective' (Wikipedia Contributors, 2014b). The citations are thus a potent conduit for the macro-social master narratives from particular socio-historical contexts to shape the content and emphasis of a Wikipedia article.

The 'Murder of Meredith Kercher' article in the English and Italian Wikipedias contained a number of citations. A quantitative summary of the total citations in the selected versions of the page history of the 'Murder of Meredith Kercher' articles is given in Table 3.4. In the English and Italian versions of the article, a small proportion of the citations were from the trial transcripts or academic books on legal matters. In contrast, 95 percent were from mainstream news sources or books about the case published by journalists. The intertextuality of Wikipedia articles is symptomatic of wider media convergence, where the dominant narratives that circulate in the mainstream news media are

Table 3.4 *Number of citations in selected versions of the 'Murder of Meredith Kercher' article in the English and Italian Wikipedias*

Date of version	English Wikipedia	Italian Wikipedia
1 December 2007	26	18
4 January 2010	101	18
3 November 2011	169	19
27 February 2014	193	20
27 April 2015	202	110

reproduced through citation of those reports. Given that the dominant narrative of Knox's guilt or innocence depended on the news values relative to the national context of the media reports used for citations, this posed a particular dilemma for the editors of the article. As one contributor said,

> We can all find reliable sources to back up our personal biases. The challenge is to try to *avoid* doing that and instead keep the article faithful to what you would get if you could put all reliable sources into a blender and then distill [sic] the result down to encyclopedic length.

The extent to which the balance in the selected citations was maintained or not, and hence the extent to which the innocence or guilt of the suspects was positioned, can be traced through analysis of the citations in each version of the article, in terms of the nationality of the publication and the representation of the suspects in the cited source.

Analysis of the Citations

A comparison of the citations based on the date of the news publication from all the selected versions of the article considered here showed that most of the intertextual materials date from the period between 2007 and 2011, which is to be expected, given that six of the versions of the article also date from that period. However, it is notable that the publication dates of the citations are not evenly dispersed across that period of time. The cited sources are taken most often from the years in which the most newsworthy events in the timeline occurred: 18 percent were published in the year of the crime itself (2007), 24 percent in the year in which the first convictions occurred (2009) and 31 percent in the year in which Knox and Sollecito were acquitted (2011). When the publications are disaggregated by the nationality of the publication outlet, further differences over time emerge. The majority of the British sources (which position Knox as guilty) date from 2007–09, the period running up to the first

Table 3.5 *Names in news reports, by nationality of news source, calculated to a relative frequency per million words*

Name	British news publications	American news publications	Italian news publications
Kercher	15 634	611	18 018
Knox	15 192	21 808	13 514
Sollecito	1327	0	13 795
Guede	2360	0	11 543

conviction. In contrast, the majority of the American sources (which position Knox as innocent) date from 2010–13, the period in which her alleged guilt was contested. The frequency of publications from Italian sources is different, once again. The majority of citations from Italian news outlets were published in 2015, after Knox and Sollecito were finally exonerated.

Further differences emerge when the citations are disaggregated according to the versions of the article in which they occurred. In the English Wikipedia, the majority of citations were from British news sources in all except for the version revised one month after the acquittal of Knox and Sollecito in December 2011. The relative proportion of citations according to their national publication shifted at this point so that 71 percent of the cited sources were from an American context. In contrast, in the Italian Wikipedia, American sources were used rarely, only occurring in the versions dated after Knox and Sollecito's acquittal, and then in the minority (as 5 percent of the citations in each article or less). In the Italian Wikipedia article, Italian citations only began to dominate after the second conviction of Knox and Sollecito in 2014. Until that point, most of the citations were from British publications dating from before 2009.

The differences in the news publications used for citations are important because of the relative news values that were assigned to Knox and Sollecito in different national contexts. The relative news values of the four figures were compared by quantifying the relative frequency (per million words) with which their names (occurring as first name, surname, first name + surname) occurred in a dataset comprising the citations compiled for each of the selected versions of the article. This is summarised in Table 3.5. As the results indicate, the suspects were mentioned most frequently in the publications that corresponded to their nationality, where Knox is named more often in the American news than in the British or Italian publications and Sollecito is named more often in the Italian publications than in the British or American news. This suggests that the representation of the suspects used in the citations was driven in part by the news value of proximity. The results also suggest that the news value of proximity intersects with master narratives of gender. Of the three suspects, Knox is the most frequently mentioned in both British and American sources. Even in British publications, the relative frequency of her name outranked the names of the male suspects, with a ratio of 7:1 in the case of Guede and 11:1 in the case of Sollecito. It seems that the news value of negativity is shaped by gendered asymmetry: discourses of female criminality appear more newsworthy than those invoked in relation to the male figures in the examples of the British press coverage of this case. In the American news sources, the male suspects are of even less interest: they are not mentioned by name in any of the headlines cited.

The differences in the positioning of Knox in relation to the master narratives of 'trouble' played out in the news sources are evident in the analysis of the lexico-grammatical patterning in the different news headlines. As a starting point, I analysed the headlines in which Knox was mentioned by name in terms of the relative agency with which she was represented. The choice of whether to activate or passivate (van Leeuwen, 2008) a participant's representation is realised according to the transitivity role (Halliday, 1994) in which they are cast. For each of the headlines where it was possible to infer a process and participant, I counted the number of times in which Knox was represented as the do-er (the actor, senser or sayer) versus the the done-to participant (the goal), or was characterised using an attributive verb and complement. Based on this analysis, she was represented in the most agentive role (the actor) twice as often in the headlines from British news sources (17 percent of all the participant roles, N = 24) as she was in the headlines from the American news sources (8 percent of all the participant roles, N = 12). In contrast, in the American news headlines, the representation tended to emphasise Knox's position as the done-to participant, where she was represented in the passivated role of goal in 21 percent of all participant roles (N = 30). In the British news headlines, the activated representation of Knox clearly aligned with a meta-narrative of deviant behaviour, which sexualised female criminality:

Amanda Knox wrote stories about rape (*Daily Telegraph*, 7 November 2007)

Amanda Knox tries to ban 'prurient' book on her love life (*The Times*, 13 January 2009)

Amanda Knox did cartwheels and splits at police station after Meredith Kercher murder (*Daily Telegraph*, 27 February 2009)

These sexualised narratives of Knox's behaviour most notoriously named her in the tabloid press using the nickname 'Foxy Knoxy':

Foxy Knoxy: Inside the twisted world of murdered Meredith's flatmate (*Daily Mail*, 6 November 2007)

Murder suspect 'Foxy Knoxy' spends Christmas in an Italian jail 'singing carols and watching Kung Fu Panda film' (*Daily Mail*, 25 December 2008)

The naming choice 'Foxy Knoxy' occurred in 7 percent of the British news headlines used as citations in the selected articles, but never in the American news reports. Instead, the sexualised representation of Knox was almost entirely absent in the cited American publications, referred to only once in a report which was used as a citation to verify Wikipedia's content about the convicted suspect, Rudy Guede. In contrast, the passivated representation of Knox in the American headlines emphasised a narrative where Knox was cast as the wronged victim:

Amanda Knox: Italian Civil Court awards Knox $55,000 in damages for violation of privacy (*ABC News*, 22 March 2010)

Amanda Knox's grueling day: Called 'She devil,' shown roommate's wounds (*ABC News*, 26 September 2011)

The representation of the two male suspects contrasted with the representation of Knox in terms of the relative balance between activation and passivation. In both cases, Sollecito and Guede tended to be passivated, and their agency was downplayed. Sollecito was not activated in any of the headlines from British news reports. In the Italian news reports, he was passivated in 61 percent of the roles and activated in only 26 percent. Where he was represented in an agentive role, none of the processes implied any sexualised behaviour, but rather emphasised the reclamation of his innocence:

Raffaele Sollecito ai giornalisti: «Non chiamatemi mai più assassino» (*Corrier dela Sera*, 30 March 2015)

Similarly, Guede was passivated over twice as often as he was activated in the British and Italian news headlines used as source material in the Wikipedia articles. Where he was represented in an agentive role, this implied his guilt, but in a monstrous rather than sexualised manner:

Rudy Guede: engaging drifter who boasted 'I will drink your blood' (*The Times*, 28 October 2008)

Intertextuality and Reported Speech

Lastly, the analysis of the quotations from the source material in the Wikipedia articles indicates further, gendered differences in the ways that the suspects were presented. Citations in a Wikipedia article can recontextualise content from their sources either indirectly (for example, paraphrased or summarised) or directly (as a quotation). The intertextuality of the article in terms of the micro-level choices of whether to quote material using reported speech is another key indication of ideological positioning. In Wikipedia, the use of reported speech can indicate that the subject matter is controversial. Wikipedia's (Wikipedia Contributors, 2014c) guidelines for quotation say, 'Editors of controversial subject should quote the actual spoken or written words to refer to the most controversial ideas'. More generally, Caldas-Coulthard (1992, p. 76) points out that the heightened vividness and ability to verify the words reported in direct speech can be used by news reporters to 'reiterate and reinforce their primary discourse'. The primary discourse as indicated by the use of quotation in the Wikipedia articles for the 'Murder of Meredith Kercher' placed Amanda Knox at the heart of the controversy. Her words accounted for 35 and 31 percent, respectively, of all reported speech in the versions of the English and Italian articles considered here. Other people were quoted less often: the other suspects only once each, with the remaining quotations attributed to the police, judges, legal personnel, witnesses and journalists. The reported speech associated with Knox also contrasts with that of the other quotations, in that Knox's words were used to retell some of the reported events, whilst other people's were used more often to provide evaluation of those events.

The attention to Knox's reported words is perhaps unsurprising, as in both the police investigation and the media coverage, the inconsistencies in her testimony were treated with suspicion. Changing a statement can suggest that a witness is unreliable. When that witness is accused of a crime, retelling events in a different way can be interpreted as a signal of guilt. Similarly, although different parts of Knox's statements, testimony and reports were quoted in different versions of the articles, these quotations often signalled occasions when her words were subject to misinterpretation, or offered as evidence of her instability. It is no surprise to find that the version of the article which is most strongly aligned with a meta-narrative of her innocence (one month after Knox's acquittal in 2011) also contains the least reported speech (only 2 percent of the article), and that the version where her words occur most prominently (11 percent of the article) occurred following the crime in 2007.

In the Italian versions of the article prior to 2015, there were no instances of reported speech that supported a narrative of Knox's innocence. Only after the exoneration of Knox and Sollecito does any reported speech portray Knox in a positive light, when her letter to the Foundazione Italiane USA (written in 2011, but only included in the Wikipedia article in 2015) was quoted to express her gratitude for Italian support. In contrast, in all the previous versions of the article in the Italian Wikipedia analysed here, the words attributed to Knox were associated with her guilt. In particular, the article quoted from a text message she had sent to Lumumba on the night of the murder. This message was significant particularly in an Italian context, as Knox's words were the subject of misinterpretation when translated into Italian and led to the slander of the Italian bar owner, who later was awarded damages for his alleged involvement in the crime. Knox's conviction for slander is also significant, as within the Italian Wikipedia article this was strongly associated with her guilt for the murder. The text of the article makes this clear, referring to 'dal nesso incontrovertibile tra la calunnia per la quale la Knox è stata definitivamente condannata e l'omicidio' (the indisputable link between the calumny Knox was found guilty of and the murder).

In the English versions of the article, the reported speech attributed to Knox was similarly associated with her guilt, or at least her instability as a narrator. In the 2007 version of the article, the lengthiest instance of her reported speech was foregrounded in an inlaid template and consisted of a 150-word extract, directly quoted from the statement which placed her at the scene of the crime. She went on to withdraw this statement, but it was later presented as the grounds for her conviction for slander. Sollecito also retold the events of 1 November in multiple statements to the police, but in the Wikipedia article these retellings are not quoted directly, but only summarised as a brief narrative report: 'He has changed his recollection of the evening.' The primary discourse at the time of the crime was clearly one in which Knox's unreliability (although not Sollecito's) was made the main focus.

The later versions of the article in the English Wikipedia show how the quotations from Knox's speech were repeatedly recontextualised. In the version available after her acquittal in 2011, Knox's retracted witness statement was recontextualised as evidence of her victimised role. The quotation from the statement in the later version was less prominent, reduced from 157 to 36 words and embedded in a longer portion of testimony taken from her trial, in which she qualified the instability of her account on the grounds of psychological pressure caused during police interrogation. The dominant narrative of Knox's innocence and role as victim was reinforced by other quotations in the 2011 version of the article, such as the report by the appeal judges 'that the statements she made incriminating herself during interrogation were evidence of her confusion while under "great psychological pressure"'. However, in line with the shifting away from a narrative of Knox's innocence and return to one where her instability was deemed suspicious, in the version of the article current after Knox's reconviction in 2014, these references to her retracted statement were no longer included.

Knox's words provide the closing point for the version of the article in the English Wikipedia one month after her exoneration in 2015. As observed in the analysis of the narrative structure, the English Wikipedia article concluded with sections that documented the final legal outcomes of the eight-year trial. Within the concluding section, citations drew on multiple American news reports, including a statement to the press in which Knox was quoted as saying, 'The knowledge of my innocence has given me strength in the darkest times of this ordeal'. However, alongside this declaration of her innocence, the use of direct speech to characterise Knox as an unreliable narrator persisted. Although no longer currently present in the article, in 2015, the final sentences returned once again to reiterate the controversial statement that Knox made about the crime and for which she was convicted of slander.

Conclusion

The analysis of the stories in this Wikipedia article showed that sharing as a form of telling is not neutral. Instead, some versions of events are promoted, whilst others are not. The analysis of the multiple stories narrated in the 'Murder of Meredith Kercher' article suggested a contrast between the different versions that appeared over time in the English and Italian Wikipedias. The differences in these versions reflect the relative dominance of narratives that positioned particular suspects as more or less guilty over time and according to national context. Whilst some narratives stayed relatively stable as a shared story (such as Guede's guilt), the narrative of Knox's innocence (or her guilt) was volatile, most notably in relation to the English Wikipedia during the period between her first conviction and her first acquittal. In part, this volatility is related to the journalistic nature of the intertextuality that was used in the service of Wikipedia's core policy of Verifiability, where the news value of negativity particularly shaped Knox's representation in the British press in line with the sexualisation of female criminality. The importance of intertextuality as a source of ideological positioning is not limited to this article, but has relevance to the multilingual diversity of Wikipedia more generally.

The differences that can be traced in the narratives produced within these Wikipedia articles (evident in the biographical stories, the representation of agency, the balance of citations and the reported speech) suggest that the policy of NPOV is idealised. In practice, neutrality is impossible to achieve. In Wikipedia, the policy of Verifiability locates the ideological nature of an article's content within the reliable sources that are the conduit for representing events, people and places in a particular light. Given that reliable sources include the mainstream news, we should expect to see representational differences within Wikipedia that are rooted in the news values of various national and political contexts. This is true for the 'Murder of Meredith Kercher' articles, but is also applicable to Wikipedia more generally. Given the continued frequent use of Wikipedia as a source of information, supported by its congruence with Google search engines (Van Dijck, 2013), the importance of developing a critical understanding of the site's relationship with the mainstream news and thereby questioning its potential for 'neutrality' cannot be underestimated.

4 Co-tellership in the Context of Wikipedia Talk Pages

Introduction

In Chapter 3, I questioned how far sharing could be seen as a neutral endeavour, using the changing narrative representations of the suspects in the 'Murder of Meredith Kercher' article in the English and Italian Wikipedias as a case study. The analysis of the participants within the 'tale world' of the articles showed how shared stories could become a site of struggle. Instead of narrating a single, unified version of events, the Wikipedia articles contained multiple versions of them. Rather than following the core content policy of Neutral Point of View (NPOV), these multiple versions were not represented equally. Instead, some were presented at greater length than others, more prominently than others or in ways that promoted the guilt or innocence attributed to one suspect rather than another. In this chapter, I continue to focus on Wikipedia as a site for shared stories. However, I move from the analysis of the shared story's tale world as represented within the article to consider the 'telling world' of the narrators and their interactions with one another. In this way, I move from the first level to the second level of the shared story.

In this chapter, I continue to question how far sharing can be equal, focusing on the relative balance of co-tellership activities as documented on the talk pages of Wikipedia. The analysis of the co-tellers and their contributions to Wikipedia is important for narrative scholars, for it brings to light under-explored, sensitive narrative practices, such as removing the contributions of another teller. More broadly, my analysis of the co-tellership practices critiques the notion of Wikipedia as a democratic project. I argue that the construction of Wikipedia as separable from its wider socio-cultural contexts is an idealised notion, for when co-tellers tackle controversial topics, such as the 'Murder of Meredith Kercher', socio-cultural tensions can emerge, where the contributions of some tellers can be suppressed by others.

The exploration of the co-tellership of Wikipedia articles takes a contextual approach to analysing the narrative practices documented on the talk pages of the 'Murder of Meredith Kercher' article. First, I explain how the co-tellership rights for the tellers who contribute to Wikipedia (the editors) are shaped by the core conduct policies of the site. Second, I use a quantitative comparison of the editors' interactions with the 'Murder of Meredith Kercher' article to question whether some editors contributed more than others. Third, I examine how intertextuality functioned as an important ideological resource. Following the nexus approach of mediated narrative analysis, I combine corpus approaches with qualitative discourse analysis of the 'Murder of Meredith Kercher' talk pages to show how debates about reliable sources were used to position the tellers in antagonistic debates. Finally, I argue that the Wikipedian practice of reverting was central to the tensions between the editors, and was used by the editors to index the wider socio-cultural debate about the Kercher case that was played out along national lines of difference.

Core Conduct Policies: The Representation and Responsibilities of Co-tellers

Wikipedia is a collaborative project which necessarily involves the contributions of multiple tellers, who, as editors, co-construct articles. The Wikipedia community has developed a number of policies that shape the representation, roles and responsibilities of its editors. These policies fall into two main categories (Wikipedia Contributors, 2015b): core content policies (which include Neutral Point of View (NPOV), No Original Research (NOR) and Verifiability) and core conduct policies (which include Civility, Consensus, Edit Warring and User Name Policy). Both sets are important for understanding how co-tellership operates in this context.

The core content policies shape the rights and responsibilities of the editors. As discussed in Chapter 3, the articles created in Wikipedia are inherently intertextual, for under the policies of NOR and Verifiability, editors must synthesise content produced by reliable sources, rather than reproducing source material that they have authored elsewhere. Authors of cited sources are usually prohibited from directly generating the text of a Wikipedia article. Self-published sources are not allowed, in line with Wikipedia's policy of NOR. On the one hand, then, authors of cited material are necessary as the sources used for Verifiability, but on the other, they are precluded from actively contributing to an article directly. The core content policies also influence the stance that co-tellers can express. Editors who reproduce cited material are supposedly neutral: they should comply with Wikipedia's policies for neutral and nonpersonal contribution. Authors of cited sources are under no such constraints.

The core conduct policies shape how the identities of the co-tellers are represented, particularly as set out in the guidelines for User Names in Wikipedia. When an editor sets up a profile within Wikipedia, they have relative freedom about how they choose to represent their identity. They can create a user name which is pseudonymous or which reflects their 'real name'. However, in the guidance offered to Wikipedia editors, to incorporate their personal information in their user name is presented as risky, and likely to attract 'harassment'. In line with this, to disclose a Wikipedia editor's offline identity is considered unacceptable, and a form of 'personal attack' that is precluded within the conduct guidelines. As a result, within the talk pages, the editors tend to emphasise their activities and expertise within Wikipedia's community rather than any personal information that might identify them in the outside world.

The rights and responsibilities of the editors as they interact with one another on the talk pages are shaped by Wikipedia's conduct policy of Civility, which includes a number of suggestions that shape how co-narration might be shared successfully. First, the policy of Civility recognises that differences of opinion between editors are inevitable in the context of collaboration. Disagreements in talk pages are not unexpected, and may not be dispreferred. Instead, the purpose of the disagreements is framed with the expectation that they will result in consensus between editors and a balanced synthesis of different perspectives within the article. Second, the guidelines for Civility govern how discussions and disagreements should be expressed. From a Wikipedian perspective, the language used on talk pages must be 'polite', avoiding 'direct rudeness' such as insults. As part of the guidelines to 'be polite', editors must avoid personal attacks; this is expressed broadly as the imperative to focus a disagreement as a comment on the content of an article, not on the contributor or the editor's identity.

In summary, the core conduct and core content policies shape the rights and representation of editors as co-tellers within Wikipedia. Together, the lack of emphasis on an individual teller's offline identity (seen in the User Name Policy and No Personal Attacks) and the emphasis on consensus as an ideal model for decision-making promote the democratic aspirations of the community. From this perspective, sharing is ideally characterised as impartial in the creation of content and the ways in which tellers relate to one another. In order to maintain this idealised impartiality, the core conduct and content policies mean that the tellership rights of Wikipedia editors as co-tellers are quite different from those that have been observed in the conversational or journalistic antecedents of the shared story, where personal experience and authenticity are valued as entitlement claims and where the corresponding narrative production might function to depict the identity of the individual narrator. In Wikipedia, the entitlement rights of the tellers downplay the editor's identity outside the site. In so doing, the tellership rights project an idealised separation between the representation and roles of the tellers within the context of Wikipedia and the wider socio-cultural contexts in which the tellers are also positioned.

Frequency of Contributions: Are All Tellers Equal?

In line with its democratic nature, Wikipedia characterises itself as operating with a 'very flat hierarchy'. In principle, anyone with access to the Internet can edit the pages of Wikipedia, even if they do not create a profile in the site. Any person who interacts with the site in this way is considered as an editor. 'Editing' can involve adding, altering or removing content from an article. However, there are asymmetries between the tellers as editors in terms of how often they interact with an article. Like many other kinds of shared story, the co-tellership of Wikipedia articles is not evenly distributed, as some editors may contribute more often than do others by making changes to an article. The community of volunteers who support Wikimedia has developed a number of tools, providing considerable amounts of quantitative data which measure how often a site member has interacted with Wikipedia. At the time of writing, the 'Murder of Meredith Kercher' articles in the English and Italian Wikipedias are linked to a revision statistics tool developed at the Wikimedia Labs. This tool itemises the number of edits per user over time, making it possible to compare the frequencies with which editors contributed to the English and Italian 'Murder of Meredith Kercher' articles.

A quantitative comparison generated using the revision statistics tool of Wikimedia Labs shows that the editors who created the English and Italian versions of the article did not share the activity evenly. Instead, in the English version, 81 percent of all edits (a total of over 9000 edits at the time of writing) were generated by the top 10 percent of the editors. The distribution of participation in the Italian version was also asymmetrical, with one editor responsible for making 33 percent of edits. The revision statistics tool itemises the thirty most frequent contributors to any given article by user name, and links to the editor's profile within Wikipedia (known as their User Page). Based on this information, the most frequent contributors to the English and Italian 'Murder of Meredith Kercher' articles appear to be more or less distinct communities, with only two editors in common during the period 2007–15. In line with the guidelines for representing an editor's identity, the editors listed as the 'top editors' did not always provide personal information on their User Pages. However, some contributors did include information about their national identity, for example, by stating explicitly that they originated 'from London' or 'ma sona nato a Roma'. Other contributors used Wikipedia's categories to indicate their national identity, for example, by using templates to identify that 'This user lives in England' or that they were an 'Utente Veneti'. Based on this profile information, of the contributors to the Italian 'Omicidio di Meredith Kercher' article who disclosed their national identity, one was from England and all others were from Italy.

The national identities of the editors of the English-language 'Murder of Meredith Kercher' varied more widely, including editors who self-identified as

American or as British. The national identity of the editors is important for the English-language article because the pro-innocence and pro-guilt debate that centred on the evaluation of Amanda Knox (see Chapter 3) was often differentiated according to nationality. In this stereotypical contrast, a pro-innocence stance was associated with American editors and a pro-guilt stance with European – and, more specifically, British – editors. Of course, the stance taken by individual editors cannot be mapped unequivocally on to their self-disclosed national identity. However, the indexical relationship between nationality and a pro-innocence or pro-guilt stance was inferred by editors who used this association to argue that the neutrality of the article was disrupted by those in the opposite camp.

Comparing the editors' activity quantitatively is therefore important, because it indicates the extent to which certain tellers were more centrally involved in creating the article as compared with others. When the known nationality of the editors is taken into account, ten of the thirty most frequent editors of the English-language 'Murder of Meredith Kercher' article were American, five were British and the remaining fifteen did not disclose their national identity. More importantly, the majority of the American editors who were listed amongst the top thirty contributors to the article contributed most often during 2011 (the period in which Knox's innocence was debated in relation to the acquittal process, and in which the representation of Knox in the article shifted most strongly towards a pro-innocence stance, using American news sources) and then ceased contributing by the end of that year. In this case, the pattern that emerges suggests that the most frequent contributions from the American editors co-occurred with the period in which Knox was represented most favourably in the English Wikipedia article, and in which the majority of citations were from American news sources. After 2011, the representation of Knox changed to become more ambivalent and the frequency of the interactions from this group of American editors decreased. This generalised picture can only take us so far, and does not describe the interactions of the individual editors in detail. In order to examine more fully how the editors positioned their identities relative to their interactions with the article, their interactions with one another and the broader socio-cultural contexts that shaped perspectives on the 'Murder of Meredith Kercher' article, we must turn to the stories that the editors told on the article's talk pages.

Data and Methods: Exploring the Stories in the Talk Pages

As a context for shared stories, the talk pages contrast with the articles of Wikipedia in their purpose and structure. Talk pages exist as a forum in which to discuss improvements to an article, not to discuss the topic of the article itself. There is no chronological architecture to structure the talk pages, but instead discussions between the editors are organised as threads in which conversation-like exchanges emerged. Within these conversational threads, the stories told entextualise the process of narration (reporting on the editors' previous or potential narrative actions) and recontextualise content from the article in order to discuss how that content might be further developed.

Both the English and the Italian Wikipedia had talk pages which functioned as forums allowing the editors to discuss the 'Murder of Meredith Kercher' and the 'Omicidio di Meredith Kercher' articles. However, the talk pages for the two articles were very different in size. There were relatively few interactions to be observed in the talk pages for the Italian article. The single archive for its forum totalled 1045 words, consisting of eleven threads, of which ten did not include any replies. In comparison, the talk pages for the English Wikipedia article were extensive, consisting of 752 threads and 9169 replies, totalling 762 815 words. The size of these talk pages is advantageous, for they provide many examples of stories where the editors debated the co-creation of the article. However, it also prohibits manual analysis of the posts in their entirety. In the discussion that follows, the analysis of the talk pages draws on corpus-assisted discourse analysis. In order to prepare the talk pages for analysis, the metadata appended to each post (including the time-stamp and the user name or signature) were removed so as not to distort any keyword comparisons. Any remaining references to editors' names or to dates are those that are contained in the main body of the post to the talk page itself (for example, as a format-tying resource of addressivity, or the date given for a cited source).

I used corpus methods to explore the talk pages in both inductive and deductive ways. First, I used keyword analysis to identify the most prominent topics discussed in the forum threads, and second, I searched for lexical terms associated with a particularly controversial type of narrative action, in which one editor removes the text written by another (known in Wikipedia as a 'revert'). In both cases, the corpus methods were used to identify particular posts within the forum threads where the search terms in question appeared. These posts were then analysed in their interactional context in order to assess how far the participants aligned with or distanced themselves from one another.

Reliable Sources as Keywords

In order to identify the distinctive lexical focus of the 'Murder of Meredith Kercher' talk pages, I generated a keyword list in Antconc, using the 100 million-word British National Corpus as a reference corpus. Given that the talk pages were written posts structured as quasi-conversational exchanges between the editors, both the written and spoken sections of the British National

Table 4.1 *Top thirty keywords from the 'Murder of Meredith Kercher' talk pages as compared with the British National Corpus*

Rank	Raw frequency	Keyness	Word
1	4175	37 502.24	knox
2	5509	36 007.47	article
3	1513	14 378.52	guede
4	1584	13 034.1	amanda
5	1345	12 781.96	sollecito
6	1205	11 451.5	kercher
7	1157	10 995.34	wikipedia
8	2066	10 380.72	trial
9	1154	10 173.6	wp
10	1856	8934.335	sources
11	928	8819.077	ledrush
12	1614	7890.578	murder
13	1839	7803.661	source
14	1061	6042.55	reliable
15	1261	5869.11	italian
16	612	5816.029	formerip
17	591	5616.46	bluewave
18	772	5179.708	editors
19	1614	5129.183	april
20	530	5036.758	npov
21	15 916	4988.849	that
22	498	4732.651	mignini
23	669	4720.897	edit
24	14 784	4707.135	is
25	498	4676.676	blp
26	11 709	4555.233	i
27	479	4552.088	wikid
28	703	4381.031	meredith
29	2300	4363.68	case
30	1466	4212.582	march

Corpus were included in the reference corpus. The first thirty keywords in this list are given in Table 4.1. The thirty most frequently overused words in the talk pages included, unsurprisingly, lexical words related to the topic of the article, such as the names of the persons involved in the crime (*Knox*, *Sollecito*, *Guede*, *Kercher*, *Amanda*, *Meredith*, *Mignini*), the topic of the article (*trial*, *murder*, *Italian*, *case*), the names of some of the editors (*Ledrush*, *FormerIP*, *Bluewave*) and words related to Wikipedia (*article*, *source*, *sources*, *Wikipedia*, *reliable*, *npov*, *blp*, *edit*, *editors*). Given that the article reported the narrative of the crime and its aftermath, and that narratives typically over-represent the names of the participants (see Toolan, 2016), the analysis of the keywords relating to the figures in the trial is not the focus for discussion here. Instead, I focus on the keywords relating to Wikipedia and how these reflect the use of core policies by the editors.

Having disregarded the names of people, the first and most frequent keyword was *article*. The overuse of this word points to the main function of the talk pages: namely, to discuss improvements to the article, 'not general discussion of the article's *subject*' (Wikipedia Contributors, 2017a, my emphasis). It can also be explained by the various uses of the word by the editors to refer to both the Wikipedia articles and the source material (such as 'news articles'). In order to test how far the overuse of *article* was typical of Wikipedia talk pages more generally, I generated a second keyword list, using a specialised reference corpus of Wikipedia talk pages (in size, 1 173 919 words). The first thirty items on the keyword list for the talk pages of the 'Murder of Meredith Kercher' article as compared to this specialised corpus are given in Table 4.2. Words relating to the crime and the trial account for the majority of the items on this list (which now also include *appeal*, *crime*, *dna*, *evidence*, *Italy*). The keyness of *article* in a comparison of the 'Murder of Meredith Kercher' talk pages with Wikipedia talk pages more generally is considerably reduced versus the keywords generated in relation to the British National Corpus word list, with a keyness value of 27.019 as compared to 36 007.24, and ranked 767th rather than second in order of keyness.

Analysing the discussions that contained the keyword *article* will only get us so far in understanding what is distinctive about the 'Murder of Meredith Kercher' talk pages and the behaviour of the editors. The one remaining keyword from the talk pages of the 'Murder of Meredith Kercher' as compared with the Wikipedia talk pages more generally is *sources*. Discussion of *sources* can therefore be considered distinctive both to the talk pages of the 'Murder of Meredith Kercher' article and to the discussion of Wikipedia talk pages in general.

The importance of *sources* as a focus for the discussions on the talk pages reflects the value that secondary material serves within the context of Wikipedia. Sources are the means by which editors can support their choice of content reported within an article under the policy of Verifiability. The contexts in which the keywords *source* and *sources* occurred show that within the 'Murder of Meredith Kercher' talk pages, discussions of *sources* were embedded in debates. I used the cluster function in Antconc, set to minimum range of 4 and a minimum frequency of 5, to examine the repeated phrasal patterns in which the reference to a *source* occurred. The two most frequent clusters were 'is a reliable source' (N = 49) and 'is not a reliable source' (N = 25). These phrases occurred in claims that the editors made about particular source material, as in the following examples:

Table 4.2 *Top thirty keywords from the 'Murder of Meredith Kercher' talk pages as compared with a specialised reference corpus of Wikipedia pages*

Rank	Raw frequency	Keyness	Word
1	4155	5928.395	knox
2	2056	2793.292	trial
3	1573	2244.372	amanda
4	1610	2163.27	murder
5	1513	2158.763	guede
6	1339	1910.498	sollecito
7	1186	1692.196	kercher
8	1258	1615.88	italian
9	1199	1600.247	police
10	2062	1485.343	she
11	45 988	1478.992	the
12	2216	1438.753	her
13	926	1321.226	ledrush
14	1540	1234.179	evidence
15	1078	1220.986	court
16	2300	1083.173	case
17	705	992.13	prosecution
18	679	968.804	meredith
19	18 320	892.288	of
20	610	870.354	formerip
21	653	855.948	dna
22	589	840.391	bluewave
23	655	775.688	appeal
24	594	773.271	italy
25	607	732.933	crime
26	871	723.931	media
27	496	707.698	mignini
28	14 777	701.713	is
29	478	682.015	wikid
30	1851	646.383	sources

The reason I ask is that I'm surprised that CNN is not a reliable source.

The Times is a reliable source.

The ideological importance of the intertextual references to source material reflects, in part, the potential of those sources to represent the events of the crime and trial differently (see Chapter 3). The ideological importance of the reliable sources was also important as a means of positioning the editors relative to one another. The *sources* functioned as stance objects (Du Bois, 2007); that is, as texts which the editors evaluated as either *reliable* or *not reliable*.

As stance objects, the intertextual references to the sources were extremely important, for they also allowed the editors to align with one another about those sources. Du Bois (2007, p. 163) explained the interpersonal dimension of stance-taking with the formulation, 'I evaluate something, and thereby position myself, and thereby align with you'. Similarly, I argue that the editors who evaluated the source material thereby also positioned their stance relative to the addressees within the forum of the talk pages. The use of *sources* as stance objects that allowed editors to align with one another is most evident in the co-textual exchanges, where one editor disagreed with the evaluation made by another in a preceding post. An illustrative example follows.

Post 1:

> Your personal docstoc page is not a reliable source. Italian news articles are. Please provide reliable sources.

Post 2:

> Only Italian news articles are reliable? How interesting. [Name] is just providing a translation of Raffaele's appeal. She is right it is not in any sense different than the translation of the Massei report. What are we supposed to do? Use an unreadable Google translation? Be sensible.

The use of *reliable sources* as stance objects is vital, because it shows how the editors inferred ideological positioning as indexed by the stance object and applied this to the editors who were interpersonally aligned in these evaluations. This strategy allowed the editors to maintain the idealised separation of Wikipedia as a generic context from its socio-cultural contexts, and appears to comply with the core conduct policy's instruction to criticise the article (and its reliable sources) and not the other editors. However, the idealised separation of Wikipedia from its socio-cultural contexts could not always be maintained. Some editors used the ideological association of the intertextual sources (as pro-innocence or pro-guilt, based on the nationality of the publication) to criticise the lack of neutrality in the article and the behaviour of particular editors. An example of this more explicit expression of stance follows:

> You said it yourself, that you write especially for the US side, which sees things very different from the Italian/English side. Therefore it makes your 'side of the story' not more reliable, if you always back it up with these kind of sources. All you achieve is a biased side of the article which for sure provokes someone from 'the other side' to write something just as biased or delete your edits.

At their most aggravated, the debates about the use of source material culminated in 'personal attacks' that directly identified the nationality of individual editors in ways that infringed Wikipedia's guidelines for Civility (for example, referring to a site member as a 'British editor').

In summary, Wikipedia's core content policies of Verifiability and NOR mean that intertextuality in the form of 'reliable sources' became an ideology-laden object by which the editors as co-tellers could indirectly take stance towards a topic. As stance objects, these intertextual references also became interpersonal resources that allowed editors to align with one another as they evaluated the sources. When editors did not align with one another, but disagreed about source material, debates ensued. The more heated the debate, the more directly and explicitly the editors made the ideological association between the stance assumed in the source material (pro-innocence or pro-guilt; American or British) and their attribution of those identity characteristics to the editors who were the target of the disagreement. In the case of controversial articles, such as the 'Murder of Meredith Kercher', the socio-cultural contexts which shaped the media coverage of the topic also bled into the editing practices.

Reverts and Stance

The ways in which the co-tellership might become unequal can also be observed through the analysis of a particular type of interaction. In Wikipedia, when one editor undoes the work of another, this is called a 'revert'. In theory, any editor can revert the contribution made by another. There are no limitations on what kind of contribution can be reverted. Examples of a reverted edit can include correcting mistakes in factual information or presentation (such as spelling). Larger-scale reverts can include removing entire sentences or citations. Removing the contribution of another editor is a sensitive matter, and reverting practices are most fully codified within Wikipedia's communities in the core conduct policies for the frequency of reverting: the Three Revert Rule (3RR). This policy constrains how often an editor can repeatedly revert the same content on a single page to no more than three times within a 24-hour period. Reversions are particularly important as a type of interaction, as if they occur repeatedly between editors, then they can escalate into 'edit wars', where one editor repeatedly over-rides the actions of another. Within Wikipedia, edit wars are undesirable as they work against the community's goal of consensus.

More generally, reverting practices are particular potent as they may function as 'arguable actions' (Hutchby, 1996, p. 24) that aggravate opposing stances between particular editors. Like reliable sources, reverts involve an editor's stance towards an object (the text in the article that is removed). Reverting the content implies that the content was incorrect or should not be included in the article. For example, on 1 October 2016, one editor incorrectly altered the age of Meredith Kercher as given in the English Wikipedia article. Within an hour, another editor had reverted the change to the age previously given, pointing out the error in the first editor's contribution. Reverts can also imply interpersonal alignment: for example, that one editor does not agree with the contribution of another. Where the reverted content is large-scale or where there may be alternative viewpoints that need to represented to maintain NPOV, removing content associated with a particular side of an argument (which in the 'Murder of Meredith Kercher' article included pro-innocence and pro-guilt representations of Knox) can also take on ideological significance, and is assumed to index the stance of the editors involved.

The practices of reversion can be observed through scrutinising Wikipedia's archives. Reversions can be traced by comparing one version of an article with another in the page history. However, for articles like the 'Murder of Meredith of Kercher' in the English Wikipedia, which has been edited on thousands of occasions, tracking the patterns of reversions in this way can be unwieldy. In the digital humanities, computer scientists have begun to develop algorithms that can process and measure editing patterns. One such enterprise is the revert graph, developed by Yasseri et al. (2012) to measure patterns of reversion across several million Wikipedia articles. In their study, Yasseri and his colleagues showed that the patterns of reversion signalled the potential levels of controversy associated with particular articles. Alongside large quantitative comparisons of many Wikipedia articles, the revert graph can also present insight regarding the patterns of reversions between particular editors for individual articles. A network generated for the English Wikipedia article 'Murder of Meredith Kercher' visually documents how the editors who were involved up until 2011 carried out reversions.[1] I cross-referenced this network with the list of the editors most frequently involved in editing the article available through the Wikimedia Revision Statistics tool (as discussed earlier in this chapter). These two sets of information suggest that the editors who interacted with the article most frequently did so in a way that reverted the content of others. Comparing the revert graph with the profiles of the top editors of the article was revealing, as this allowed me to compare the editors' known nationalities from their profiles with their reverting patterns and so examine whether editors of one nationality (American or British) were removing the content created by others. The network in Figure 4.1 represents the patterns of reversion in the 'Murder of Meredith Kercher' article, where the edges (lines) between nodes (points of intersection) indicate that one editor has undone the work of another. The thickness of the edges represents visually the frequency with which reverts occurred (the thicker the edge, the greater the number of reversions), and the direction of the arrow at the end of the edge, the agency of the editors within the interaction. If two editors reverted each other's work, the edge between the two nodes is represented with arrows in both directions, whereas if one editor only reverted the work of another, the edge is unidirectional. The network shows that the reversions made by the editors varied. Some editors carried out isolated reverts. Other editors carried out many reverts but did not have their work

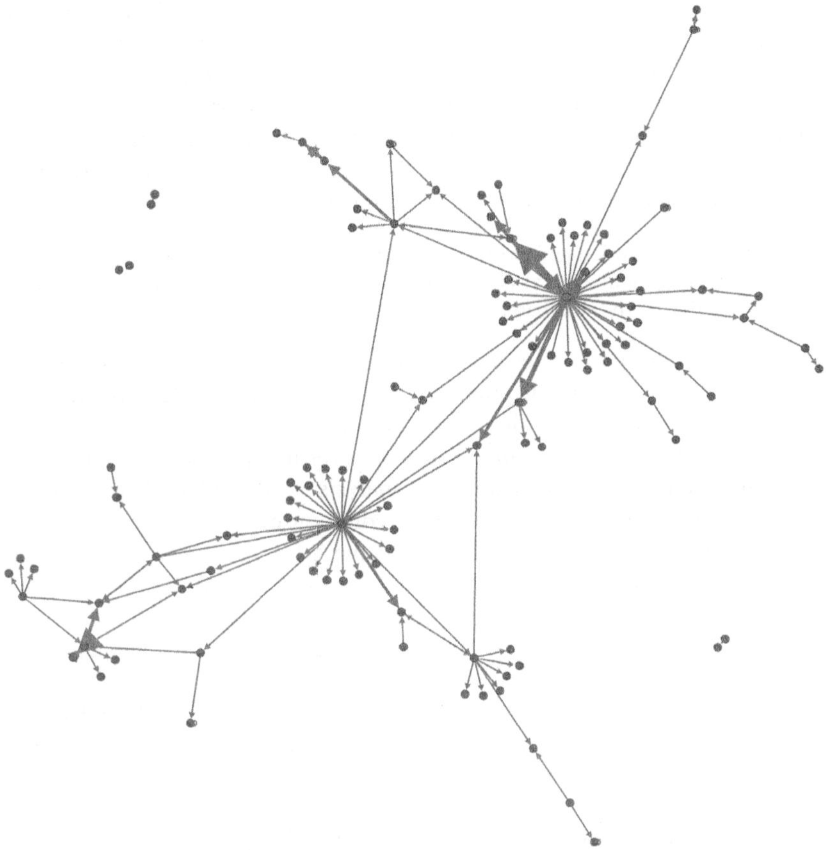

Figure 4.1 Revert graph for the 'Murder of Meredith Kercher' talk pages in 2011

reverted in return. At least two of these identified as British editors (Rothorpe and Cumulus Cloud). In other cases, the revert graph network indicated that particular editors frequently reverted each other's work (like FormerIP (British) and Pilgrim Rose (American)), suggesting that particular conflict had arisen over the content each editor had added and removed.

The network produced by the revert graph is a powerful example of how the metadata available in the interactional context of shared stories can provide us with insights that would be very difficult for a single reader to observe and represent. However, this network cannot provide the full picture of what the patterns of reverting meant in the multilayered context of Wikipedia as a site for shared stories. The network cannot show us exactly which content was reverted, or what the editors' evaluations of the reversions might have been.

Some reverts may be highly appropriate, if the action was taken in order to undo vandalism or to correct factual or typographic mistakes. Other reversions might be considered more contentious, if the same editor repeatedly removed and replaced the same material, especially within a short period of time, as codified by the conduct policy in Wikipedia, listed in the 3RR. One editor who contributed to the 'Murder of Meredith Kercher' article neatly summarised the sensitive and interpersonal nature of reverting, saying:

> People are trying to work together to write the encyclopedia, and rapidly deleting someone else's carefully sourced text is likely to offend that person, as being attacked by a rude, callous, destructive and barbaric action.

In order to understand the varying potential for reverts to function as arguable actions, we need to turn to the pragmatic analysis of the co-tellers' interactions with one another where they discussed reverting practices on the talk pages.

I analysed the editors' stance towards reverting practices using corpus approaches combined with qualitative analysis of the editors' interactions. First, I identified all the instances where editors used the lexeme 'revert' (as either a noun or a verb) in the talk pages of the 'Murder of Meredith Kercher' article using a concordance search for this term. There were 252 occasions when the editors discussed reverting edits. I then analysed each mention of 'revert' in the context of the post in which it occurred and its adjacent posts within a thread.

Reverts can be more or less overtly used to express stance. Based on the co-textual analysis of the 252 occurrences of *revert* in the talk pages, just over half (52 percent) were part of a post where the editor explicitly indicated stance towards the reversion, as evidenced from the evaluative language in the adjacent co-text. For example, statements of agreement and approval indicate that the editors were aligned with the editorial action, as in:

> I agree with TMCk's revert.

> Yes, a good revert – I was considering restoring the original text myself.

In contrast, other reverting edits were evaluated in negative terms, suggesting that the editors were not in agreement with the previous reversion:

> Arbitrarily reverting the move will not help.

> But it's distressing that my initial good faith edit was reverted two minutes after it was made.

Based on this analysis, as stance objects, reverts were evaluated more often negatively than positively on the 'Murder of Meredith Kercher' talk pages. Amongst all mentions of reverts, 42 percent were evaluated negatively, whilst 10 percent were embedded in co-texts where the editor expressed agreement with the reversion. Reverting in and of itself thus cannot be interpreted unequivocally as a negative narrative action, but there seems to be evidence that this is more often the case than not.

The potential for reverting practices to provoke disagreements between editors also depended on how the agency of the participants was represented. Reversions are the result of an editor's actions. In the talk pages, editors could report their own reverting actions, as in this example,

> And I just reverted again per BLP [Biography of Living Persons], this is a SPS [Self Published Source], per BLP it cannot be used.

Alternatively, editors could report the reverting actions carried out by another:

> You have made numerous reverts and removals and are violating 3RR.

Where an editor reported the reversion of a second party (that is, another editor), this was evaluated negatively three times more often than reports of an editor's own reversions, as in these examples:

> [name] has now reverted my tags. Apparently I'm not even allowed to question the relevance of specific statements.

> Did you see what I placed there before you hastily reverted again? Two more sources were found. Did you not even notice that? Or maybe those sources were somehow not good enough? Just curious.

The negative evaluations of reversions by another editor provoked tit-for-tat disagreements where a claim made by one editor about a reversion was followed by a counter-claim by another. Typically, the target of the disagreement moved away from the content of the article (the text which had been reverted) and moved increasingly towards evaluation of the editor and their character, thereby breaching the code for Civility. When this happened, the reversions were also interpreted as ideologically loaded. The reverting practices were interpreted in line with an assumed stance towards the reported events of the Kercher case, not the content of the article. Once again, the idealised separation of the 'telling world' of Wikipedia and the broader socio-cultural context in which the editors were positioned was eroded as the editors attributed stance to one another via their evaluation of the reverting practices, for example, as 'pro-guilt edits'.

At its most extreme, some editors interpreted the reverting as a way to silence the contributions of particular editors and so create a biased rather than neutral account of events in the article. For example, one editor described the practice as a form of 'censoring', saying:

> I don't agree that this edit should have been reverted. Condensed or summarized, sure, why not, that would be a perfectly ok editorial revision. But censoring the views of prominent journalists and newspapers because it doesn't fit an agenda, is the precise opposite of NPOV.

In the ideological interpretation of the editing practices, reverting was recast within a national narrative of anti-Americanism. The American editors argued that the reversions to the article removed the pro-innocent representation of Knox. As the analysis of the article's content in Chapter 3 suggested, until Knox's first acquittal, her representation within Wikipedia was imbalanced in ways that implied her guilt. This could be because the editors who tried to introduce a pro-innocence representation of Knox had their work removed. The analysis of the revert graph in Figure 4.1 suggests that in some cases, this explanation may hold some sway, for the editors whose work was most repeatedly reverted (Pilgrim Rose and Wikid77) both identified as American. More extensive analysis of the reverting patterns would be needed to assess how far this held true over time. What is clear is that the majority of American editors who contributed to the article ceased to do so after 2011, and after this time, the representation of Knox in the article returned to its rather more ambivalent form. Repeated reverting could lead to blocks and bans, or to an editor withdrawing from actively working on an article through their own choice. These outcomes show that reverting is a powerful narrative strategy that can result in negative alignment between editors, with potential to create inequality between the co-tellers of a story in a way that is quite at odds with Wikipedia's democratic ideals.

Conclusion

In this chapter, I have shown how co-tellership is shaped strongly by its contextual norms. The contextual norms as established in Wikipedia's codes of conduct suggest an idealised separation between the generic context of Wikipedia as a site for interaction and the broader socio-cultural contexts in which the production of shared stories takes place. This separation shapes tellership rights in ways that are quite different from other contexts, and which downplay personal experience and expertise on the part of the teller, and consequently also background their identity as members of particular national or political groups. This could be seen as Wikipedia's preferred view; one that opens up a more democratic opportunity for contributing to a shared story that is not limited to those tellers with offline forms of authority or expertise. However, this does not mean that co-tellership within Wikipedia is equal or always equitable. Quantitatively, some tellers contribute more often than do others. Qualitatively, some tellers carry out different kinds of actions that impinge on the tellership rights of others, for example, by reverting content from an article.

Within the talk pages, the idealised boundaries of Wikipedia as a self-contained site for interaction are maintained through the code of conduct for Civility, which guides editors to focus on discussing the content of an article, not other editors and their attributes. However, the inevitably ideological nature of the source material used in the articles to support the policy of Verifiability blurs the boundary between these site-specific and broader socio-cultural values. The use of reliable sources as stance objects points to the importance of intertextuality as an ideological resource within shared stories which opens up dialogic positioning between editors vis-à-vis the more explicit stance attributed to the use of the sources by particular members of the site. Similarly, the use of reversions as a stance object showed how editors used reversions to negatively position the actions of other editors, and vis-à-vis the editor's actions with the text, attributed the reverting editors with ideological stance rather than the neutrality required for encyclopaedic co-tellership.

The idealised separation of Wikipedia from its wider, socio-cultural context is illusory. The connection between Wikipedia and its cultural contexts is indirectly mediated through its intertextuality and through the interactions between its editors, shaping the shared stories which emerge in the articles. The connections between the socio-cultural context and the editorial practices in the case of the 'Murder of Meredith Kercher' English-language article were fiercely debated between the editors of the article. In its own way, this debate was a counter-narrative that attempted to contest the neutrality of Wikipedia as an encyclopaedic project open to editing by all. The extent to which this counter-narrative gave voice to the editors who made claims for national partiality is limited, for at least some of those editors ceased editing the article in 2011.

The analysis of the co-tellership in this chapter is important for our understanding of the shared story, as it signals the ways in which particular sites (here, Wikipedia) can constrain tellership rights and representation. In order to trace the mediated ways in which narratives were expressed, negotiated and silenced, the analysis must take into account multiple layers of the shared stories' context. This includes the generic context and its codes for conduct; the architecture of the site, which positions the talk pages for the article as a subordinate context behind the main article; the metadata present in the interactions, which here identified the patterns of reverting in the article; the co-textual exchanges which positioned the editors within disagreements about stance objects; and the wider socio-cultural context which was implied through the editors' use of nationality to characterise their own and other editors' identities. Wikipedia is a highly ratified context, in which the norms for co-tellership are explicitly documented through the extensive policies that the community continues to develop and enforce. The extent to which co-tellers can subvert, negotiate and rework the resources for sharing stories in other social media sites might be somewhat different. These alternative contexts are explored in the next two chapters, which turn to the international social network site, Facebook.

NOTE

1 In Figure 4.1, the revert graph has the names of editors removed. However, the graph is usually produced with the individual usernames of each Wikipedia editor next to each node, which allows the researcher to cross-reference between the graph and the individual profiles of those who interacted with a particular article. The network of reverting patterns was generated by Taha Yasseri for the analysis in this chapter. I am grateful for his time, effort and assistance in creating this network, reproduced with permission here.

5 Shared Stories and Bonding Icons in Facebook Community Pages

Introduction

In the previous two chapters, I argued that sharing was not neutral, but instead could promote selective versions of events (Chapter 3) and produce inequalities between the co-tellers who interacted with one another (Chapter 4). In this chapter, I continue to explore the complexity of sharing by asking how far shared stories can bring tellers together and create common ground. I explore this in relation to the community pages of Facebook as a relatively new development within the international social network site, focusing on the use of these pages as a site for online mourning of public figures. The stories I analyse are found on the community Facebook pages that were created after the death of two landmark political leaders: Margaret Thatcher and Nelson Mandela. The stories are important, for they show how mediated narrative resources can be ambiguous and lead to multiple interpretations that may or may not be shared between the co-tellers. The analysis of the multimodal content of the Facebook posts (words and images) suggests that we need to look beyond the surface meanings of the narrative content and explore the wider range of indeterminate but implied meanings that may draw together or polarise the tellers of the story. I explore the responses to these stories by examining the use of the 'like' button as a mediated resource for narrative interaction that can also be framed as more or less ambiguous. I argue that beyond its surface meaning of endorsement, 'liking' can create shared social identities that aggregate the tellers into collective groups that compete with one another for visibility within the context of Facebook.

The mediated narrative analysis in this chapter uses interactional pragmatics to bring focus to one of the emerging concepts in the social semiotic analysis of online interactions: bonding (Zappavigna, 2014a). Bonding is an intuitively attractive concept which implies shared values, interpersonal alignment and mediated connections between the tellers as a form of building common ground. Yet, as an analytic concept, it remains fuzzy, conflates the different aspects of sharing (representations of stance and interactional alignment) and tends to emphasise a single outcome of like-mindedness. I develop the research about bonding by arguing that it is a scalar concept, where the figure or object that is the focus for the evaluation (the *bonding icon*: Stenglin, 2004; Tann, 2010) can be more or less 'bondable'. The extent to which a figure prompts bonding is determined by the extent to which their representation within a narrative is straightforward or ambiguous, where the greater the potential for the narrative to prompt multiple interpretations, the less likely that a shared stance – and, therefore, bonding – might occur.

Bonding, Sharing and Stance

Bonding is a concept from Systemic Functional Linguistics that has transferred readily into the analysis of online interactions, particularly social network sites. However, as a key term, bonding pre-dates the mainstream use of social media; it was first proposed by Stenglin (2004) in her study of an offline context: the interactions of visitors and museums. Stenglin (2004, p. 402) said:

> bonding is about making visitors feel welcome and as though they belong, not just to the building and the physical environment – but to a community of like-minded people, people who *share similar values* . . . and enjoy participating in the *shared activities* that the institution offers. (my emphasis)

In its emphasis on the community-building potential of shared attitudes, bonding is a concept that has much to offer shared stories. Although it can apply to any kind of interaction, it has particular relevance to narratives and illuminates two aspects of the shared story, namely intertextuality and stance as a means for positioning the co-tellers relative to one another. This builds on earlier systemic functional research, where bonding has been approached through the ways in which in-group knowledge is invoked; for example, through allusions (Caple 2010), and through the analysis of evaluative language as an interpersonal resource (Zappavigna, 2014a, 2015). In her discussion of bonding, Zappavigna (2014a, p. 146) explains that 'in order to adopt an evaluative stance, around which we might affiliate (or not), we must construe attitudes *about* ideation (people, places, things etc.).' Zappavigna's explanation echoes the interconnections that Du Bois (2007, p. 163) makes in his discussion of the stance triangle, whereby bonding, like stance, has two separable but interconnected dimensions. As we saw in Chapter 4, according to Du Bois' model, the stance-taker evaluates something, or expresses a stance *about* an object (person or event). In so doing, that person positions his- or herself, and thereby aligns with another person. In the same way, bonding as a form of stance-taking allows tellers to align with one another, by means of expressing an opinion about a stance object. The analysis of bonding vis-à-vis the stance triangle is an important first step towards separating the different aspects of bonding. However, one further piece of the puzzle is missing in understanding bonding as a form of stance-taking. This concerns the apex of Du Bois' triangle: the representation of the stance object itself.

This chapter examines what factors make the representation of a stance object more or less bondable, and therefore more or less likely to create alignment between the co-tellers of a shared story. I focus on key figures as particularly important stance objects. Tann (2010) describes these figures as bonding icons, whose representation occurs in semiotic phenomena that recur across different texts, for example in images, slogans and stories. Examining the construction of bonding icons within shared stories allows us to analyse more clearly the narrative practices used by tellers who position these figures within reported events or as intertextual points of reference, and thereby discursively construct the common ground assumed by the notion of 'bonding'. I examine two contrasting political leaders whose representation as bonding icons was narrated in a specific mediated context: Facebook community pages used as online memorials.

Facebook Community Pages as a Site for Bonding through Shared Stories

Facebook community pages are a prime site for sharing stories about a bonding icon. Facebook groups and community pages were developed in 2010, several years after Facebook was first launched in 2004 as a social network site. The rhetoric which the Facebook developers used to describe community pages evoked the notion of homophily, which is so important for the shared story as a genre. For example, Facebook's introduction to community pages by Hicks (2010) said:

> Community Pages are a new type of Facebook Page dedicated to a topic or experience that is owned collectively by the community connected to it. Just like official Pages for businesses, organizations and public figures, Community Pages let you connect with others who share similar interests and experiences.

Unlike personal Facebook profiles, where the network of connections between the participants centres on the individual as the account owner and their Friend List, the connections between the members of community pages centre on the interest of the page. The networked connections which are created via the community pages also differ from personal Facebook pages that use semi-private settings. For a semi-public personal profile, access to the content is gained by becoming 'Friends' with the account owner, whereas a Facebook member can show their connection to a community page merely by clicking the 'like' button. The page owner's identity is often not disclosed, and their contributions are pseudonymous, represented by the page and not the person's individual profile within Facebook. The network of connections associated with the page is facilitated via the interactions with the textual content on the page, not through the reciprocal network of 'Friending' relationships between the members who might have 'liked' the group. As a result, the theme or interest for the community page is positioned as the focus around which the participants bond.

There are many kinds of interactions that take place as Facebook members post and respond to content on community pages. Amongst these, stories can be shared on Facebook community pages as they are embedded in individual posts or comments, or may be episodically distributed across posts as they are published in the timeline or between posts and the comments which respond to them. Many tellers can contribute to the shared story, including the page owner and the Facebook members who join the page. The stories that are told in the posts and comments are multimodal, including written captions, images and uploaded video clips. Facebook's templates include a number of mediated resources for narrative interaction, including the 'like' and reaction buttons. Stories can also be redistributed outside the community page and recontextualised with further responses as they are reposted when members click the 'share' button.

Shared stories can be found on any kind of community page. However, community pages which focus on a public figure as a shared interest typically use stories as a resource to discursively construct that figure as a bonding icon. Examples of community pages which focus on public figures include fan pages for celebrities and outreach pages maintained by or on behalf of politicians. A distinctive use for Facebook community pages has included public memorial pages (Forman et al., 2012). These pages can be understood within the emerging transformation of public rituals for mourning in online spaces, which also include Twitter (Sanderson and Cheong, 2010) and MySpace (Brubaker and Hayes, 2011). Most of the research literature to date has considered Facebook memorial pages that mark the death of private individuals (Giaxoglou, 2015a; Marwick and Ellison, 2012), although in Kern et al.'s (2013, p. 7) survey, just under 17 percent of their sample of memorial pages paid tribute to celebrity figures. The use of community pages for online memorials of public figures is to date relatively under-researched, but it has importance as a forum in which bonding icons are discursively constructed in a particular mediated context (of the Facebook community pages) which is also constrained by the socio-cultural norms for appropriate conduct during a time of public mourning.

Margaret Thatcher and Nelson Mandela as Bonding Icons

The discussion in this chapter examines two iconic leaders who functioned within narratives of national identity for their respective countries. Margaret Thatcher and Nelson Mandela were landmark political leaders. In 1994, Mandela became the first democratically elected President of South Africa. In 1979,

Thatcher was the first woman to be elected as Prime Minister of Britain, and served the longest term of any British Prime Minister in the twentieth century. However, both figures might be considered controversial, although for very different reasons. Mandela's activism in contesting the racism and inequality of apartheid included his involvement with the African National Congress (ANC), which led to his imprisonment by the government of the time (but from which he was later released). The activism of the ANC included violent activities such as bombings. The extent to which biographical accounts of Mandela either made reference to these events or legitimised the violent activities of the ANC as justified in the fight for equality varied. On the one hand, the dominant discourse presented Mandela as an iconic, humanitarian leader who symbolised unity. On the other, references to Mandela's involvement with the ANC meant he could be interpreted by some as a 'terrorist'. Thatcher's status as a controversial figure was not associated with her activities prior to becoming Prime Minister, but rather related to her style of uncompromising leadership, her economic policies (which privatised public services and introduced additional taxation regimes) and international associations that led to military intervention in Argentina and in the Middle East. On the one hand, her actions contributed to the recovery of the British economy during the 1980s. On the other, this recovery was gained at the expense of taxation programmes and privatisation that was resisted by many (as evidenced in the riots and trade union action in this period). As iconic figures, these political leaders had the capacity to function as bonding resources, or to polarise the tellers.

The bonding potential of an iconic figure is heightened at key points in their biography, particularly at their death, whereby the stance that might be taken towards the figures is constrained additionally by the social norms for expressing collective grief. As with other public figures, the news of Thatcher's death on 8 April 2013, and that of Mandela's on 5 December 2013, each prompted a media spectacle (Kellner, 2009), where responses and reactions were published widely across international mainstream media outlets (television and news reports) and across social media sites. The social media responses included posts to the micro-blogging site Twitter, the creation of YouTube videos, the dissemination of songs in music-sharing sites, the posting of images to the photo-sharing site Flickr and the content-sharing site Pinterest, and the creation of memorial pages on the social network site Facebook. The iconic status of Mandela and of Thatcher is reflected in the many eulogies that were given from international political leaders, broadcast through mainstream media such as television and news reports. In South Africa, Mandela's death was followed by a ten-day period of public mourning, with high-scale public gatherings, a day of national prayer and a state funeral. In the United Kingdom, Thatcher was given a ceremonial (not state) funeral, but the decision to do so was greatly contested. Indeed, the polarised evaluations of Thatcher led to debates in the mainstream

Table 5.1 *Summary of the data from the Facebook memorial pages for Margaret Thatcher and Nelson Mandela*

	RIP Margaret Thatcher	RIP Nelson Mandela
Number of posts made by page owner	11	11
Date range of posts by page owner	8 April–10 May 2013	5–6 December 2013
Number of participants who contributed to the page	182 801	27 923
Total likes	245 971	72 975
Total comments	29 393	712

media in the days following her death about how to employ appropriate death etiquette. Hagiographic eulogies were deemed inappropriate in failing to acknowledge the negative actions and outcomes of her political leadership. Instead, there were both offline and online reactions which saw Thatcher's death as a cause for celebration, and the occasion was marked with street parties. These celebrations were also deemed inappropriate on the grounds that they violated the social interdiction to avoid 'speaking ill of the dead'.

Data and Methods

The extent to which Mandela and Thatcher functioned as bonding icons in shared stories is explored in relation to a particular social media context: the Facebook community pages that were created as memorial tributes to each leader. Thirteen pages were listed under a Facebook search return for 'RIP Margaret Thatcher' and seven pages under a search for the term 'RIP Nelson Mandela'. The analysis focuses on two memorial pages in particular: those which (according to the Facebook and Google searches) garnered the most interaction, as indicated through the number of responses to the pages in the form of 'likes' and comments. Both pages were created on the day that the death of the public figure in question was announced. The RIP Margaret Thatcher Facebook community page was created on 8 April 2013 and the RIP Nelson Mandela page on 6 December 2013. In both cases, the person who created the pages remained anonymous. The information given on each page signals their role in paying public tribute to the deceased figure, announcing the death of the political leader, and in the case of Mandela's memorial page, also inviting public contributions: 'Please show your respect and condolences by posting on the wall.' I extracted the posts published on each memorial page and the interactions appended to them using Netvizz (Rieder, 2013). A summary of the information about each Facebook community page is given in Table 5.1. In this chapter, I focus on the stories that were told by the page owners in the posts that they made to the page in question and the use of 'likes' as a mediated resource that the members of the community pages used to respond to the content on the page. In Chapter 6, I focus more fully on the comments that were appended to the posts.

Shared Stories in Posts by the Page Owner

The stories that were told on the memorial pages for Thatcher and Mandela by the page owners illustrate the ways in which sharing can be risky and open to misinterpretation. Whilst some stories prompted a shared interpretation of the figure as a unifying bonding icon, others did not. The extent to which stories prompted a shared interpretation of the figure depended in part on how far the narrative representation of that figure was ambiguous. In Gricean (1975) pragmatics, ambiguous communication is to be avoided in line with the maxim of manner. One reason that the maxim of manner might be important as a contextual norm for shared stories is that ambiguous narratives are challenging in terms of a shared interpretation, for ambiguity can give rise to multiple implicatures. These implicatures might include contrasting evaluation of the iconic figure, and can arise in a number of ways, relating to the multimodal content used in the stories; in particular, words and images. I begin by analysing the representation of the two leaders in the verbal content of the posts published on the memorial pages.

In the Mandela page, the page owner told five stories in the eleven posts published on the timeline. These were biographical accounts that narrated key events from Mandela's life, and which emphasised his role within a national narrative of South Africa's history. For example, one post read:

> Mr. Mandela spent 27 years in prison after being convicted of treason by the white minority government only to forge a peaceful end to white rule by negotiating with his captors after his release in 1990. He led the African National Congress long a banned liberation movement to a resounding electoral victory in 1994 the first fully democratic election in the country's history. R.I.P.

There is little that is ambiguous about the narratives posted by the Mandela memorial page owner. The posts consistently focused on the positive achievements of Mandela, positioning him as a superlative example of leadership. Mandela was represented in the posts in relation to his political role ('former South African President'), his iconic status ('a potent symbol' and 'moral compass'), his relationship to others ('a yardstick for African leaders', 'our greatest son'), and his legacy (he 'achieved more than could be expected of any man'). Where events in Mandela's history might be open to critique, these were sequenced so that his transformation to more positive roles was emphasised; for example, 'he went from a militant freedom fighter to a prisoner to a unifying figure to an elder statesman'. The verbal narration of Mandela in the posts to the memorial page thus seems in line with the heroic representation of an iconic figure, to which the page owner seemed to 'bond'.

In contrast to this, the narratives posted by the Thatcher memorial page owner were more ambiguous in the representation and evaluation of their subject. There were two narratives told in the eleven posts published on the page. In the first post, the ambiguity arose from the representation of Thatcher's agency. The post read:

> R.I.P Margaret
>
> Her legacy had a profound effect upon the policies of her successors, both Conservative and Labour while her radical and sometimes confrontational approach defined her 11-year period at No 10.

In this account, the exact nature of Thatcher's legacy and its 'profound effect' was not specified. The use of noun phrases ('her legacy' and 'her approach') meant that Thatcher's actions remained un-narrated and only inferred. The qualified evaluation of her approach as 'radical and sometimes confrontational' did not necessarily lead to a positive evaluation of her actions or identity. Instead, by backgrounding Thatcher's actions and hence her agency, the page owner left the representation of the figure open to varying interpretation. Affiliated support and polarising disapproval were simultaneously available as interpretive responses to this post.

The second narrative told by the page owner, posted a day after Thatcher's state funeral, was more ambiguous still. This post read:

Lovely funeral yesterday

Please take a second of your time to like the page to show your respect

R.I.P The Iron Lady.

The narrative content in the post was brief, inferred from the elliptical reference to the event: 'Lovely funeral yesterday'. No biographical account of Thatcher or her political actions was given, but her identity was positioned through the ambivalent metaphor with which she was associated: 'The Iron Lady'. The brevity of this narrative fragment is in line with the 'breaking news' found in updates on Twitter and Facebook that similarly tend to omit either the actor or the verb phrase reporting particular actions (Page, 2012a). However, this brevity gives rise to ambiguity, for the story seems not to say enough. It is in danger of failing to fulfil Grice's (1975) maxim of quantity; that is, to give as much information as is required. This under-narration is an apt strategy for positioning an icon whose actions might polarise rather than unite an audience. Instead of relying on what was told explicitly in the verbal content, this kind of shared story relies on an assumed shared knowledge between the tellers. In the case of this post, the shared knowledge involved knowing whose funeral had occurred and to whom the moniker 'The Iron Lady' referred. For the audience that shared knowledge of the controversy around Thatcher's funeral (which debated the use of public funds to pay for the event), the evaluation of the funeral as 'lovely' might be interpreted as controversial, shared by her supporters but rejected by her opponents.

The narratives posted by the page owners also included images accompanying the verbal content. These images opened up different kinds of bonding potential for the shared stories, which like the verbal content of the posts could be more or less ambiguous in the representation of the iconic figure. The ambiguity of images as a resource for shared stories arises in part through their transpositional implications (Blommaert et al., 2016). None of the images were visual representations of the events that were reported in the verbal content of the post. Instead, the images on both memorial pages had been recontextualised from prior sources, and were available in many hundreds of contexts across the Internet, as indicated by the search returns for these images in Google. As images that had been shared many times prior to their use in these memorial pages, they might seem to open up a range of shared interpretations for the audience, which was more or less able to recognise the events and prior uses of the images. As such, the discourse itineraries (Scollon, 2008) of the intertextual images used in these shared stories could invoke more or less explicit contextual knowledge about the iconic figure for the viewing audience.

The potential for the images to create ambiguous stance towards the bonding icon also related to how far the visual representation was consistent with other co-textual representations of the figure, such as the other images on the timeline, or the verbal content accompanying them, in the form of captions or written posts. Where the images represented the iconic figure with similar referential content that was consistent across the contributions to the community page, the visual representation of the bonding icon was likely to prompt shared interpretations from the audience and thus to be highly 'bondable'. In contrast, where the visual representation was inconsistent, and mismatches were created within its co-textual and intertextual uses, the discursive representation of the iconic figure was less likely to prompt a single shared interpretation. The two community pages differed in the ways in which their images used their interdiscursive context and localised co-texts to generate shared interpretations of the bonding icons.

The images that depicted Mandela in the posts to the memorial page were consistent in the content and composition used to depict the leader. The nine images which occurred in the posts were all portrait shots which showed Mandela's face in full focus and occupying the central position in the frame. In terms of Kress and van Leeuwen's (1996) visual grammar, the images were not narrative representations, for they did not contain any vectors. Each image represented who Mandela was, rather than showing him carrying out an action.

All of the images showed Mandela smiling and formally dressed, emphasising his status as a public figure at a 'frontstage' performance. Several were taken from key events in his political career, such as his inaugural speech as President and his last public appearance at the 2010 World Cup held in South Africa. Of these images, his iconic national status was most clearly reflected in the photograph used as the cover image for the page, in which the South African flag appeared as the backdrop. In terms of their discursive itineraries, the sources for these images reinforced Mandela's iconic position as a landmark leader. Although there are many previous online contexts in which these portraits of Mandela appeared, many of them occurred in sources that purported to a historical purpose, such as the *Encyclopaedia Britannica* or the Nelson Mandela Foundation. In summary, the visual content of the posts consistently depicted Mandela in a positive light, emphasising his characteristics as a landmark public figure, all of which supported the eulogies narrating his life found in the verbal content of the posts.

The eight images that were posted to the Thatcher memorial page similarly represented the deceased figure, but when compared with the visual representation of Mandela as an icon, appear heterogeneous in their content and composition. Some images were portraits, whilst others showed Thatcher taking part in actions. The affective representation of Thatcher also varied. In some images, she was shown smiling, but in others her facial expression appeared more thoughtful and serious. Like the visual positioning of Mandela, the images were associated with key events in her political career, such as when Thatcher launched the Conservative manifesto in 1983. However, unlike the images used on the Mandela memorial page, not all of these images led to an unequivocal interpretation of Thatcher's leadership in a positive light. Whilst Mandela was depicted visually as a unifying icon, the events selected from Thatcher's career were controversial, with the potential to provoke dissenting criticism from her opposition or endorsement from her supporters. For example, one image showed her being awarded the Medal of Freedom by George H. W. Bush in 1991. The image represented an event that marked the international significance of Thatcher's achievements, but for an audience familiar with the history of Britain's relationship with the United States of America, it selected controversial leaders whose military interventions in the Middle East were to leave a debatable legacy in the decades that followed.

The inconsistency in the visual representation of Thatcher in the images posted to the page was further complicated by the dissonance between the messages conveyed in the visual and verbal elements in the posts. Each of the images was accompanied by verbal content written in the post. In some cases, the images were also altered by the addition of a superimposed caption. For example, the image of Thatcher being awarded the Medal of Freedom was annotated with a header that said, 'Like if you're glad she's dead, share if you'll miss her', suggesting that the intended audience of this image would include both opposition and supporters.

The shared knowledge of the image and its previous contexts of use also opened up inter-discursive mismatches, where both positive and negative evaluation of Thatcher was possible. A good example of this was found in the cover photo of the page, which showed Thatcher in the foreground against the backdrop of Chequers, the country retreat of the Prime Minister in post, taken during 1993. Whilst the visual content indexed Thatcher's professional status as the then-current Prime Minister (through the selection of Chequers as the backdrop), the quotation superimposed on the image had little to do with Chequers per se, and was a recontextualised quote from Thatcher published in the *Observer* newspaper in 1980. The quote, 'I don't mind how much my ministers talk, as long as they do what I say', depicted her authoritarian disregard for consensus. The potential for the image and its caption to generate interpretations that cast Thatcher in an unfavourable light is strengthened when the other contexts in which the image was used are taken into consideration. A search in Google Images showed that it occurred in at least 150 other Web pages, including news reports which dubbed Thatcher the 'Prime Minister of Property', alluding to her decision to allow council house tenants to purchase their own home; other reports at the time discussed the outcome of this decision in terms of exacerbating an economic and class divide. The use of the image can be taken as an allusion to the economic and class divide between Thatcher and at least some of the constituents under her leadership that is ironic and controversial.

Scholars in narrative theory have drawn attention to the inherent ambiguity of images as narrative resources. Working from a pragmatic perspective, Forceville and Clark (2014) point out that in the absence of a clear, codified visual grammar, images are likely to prompt a wide range of weak implicatures (that is, to open up a larger number of possible interpretations of intended meaning over and above their representational content), rather than a narrow range of explicitly conveyed meaning. This is true of all images. However, some seem more ambiguous than others. In the data considered here, the image which most exploited the potential of implicatures to position Thatcher in ambiguous terms was the photograph which accompanied the breaking news story, 'Lovely funeral yesterday'. This image was a publicity shot from *The Iron Lady* (2011), which showed the actress Meryl Streep playing Margaret Thatcher.

The ambiguity of the image arose from the shared knowledge that was required to recognise its intertextual nature. *The Iron Lady* was a particular, selective account of Thatcher's life; one which provoked criticism at the time it was screened for showing Thatcher's later decline into dementia. The interpretive gaps between what is shown in the image (Streep playing Thatcher) and the additional implicatures that might arise based on the audience's knowledge of the biopic (as a controversial film) are further increased by the relationship between the image and the verbal content of the post, which was itself under-narrated. The post referred to 'The Iron Lady', and so to Thatcher and to the film, and hence to Streep herself when playing the titular role. This ambiguity of reference was problematic given the under-narrated story within the post: 'Lovely funeral yesterday'. It was unclear whether Thatcher or Streep was assumed to have died. Indeed, one commenter asked, 'Is Meryl Streep dead?'

The ambiguity of the publicity shot from *The Iron Lady* was all the more marked given the contextual incongruity of this image within the Facebook page. In terms of social distance, the image showed Streep in the titular role in close distance to the camera, making direct eye contact with both it and the audience. In Kress and van Leeuwen's (1996, p. 117) visual grammar, this could be interpreted as a form of direct address between the subject of the image and the viewing audience. All other images posted by the page owner were taken at longer distance, and none showed Thatcher making direct eye contact with the camera. The co-textually unusual directness of the visual composition, along with the shared knowledge that the image was not of Thatcher but of an actress (Streep), prompted questions from the commenters on the page about the use of the image by the page owner. In terms of the contextual norms for collective mourning, the use of an image of an actress (who was still alive) rather than of the deceased leader was deemed inappropriate conduct. There is evidence from the comments that the responding tellers interpreted the image in different ways. Some reactions clearly interpreted the choice as inappropriate, making rapport-threatening criticism of the page owner, such as:

Shocked that you have a picture of meryl streep rather than the Baroness! Very odd! That aside a true inspiration and liberator

Can't you find a picture of Lady Thatcher? Shame on you.

Other reactions suggested that the effect of the image was not one of offence, but that it was intended to be taken as a joke, and projected rapport-enhancing appreciation of the page owner's choice:

Ha! Ha! Meryl Streep!!!!

The use of the image resulted in responses that polarised the relational work amongst the tellers, rather than facilitating their collective affiliation towards Thatcher. As a stance object, the image did not create bonds of alignment between the tellers. Rather, it positioned individual commenters in different ways relative to the page owner, either as condemning the page owner's behaviour through rapport-threatening criticism or as signalling humorous appreciation of the page owner's choice of image in ways that were potentially rapport-enhancing.

In summary, the analysis of the stories posted to the memorial page shows how the multimodal representation of the bonding icons can be more or less consistent. In the stories told about bonding icons, the narration can be straightforward and consistent in the use of words and images to represent the key figure. The narration of Nelson Mandela in the multimodal stories found in the Facebook posts on the Mandela memorial page illustrates this use of stories to project a shared representation which opens up interpretive opportunities for shared stance. However, the narration of shared stories can also be ambiguous. The analysis of the multimodal stories found in the Facebook posts on the Thatcher memorial page illustrates the forms of ambiguity that might occur. Ambiguity was created through under-narration in the verbal content and through the use of images that generated multiple implicatures. In particular, the images were not consistent with the other visual content that was present in the co-text of the Facebook page or with the inter-discursive context, which drew on wider socio-cultural knowledge of Thatcher and her representation in other mediated contexts. Where the shared knowledge might polarise the tellers, there was less likelihood that bonding about the iconic figure could take place. Instead, the discursive representations of Thatcher allowed multiple, polarised responses to the page owner's stories to emerge. Thus far, I have claimed that ambiguous narration, as a form of 'sharing as telling', made bonding less likely between tellers. In the next section, I provide evidence to support that claim, by analysing the interactions that responded to posts on the page using Facebook's 'like' button.

'Liking' as a Resource for Shared Stories

'Liking' is a practice that is ubiquitous within Facebook, whereby members of the site can click on a 'like' button in response to an object within Facebook's network, such as a page, a post or a comment. 'Liking' is a key resource for bonding, for it can indicate stance towards the object to which the 'liking' responds. Similar to other kinds of stance, 'liking' is interpersonal, which is mediated in that it creates connections within Facebook between the profile of the person who clicked the button and other members of the site, such as the person who created the object and those who have also clicked the same 'like' button. The interpersonal, mediated forms of 'liking' create shared social identities for the tellers, such as a person's membership of a particular community page based around a particular shared interest. However, the semantic range of 'liking' is not as straightforward as it might seem. Although 'liking' conveys a stance of endorsement, similar to the narrative function of evaluation, the 'like' button is discursively flexible and can be reframed as a form of 'forced stance-taking' West (2015), or can be used as a minimal form of response within the context of private Facebook wall pages (Page et al., 2013). 'Liking' as a form of interacting with a shared story cannot be read simply as a measure of endorsement. Instead, 'liking' can be repurposed to create divisions between the co-tellers, rather than a single shared stance.

'Liking' a Page: Bonding with What or Whom?

The social identities that are created through 'liking' as a mediated resource in shared stories vary according to the object to which the member of Facebook responds. Within Facebook, the 'like' button is available as a response to posts, replies to posts and entire pages. 'Liking' a page is an interaction that connects a Facebook member with the page as a whole, as an act of collective identification that affiliates the member with the shared interests of the page and the page owner. By creating this connection, the page also appears in the individual Facebook member's profile information, and potentially provides a form of semi-public identification with the 'community' and its interest. In contrast, 'liking' a post or a comment is a response to an individual textual object, which connects the 'liker' to the creator of that object (the post or reply) and a subset of potential other members of the page who might also reply to the object by the automated notifications sent from Facebook within its network. This connection does not appear in the timeline or profile information of the 'liker', and is thus a more temporary, and individual, opportunity for bonding.

'Liking' practices were taken up differently in relation to the Facebook memorial pages for Margaret Thatcher and Nelson Mandela. These differences are related to the varying bonding potential of these iconic figures. As the analysis of the posts made by the page owners suggests, Mandela was represented in ways that made it more possible for people to bond in a shared stance towards him. This is reflected in the frequency with which members used 'likes' as responses to the page, posts and comments for the Mandela memorial Facebook page. A summary of the 'liking' patterns for the Mandela and the Thatcher memorial pages is given in Tables 5.2 and 5.3. For the RIP Nelson Mandela page, on average, likes were more often used by Facebook members to connect to the page as a whole rather than to individual posts or comments. This is suggestive of Mandela's status as a bonding icon, where connecting to the page was interpreted as communal identification with collective mourning. In contrast, for the RIP Margaret Thatcher page, on average, 'likes' were used more often to respond to individual posts, rather than to connect Facebook members to the page as a whole. In line with the ambiguous representation of Thatcher, which did not generate a single, shared stance, 'liking' used on the memorial page did not unite people in a single, collective response.

The more individualistic use of 'liking' to take stance towards particular posts indicates the ways in which Facebook members responded to the representations of Mandela and Thatcher on their respective memorial pages. On

Table 5.2 *Quantitative summary of the 'likes' used on the Facebook memorial pages for Margaret Thatcher and Nelson Mandela*

	RIP Margaret Thatcher		RIP Nelson Mandela	
	Raw count	Percentage of all 'likes' to the page	Raw count	Percentage of all 'likes' to the page
Likes for page	14 069	6%	27 923	38%
Likes for posts	18 1402	73%	44 322	61%
Likes for comments	50 500	21%	712	1%
Total	245 971	100%	72 957	100%

the memorial page for Nelson Mandela, the posts which gained the most number of likes were formulaic RIP statements that marked respect for Mandela, such as:

R.I.P Madiba (9941 likes)

There are few people who are as respected as Nelson Mandela. Rest in Peace (5312 likes)

R.I.P (3957 likes)

In this memorial page, the use of the 'like' button seems to reflect its surface meaning of endorsement, signalling agreement with the sentiment shared by the page owner's respectful representation of Mandela.

In contrast to this, the posts made by the owner of the Thatcher memorial page explicitly made reference to the practices of 'liking' and 'sharing', which recontextualised the meaning of 'liking' beyond straightforward endorsement as a form of shared stance. Unlike the responses to the posts on the Mandela memorial page, the post which was least 'liked' on the Thatcher memorial page was a formulaic phrase of respect: 'R.I.P Margaret Thatcher'. Instead, the frequency of 'liking' a post varied considerably across posts which framed the interactions in different ways. In some posts, 'liking' was constructed as a mark of agreement and support for Thatcher, as in the following example:

Table 5.3 *Average 'liking' patterns used on the Facebook memorial pages for Margaret Thatcher and Nelson Mandela*

	RIP Margaret Thatcher	RIP Nelson Mandela
Average likes per page	14 069	27 923
Average likes per post	16 491	4029
Average likes per comment	2	1

Figure 5.1 'Likes' and 'shares' beneath a Facebook post

How many likes for this amazing woman? Make sure you like the page to show your support!

In other cases, 'liking' was used like a poll to measure the audience response, as in the post:

Like if you would buy a Margaret Thatcher magnet for £5.

In yet other instances, the use of the 'like' button could be framed as a comparative measure of response used to align with anti-Thatcher sentiment, as in:

Like if you're glad she's dead, Share if you'll miss her.

The varying use of the 'like' button throws into question the consistency of the page owner's stance towards Thatcher and suggests that it would be misleading to take an overall, aggregated measure of the 'liking' behaviour to indicate affiliation with a single, shared stance between all members of the page.

The use of 'liking' as a choice to affiliate or not to affiliate with a conditional statement is described by West (2015, p. 56) as 'forced stance-taking', which polarises responders into competing groups. This forced stance-taking exploits a further affordance of 'liking' practices in Facebook: 'liking' is a collectivising response, for the representation of 'likes' displays such interactions as a numerical total (see Figure 5.1). As social actors, the individuality of Facebook members is obscured via their interaction of 'liking' the object, which is subsumed within the aggregated total displayed under the object in question (such as a post or comment). The aggregation of Facebook members in this way can be co-opted for the purposes of either bonding or polarising the respondents into quantifiable groups. A single numerical total unifies the respondents as collectively belonging to the same group. However, when forced stance-taking occurs, the different choices that a respondent can make are compared quantitatively (for example, as the total number of 'likes' versus total number of 'shares'). The aggregation of the Facebook members via 'likes' can result in competitive outcomes for the respective groups, where one total is judged as greater or lesser in numerical terms. This is significant for understanding how bonding can take place on social network sites, where the use of the like button relies in part on its collectivising affordances. These can emphasise connection either with a communal, shared interest, via 'liking' the page as a whole, or with individually authored content. In either case, 'liking' collectively aggregates the identity of the Facebook members so that the quantity of interactions is given particular value within the social networking site.

'Liking' as a form of forced stance-taking cannot polarise tellers into competing collective groups at the level of 'liking' a page, but only through reframing the meanings of 'liking' in the posts and comments. A comparison of the 'liking' practices on the Facebook memorial pages for Nelson Mandela and Margaret Thatcher suggests that, like the use of verbal and visual stories in the posts, the greater proportion of 'likes' appended to the page as a whole reflected collective bonding around Mandela as an iconic figure. In contrast, the memorial page for Thatcher used 'liking' less to construct a single, collective response, and more to respond to individual posts. The interpretive gaps created in the stories told about Thatcher could then be pitted against one another in forms of forced stance-taking, where the respondents were collectively positioned within competing groups compared on a quantifiable basis (number of likes). To return to an example discussed earlier in this chapter, the image which showed Thatcher receiving the Medal of Freedom used the interactions of 'liking' and 'sharing' in the caption, which instructed the audience to 'Like if you're glad she's dead, share if you'll miss her'. In this way, Thatcher's opponents could quantify their interactions as 'likes' (which totalled over 1700) and compare this with the number of 'shares' by her supporters (which totalled 283).

The social identities that were created for these opponents and supporters recontextualises the intensity of stance-taking, or bonding, in numerical terms, where aggregation is used to make judgements about the relative size of one group of stance-takers as compared with another. The value of aggregation within social media sites like Facebook should not be underestimated, for the numerical comparisons may feed into the algorithms used in the site to promote the visibility of a particular item (for example, presenting it at the top of a news feed). The competitive nature of mediated bonding is not simply a matter of one group gaining more interaction than another; it also has implications for promoting the visibility of the group and its interests within the context of the particular page.

Conclusion

In this chapter, I have shown that bonding, as a form of stance-taking, rests in part on the representation of the stance object. As stance objects, bonding icons can be represented in ways that promote a shared stance or can be evaluated in different, sometimes polarising terms. The potential for multiple interpretations to arise from the multimodal narrative content which is 'shared' is explained from a pragmatic perspective in terms of implicatures. The lower the range of implicatures generated from the narrative content, and the more singular the interpretation, the greater the potential for bonding between the tellers, who can unite in their collective identity as a single group. Conversely, where additional implicatures are generated, the interpretation of the iconic figure is no longer stable. The additional implicatures can result from ambiguous, under-narrated verbal posts, from the potential of images to generate a large number of weak implicatures or from dissonance created through intertextual mismatches between the current and previous uses of recontextualised narrative material. Sharing is not always straightforward, and bonding, like stance, is a relative concept that can result in a range of relational work, either polarising or uniting tellers.

This chapter has also examined 'liking' as a mediatised form of bonding. In part, the use of 'liking' to create collective identities that draw together or polarise participants is enabled through the affordances of Facebook, but given its ubiquity as a form of endorsement or ranking on other forms of social media sites, my observations in this chapter have wider implications for 'liking' as a narrative resource found in analogous contexts that also use ranking options. First, 'liking' as a mediatised action can create collective or individual connections within a network of users. In the case of Facebook community pages, this depends on the object to which the 'like' responds. 'Likes' are networked connections which can link an individual to a wider group of other site members who belong to the same community page. However, rather than assuming that all members of the same community page will share the same stance, members can use 'liking' to differentiate their stance from others as they interact with individual items of content on that page (such as posts or comments). In this second use of 'liking', social media sites exploit the aggregation of 'liking' interactions, which appear as a quantitative figure in relation to a page, post or comment. When the semantic range of 'liking' is restricted in a particular post, this aggregation can force respondents into competing, collective groups, where quantitative comparisons are used to measure the relative success of one group of tellers against another. In this chapter, I have argued that constructing shared ground between tellers is not straightforward, and that homophily is not the only social outcome that can arise from bonding as a form of stance-taking towards a key figure such as a bonding icon. The extent to which the competing interests of different tellers used the affordances of Facebook to tell contrasting shared stories about bonding icons is taken up further in Chapter 6, which examines the comments that were posted to these Facebook memorial pages.

6 Collective Identities and Co-tellership in Facebook Comments

Introduction

A central tenet of this book is that shared stories are never straightforward but are open to disruption in ways that exploit the mediated contexts in which they are told. In this chapter, I show how sharing was disrupted within the interactions that took place on community pages of the international social network site, Facebook. These community pages were used ostensibly for the purposes of mourning public figures. The public figures in question were political leaders, who, as bonding icons, represented macro-social narratives for their respective national contexts. In Chapter 5, I showed how the representation of the bonding icon could open up interpretations that might be shared by the co-tellers who contributed to the page or which might polarise the tellers into competing groups. In this chapter, I turn to the comments that responded to the posts and argue that far from promoting shared interests between the co-tellers, community pages could be co-opted as contexts in which rapport-threatening disagreements took place. Sharing as a means of establishing common ground between texts and tellers is always in a dialectic relationship with the processes of differentiation. As Lindgren (2012, p. 164) puts it,

> There is a constant struggle between the forces that encourage sharing and the building of relationships, and the forces that create borders and separate people. Depending on context, either of these sides may become dominant.

If this is true at a general level, then it is all the more so in cases of narration where the reported events are open to debate. In this chapter, I analyse the struggle between sharing and separation through the use of collective identities as a resource for positioning the co-tellers within in-groups and out-groups. The first part of the chapter examines the representation of the tellers as social actors (van Leeuwen, 2008), where collective identities were used to support or contest the co-tellers' entitlement to contribute to the shared story. In mediated narrative analysis, the researcher is not just interested in the representation of a story, but understands narratives as a form of social practice. The second part of the chapter turns to the intertextuality in the comments, in order to examine the various options for collective consumption and reproduction of shared stories. This is important because it extends the analysis of social actors from their representation to their participation and takes into account the multimodal forms of intertextuality that occur in Facebook, as well as in other kinds of online and mediated contexts of interaction.

Collective Identities and Shared Stories in Facebook Comments

Shared stories emphasise commonly held beliefs between the multiple tellers, from which collective identities can emerge. In social psychology, collective identities rely on a process of mental categorisation that compares the individual self with others on the basis of similarity and otherness (Duszak, 2002, p. 2), where collective identity refers to a person's self-identification as a group member, rather than in terms of their unique, personal characteristics (Spencer-Oatey, 2007, p. 642). Collective identities are important for their psychological and pragmatic outcomes, which can include a sense of inclusion within a social world. Conversely, when collective identities are used to differentiate one group from another, the exclusion of a person or group of persons is also possible, often typified as polarity between the self and other, or 'us' versus 'them'. Within Critical Discourse Analysis, the lexico-grammatical forms by which collective identities can be represented have been studied extensively, most notably in ways that extend van Leeuwen's (2008) work on social actors (see, for example, Koller, 2012; Machin and Mayr, 2013; Richardson and Langford, 2015). Work in this field has focused on the ways in which the representation of collective identities can be used strategically for ideological outcomes, such as legitimising or delegitimising a particular macro-social category, or obscuring individual identity. In pragmatics, collective identities have been considered in relation to types of face (Culpeper, 2011; Spencer-Oatey, 2007) and the different ways in which collective face can be affectively sensitive. A teller can use collective identities to represent their own or another person's social category in ways that can be rapport-enhancing and suggest alignment between the tellers when they belong to the same group. Alternatively, collective identities can be used for rapport-threatening outcomes when they delegitimise another teller, positioning them in a negatively evaluated out-group. This polarising pattern is well documented in many contexts, where collectivisation promotes the interests of the in-group to which the speaker belongs, but discriminates against the out-group (Reisigl and Wodak, 2001).

The options for representing the tellers' collective identities are construed through the lexico-grammatical choices these tellers made as they told stories. The stories that I focus on in this chapter are those that were told in the comments that responded to the posts made on the Facebook community pages created after the deaths of Margaret Thatcher and Nelson Mandela in 2013 (see Chapter 5 for a full description of the data). Like other kinds of Facebook pages, and other kinds of social media sites, Facebook posts have options that allow members of the site to respond to them by creating a comment. The comments can include written or visual content and hyperlinks to other Web pages, both within Facebook and beyond. As an interactive context, Facebook comment threads are polylogal, where a comment can respond either to a post or to another comment in a thread. Comments can be formatted as replies, where they are linked by the mediated affordances of Facebook to a particular comment, or they can be responses to non-adjacent comments. Facebook community pages are typically characterised by collapsed contexts, where the tellers need not know one another in offline contexts or be connected within the same online networks within Facebook itself. Even whilst community pages may appear to connect Facebook members with a shared interest, this does not mean that every member of a page will share the same stance towards the page's focus. The collective identities used by the site members who told stories on these pages are therefore an important resource that might reinforce a single, shared social identity that is in line with the stated focus of the page, or that might differentiate one commenter one from another. This is crucial, given the polylogal interactive context, which makes the co-construction of a story across successive comments difficult to sustain within a single thread and therefore open to disruption.

Data and Methods

The memorial pages that form the focus for analysis were chosen because they had gained the most interaction in the period following the deaths of the public leaders in question: Margaret Thatcher and Nelson Mandela. However, although the two community pages contained the same number of posts made by the page owner (11 in each case), the number of comments that responded to these posts was different. The comments to posts on the Mandela page numbered 712 (8488 words), whilst the comments to posts on the Thatcher memorial page numbered 29 393 (738 908 words). Because of the large number of comments, the methods I used to explore the collective identities combined qualitative and quantitative analysis of the verbal content. Keyword analysis was carried out for the comments made on each of the memorial pages. I treated the comments from each page as a specialised corpus, comparing the two sets with the British National Corpus as a reference, and then with each other, in order to gain an overall picture of the distinctive lexical choices used in each. I then carried out qualitative analysis of the comment threads that responded to the two narrative posts made by the page owner for the Thatcher memorial page (641 comments) and of all the comments made on the Mandela memorial page (712 comments). The analysis was used to identify the stories and collective identities within the interactional context of the comment thread as a means of creating rapport-threatening or rapport-enhancing outcomes between the Facebook members.

Keyword Analysis of the Comments

I began by generating a keyword list for the two sets of comment threads from the two memorial pages, comparing each separately with the 100 million-word British National Corpus. The first thirty keywords for each list are summarised in Table 6.1. Given that the shared interest of each page was an online memorial of its respective public figure, the keyword lists included some unsurprising items, such as the names of the deceased leaders (*Mandela*, *Nelson*, *Thatcher* and *Maggie*) and formulaic phrases (such as *RIP*). However, unlike the posts made to the pages, where the representation of Mandela positioned him in an unequivocally positive light and the representation of Thatcher was ambiguous, the items on the keyword lists suggest that the representations of these figures in the comment threads were polarised explicitly by different tellers. The keyword list for the comments made to the Mandela memorial page included the words *terrorist* and *hero* to refer to the leader, whilst the keyword list for the comments made to the Thatcher memorial page included *lady* and *bitch* as terms which referred to the former Prime Minister. Illustrative examples in which these keywords occurred include the following comments:

> To spend ones life fighting for the rights of others, that is the definition of a true hero, and Nelson Mandela was just that, may he rest in peace.

> you are actually R.I.P.ing a convicted terrorist who used the bullet and bomb to gain his political status.

> A Great Lady who stopped the Unions ruling the country. It is shame the current MPs aren't as brave!!!!!

> I grew up in the 1960s and 70s and was working full time before the bitch came along, and remember Britain very well. It was a cleaner, nicer country, with plenty of jobs, good pay, low crime and a sense of community. She destroyed all of that and we are all still paying the price.

There are other keywords which suggest the importance of collective identities within the socio-historical narratives associated with each figure, such as *country*, which appeared on both lists. In the list for the comments on the Thatcher memorial page, keywords included the generic reference to *people* and functionalised identities of particular groups, such as *miners*, *unions* and *haters*, as in the following illustrative examples:

Table 6.1 *Top thirty keywords from the comments posted to the Facebook memorial pages for Margaret Thatcher and Nelson Mandela as compared with the British National Corpus*

	RIP Margaret Thatcher comments			RIP Nelson Mandela comments		
Rank	Raw frequency	Keyness	Lexical item	Raw frequency	Keyness	Lexical item
1	12 114	18 346.43	she	184	2545.116	mandela
2	1658	15 832.38	lol	147	2034.79	rip
3	1919	11 742.68	thatcher	123	1488.728	nelson
4	1793	11 520.18	maggie	31	569.389	madiba
5	12 667	11 492.99	you	52	497.632	wounded
6	13 934	9065.577	i	68	456.157	peace
7	2898	8722.453	country	52	429.948	bomb
8	7931	8030.029	her	63	422.78	killed
9	893	6897.335	rip	67	378.224	rest
10	4342	6669.837	people	35	346.101	terrorist
11	910	5258.699	funeral	70	219.045	man
12	1378	5091.46	respect	169	169.368	you
13	3790	4797.586	your	26	164.068	pages
14	1710	4683.746	woman	197	159.079	i
15	1223	4533.878	lady	9	158.805	obama
16	2948	4395.702	did	26	156.086	u
17	706	3926.395	miners	9	151.811	plz
18	431	3696.888	ding	8	146.939	mandelasmovie
19	444	3675.066	cunt	27	139.035	africa
20	635	3469.426	amazing	11	129.717	xxx
21	379	3215.842	dong	16	126.24	bombs
22	401	3195.183	dead	13	126.036	johannesburg
23	1070	3190.927	bitch	18	120.83	hero
24	506	3183.599	unions	9	118.987	tata
25	769	3173.78	comments	6	110.204	also
26	759	3071.984	fuck	6	110.204	website
27	497	2981.146	alison	8	107.832	umkhonto
28	531	2837.328	shit	8	106.473	homme
29	508	2782.699	like	8	104.439	wimpy
30	3128	2775.65	dont	12	102.17	spells

Not all thatcher haters are uneducated, most are, the rest are left wing simpletons.

These maggie haters did they go to school??

The haters blame it all on Maggie the mines, the milk, the Falklands

The keywords are an important starting point, for they show that the representations of the political leaders in the comments were individuated, but in ways that polarised their positions within the national narratives for their respective countries. In comparison, the commenters seem to be represented distinctively within the keywords by the use of collective identities. The relationship between the co-tellers, stance and collective identity needs to be examined in relation to the interactions which took place within the comment threads. This turns the attention from the representation of the bonding icon as a stance object to the use of collective identities as a means by which the co-tellers aligned, or refused to align, with one another.

Collective Identities as a Resource for Co-tellership

The comment threads which responded to the posts on the memorial pages for Thatcher and Mandela contained a number of narratives embedded amongst other content, such as quotations, formulaic RIP statements and invitations to interact with other kinds of online content. The narratives were used by the commenters to evaluate the leader in question (Thatcher or Mandela); for example, through the selection of reported events and representation of the bonding icon. As a form of stance-taking, the narratives also opened up interpersonal possibilities for the commenters to position their own identities as more or less aligned with the other tellers. In Du Bois' (2007, p. 163) stance triangle, alignment is the axis which connects one speaker with another. In his framework of stance, alignment is realised most clearly through the successive utterances of the two speakers, where the degree of alignment is inferred through the dialogic reproduction and positioning of one utterance relative to another. In addition, I propose that interpersonal alignment can also incorporate the extent to which a speaker (or, here, teller) represents their own or other tellers' identities as members within a social group. A key aspect of this interpersonal positioning is the use of collective identities. The narratives that responded to the posts on the two memorial community pages differed both in quantity and in the ways in which the tellers represented these identities as different kinds of social actors.

The 712 comments on the memorial page for Mandela contained forty-eight examples of narratives. These included narratives which retold events from Mandela's life, such as:

> Wow just heard the news! RIP Nelson Mandela. He went through so much and always managed to fight his way through with courage and wisdom.
>
> Rip to great humanitarian icon, Mr Nelson Mandela. The world has lost a great man. Prayers goes out to his family a true legend.

In line with the keyword analysis, in the narratives told in the comments, the representation of Mandela was individualised: through his name (*Nelson Mandela*), through the use of third-person masculine pronouns (*he*, *his*) and through the use of indefinite noun phrases (*a great man*). In contrast, the commenters represented their own identities as part of a group, or what van Leeuwen (1996, 2008) referred to as 'assimilation'. Assimilation of the commenters was projected through the lexico-grammatical resources used in the comments posted on the Mandela page, which genericised the group through plural pronouns such as 'us':

A huge loss . . . He is no longer with us but his legacy will remain with us forever . . . Rip Madiba.

Some commenters collectivised their identity through the mass noun, 'an entire nation' – united by Mandela's leadership as a 'father':

Madiba, our father, was a great man!! Some couldn't begin to understand the struggles of his ppl but his words of wisdom has reached the furthest corners of the globe!!! Remember not just his family but an entire nation is grieving today!! A little respect will go a long way.

In other instances, the commenters' shared identity was spatialised as the continent:

Africa is deeply hurted . . . . . . .RIP grand father.

Based on these examples, the collective identities used by the commenters suggest a shared stance towards Mandela and a shared social identity for the tellers as a nation in mourning. However, as the keyword list for the comments to the Mandela memorial page indicated, not all the commenters chose to represent Mandela in positive terms. A small number narrated events from his life that emphasised his involvement with the African National Congress (ANC) and positioned him as a *terrorist*. For example, one commenter wrote:

It would appear that everyone has forgotten that Mandela was once the head of 'Umkhonto' or the 'MK' which just happened to be the terrorist wing of the A.N.C. (African National Congress) . . . . and was responsible for many bombings in the early 60's before his eventual imprisonment . . . so just remember that you are actually R.I.P.ing a convicted terrorist who used the bullet and bomb to gain his political status.

This narrative was repeatedly posted by the same commenter to multiple threads on the Mandela memorial page. It is this repeated duplication of the comment which explains why the words *terrorist*, *bomb*, *bombing* and *umkhonto* appeared on the keyword list for the corpus of Mandela memorial page comments. However, the representation of Mandela as a terrorist was not accepted by the other commenters. In subsequent comments, other co-tellers denied the representation of Mandela as a 'terrorist' in rapport-threatening disagreements that were directed at the original comment's author. These disagreements escalated as they moved from mitigated face threats to conventionalised forms of impoliteness, such as insults which individualised the dissenting commenter. For example, the teller of the 'terrorist narrative' was at first positioned as immature ('young') and ignorant ('haven't had the luxury of a balanced education' and 'confused'), but was later targeted by offensive name-calling, as illustrated in the following comments:

> Despite your childish words which is not a criticism as i'm assuming you're either young or haven't had the luxury of a balanced education but that isn't your fault – unfortunately you are confused. Just because someone has spent time in Jail doesn't make them a terrorist, just because you make a statement and put the word FACT next to it doesn't make it the truth. Let's hope in 50 years time you are not judged for your current level of ignorance.

> [name deleted] he was a man fighting against an oppressive government. Try having no rights or freedoms and maybe then youll understand you fucking douche bag.

> And you are a faggot and can I tell you somthing, he was a very wise man, I think he knew a bit more than you.

The resulting disagreements between commenters disrupted the interactional norms on the memorial page, where respect for the deceased was expected, and eulogised tributes were juxtaposed with instances of aggravated impoliteness. There is evidence from the responses within the comment thread that these disruptions were interpreted as inappropriate and unwanted, as in the following comment:

> [name deleted] is a little bitch whose here just to start trouble.

The negative evaluation of the dissenting teller suggests that even if bonding around Mandela as an icon and between the tellers was not univocal, the dominant eulogising view of Mandela as a positive leader prevailed. The commenter who posted narratives with a negative stance towards Mandela did not reply to his or her critics, either to deny or to defend his or her comments. It would seem that the dissenting narratives were provocations from a single teller, not a sustained positioning of Mandela that was shared by a number of tellers. This suggests that the bonding potential of an iconic figure can be measured by how far co-tellers align with one another in their interactions, where the higher the bonding potential of the figure, the greater the agreement between the participants. The bonding between commenters was reinforced by the representation of the social actors in these comments, where the dominant in-group collectivised its shared identity through the use of generic plural pronouns, assimilation and spatialisation. This contrasted with the individualisation of the dissenting commenter as an isolated member outside that group.

The comments that responded to the two narrative posts on the Thatcher memorial page demonstrated a different stance towards the deceased leader and a different use of collective identities to position the commenters within disagreements. In the 641 comments responding to these two threads, there were 196 narratives. As the items on the keyword list for these comments suggest, Thatcher was represented in some very different ways within these narratives (ranging from *lady* to *bitch*), with little evidence that the co-tellers shared a similar stance towards her as a bonding icon. In contrast to the under-specified and ambiguous narratives told by the page owner, the commenters' stories appraised Thatcher in explicit and polarised terms, as in the following examples:

for all you wingers out there who moan about your water rates your gas bills your electric bills the woman who said when these are all sold off you can expect cheaper bills and created a skills gap in this country when she done away with apprenticeship this fucking bitch did more damage to this country than hitler did in the second world war.

The great lady was voted in by the country on a mandate of tackling the unions and putting this country back on its feet, she did both. God bless her for doing it, because no one else at that time was capable.

Unlike the representation of Mandela by the commenters on his memorial page, where the majority of comments were in favour of the leader, the polarised representation of Thatcher was divided more evenly between the co-tellers, with no clear quantitative emphasis on her supporters as compared to her opponents. In a comparison of the comments that responded to the two narrative posts on the page, we find that on the day after her death, two-thirds of the comments were critical of Thatcher, whilst on the day after her funeral, 58 percent were in her favour.

The interactional positioning of the commenters relative to one another in the comment threads was similarly divided. Unlike the commenters who collectively united against the minimal dissent on the Mandela memorial page, the exchanges between the co-tellers on the Thatcher memorial page engaged in hostile disagreements. Occasionally these disagreements were framed as adjacency pairs, like this example:

Commenter 1: If she was so bad at her job why was she re-elected again and again?

Commenter 2: then kicked out by her own party.

More often, however, disagreements between co-tellers took place across non-adjacent comments that were connected by the resources of format tying, such as referring back to a previous commenter's name or quoting from their post. The target of the disagreement in these comments within the interactional order (Langlotz and Locher, 2012) focused both on the stance towards the iconic figure (Thatcher) and on the author of the post and their identity. In framing their disagreements with one another, co-tellers attacked the other narrators' entitlement claims (Shuman, 2005); that is, their credentials and right to tell the story.

Unlike the Wikipedia editors (discussed in Chapter 4), whose disputes focused on the actions of an editor (such as reverting another's additions to an article), in this memorial page, very often the attacks on other narrators invoked their assumed or stated social identity characteristics, such as their age, nationality or geographical location. Illustrative examples include the following comments:

> [name] your not scottish you have no clue what she has done to us, she was evil just utter evil

> [name] if you were young and not even in the country you need to butt out of the debate because you clearly know nothing and are not qualified to pass judgement on those who do know the real Maggie thatcher.

In previous research about conversational shared stories, a narrator's entitlement to contribute to a story rested on their personal experience of the events reported (see Chapter 1). In those studies, the shared experiences often had localised parameters to a specific time and place, and participants who were known to all the co-tellers (such as a family meal or a particular incident). In the mediated narratives about political leaders such as Margaret Thatcher, the parameters of a 'shared experience' need to be relaxed somewhat. For example, there was no evidence that any of the commenters who contributed to the Facebook memorial page for Thatcher had ever met the former Prime Minister in person. Instead, the entitlement claim to contribute to a shared story was shaped by the wider socio-cultural context. The tellers' right to denigrate or to pay tribute to Thatcher rested on the stated authenticity of their lived experience within the broader spatio-temporal context of her leadership. Without this, their right to tell authentic stories about Thatcher's action was disputed. However, even amongst the co-tellers who could claim the shared experience of living in the same period and the same country, the divisive nature of Thatcher's leadership meant that appealing to a common social identity (such as nationality or age group) shared by all tellers was not available to these participants as a rhetorical strategy. Instead, the tellers sought to validate their opposing evaluations of Thatcher through narrating their own personal experience. This held true regardless of whether the narrator sought to defend or critique Thatcher, as seen in the following comments:

> Absolute rubbish [name deleted]. I lived through the Thatcher era most of my working life and she took away our rights as workers and made it easy for employers to exploit people under the threat of losing their job. You seem to think she was some kind of fairy princess. She was pure evil.

> [name deleted], my farther was a steel worker who was forced to strike by the peer pressure of his trade unionist (NAZI) co workers. He managed to feed his family, because he believed that HE, not the fucking state should provide.

The number of narratives which occurred in the comments made to the Thatcher memorial page might then be explained by the role of personal experience in providing evidence for the co-teller's stance towards Thatcher. A quantitative comparison of the narratives in the comments posted to the two memorial pages is suggestive, where proportionately, narratives occurred over four times more often in the comment threads examined for the Thatcher memorial page than on the Mandela page (accounting for 31 and 7 percent of the comments, respectively). Comparing the narratives in the comments on the two memorial pages, it would seem that the lower the bonding potential of the iconic figure, the more likely that a collective affective response will be disrupted. As a result, there was a greater need for individual tellers to provide evidence for their opinions about Thatcher, here in the form of narratives of personal experience.

Given the polarised evaluation of Thatcher, it was impossible for the co-tellers who responded to posts on the Thatcher memorial page to use collectivisation in relation to their own identity; the co-tellers could not unify themselves as a single national group. Instead, collective identities were used to genericise the other co-tellers from whom a commenter distanced his- or herself. In these disagreements, the commenters attacked the teller's social identity, such as their political affiliation or gender. For example:

Those young lefties with brains please do your history homework

Has anyone noticed, it's mainly men that didnt like her. Perhaps it's cos she was the last Prime Minister with BALLS!!!

The use of collectivisation to position an out-group negatively relies on the stereotypical attributes and behaviours associated with the groups in questions, which like other kinds of membership categorisation (Fitzgerald and Rintel, 2013) can be used to invoke normative assumptions about the moral order. Like other kinds of adversarial interactions (Stokoe and Edwards, 2007), the collective identities that were used to position tellers in an out-group (such as 'young lefties' and 'men' in these examples) obscured the individual identity of the commenters in question and instead characterised them as generic opponents.

The co-tellers on the two memorial pages used collective identities in different ways and for different effects in their stories. Where the co-tellers shared the same sentiment and were affiliated with a dominant discourse around a bonding icon (like Mandela), they positioned their own identity within the same collective group (for example, as a nation) and used this to evaluate both the icon and themselves as similar, peace-seeking people. In contrast, where the co-tellers did not share common ground and where the deceased person was a polarising figure (like Thatcher), collective identities were used not to identify the narrator but instead to position other co-tellers as an out-group from which the narrator was differentiated. In both cases, collective identities indexed stereotypes where schematic knowledge was invoked to characterise the participants involved in the narrative interaction. However, in a context where the co-tellers were polarised rather than affiliated around shared sentiment, the collective identities of the out-group invoked negative rather than positive stereotypes. These collective identities amplified the aggravating face-attacks and impoliteness used to undermine the personal experience narratives that co-tellers used to legitimise their right to contribute to the page in the first place.

Collective Consumption: Intertextuality in the Facebook Comments

Thus far, the representation of the tellers as social actors in the comments has shown how shared stories in online contexts use collective identities to position tellers within the same shared experience (here, of online mourning) or differentiated from that experience. As with other representations of collective identities, the ideological interpretations of these choices favour the speaker; for example, by strengthening the positive associations of an in-group to which the speaker belongs (as in the case of the commenters who contributed to the Mandela memorial page), or by projecting negative associations on an out-group from which the speaker differentiates their own experience (as in the commenters who contributed to the Thatcher memorial page). However, the analysis of the shared story does not just consider the representation of participants within the telling world or the tale world of the narration. The shared story is also characterised by intertextuality and the interactions between co-tellers. In this section, I present a framework that extends the options within van Leeuwen's (2008) social actor framework for representing collective identity in order to take account of the types of collective interactions that are generated through the intertextuality of the shared story.

Within shared stories, intertextuality has an intrinsic connection to collective identity. As the existing research has shown, the extent to which an intertextual reference is recognised by others relies on their presumed shared knowledge (Caple, 2010). This can produce an in-group of participants who have access to that intertextual knowledge and an out-group who do not. The mediated forms of intertextuality that occur when shared stories are told in online contexts go beyond this, by creating opportunities for tellers to connect with or consume the intertextual content in ways that construe distinctive collective identities-in-interaction. In van Leeuwen's (2008, p. 37) framework for social actors, he makes a useful distinction between the representation of people as individuals (individualisation) and their representation within groups (which he calls 'assimilation'). The distinction depends on the lexico-grammatical resources used to construe singularity (for individualisation) as compared with plurality

Table 6.2 *Intertextual links in the comments posted to the Facebook memorial pages for Margaret Thatcher and Nelson Mandela*

	Thatcher Memorial Page		Mandela Memorial Page	
	Raw count	Percentage	Raw count	Percentage
Archive	5	4%	1	1%
Blog	15	11%	0	0
Facebook community page	26	19%	42	59%
Facebook photo	0	0%	14	19%
Music store	2	1%	0	0%
News	39	28%	0	0%
Online store	0	0%	4	6%
Petition	1	1%	0	0%
Spam	0	0	4	6%
Tumblr	1	1%	0	0%
Wikipedia	3	2%	0	0%
YouTube	46	33%	7	9%
Total	138	100%	72	100%

(for assimilation). Using mediated narrative analysis, I now apply this distinction to the contexts within which tellers were individualised or assimilated as they interacted with the intertextual content embedded in the shared story.

The types of mediatised intertextuality were identified by means of a corpus-assisted analysis of the Facebook comments on the two memorial pages. Using Antconc, I focused on the intertextuality that was indicated by the hyperlinks in the dataset, using the concordancing software to identify the comments in which a hyperlink occurred. The results of the search identified 210 links in total (72 from the comments on the Mandela memorial page and 138 from the comments on the Thatcher memorial page). I then examined every comment in which a link occurred, and checked the sites to which the hyperlinks connected. I quantified how often each page linked to different kinds of Web genres, normalising these comparisons to a percentage of each type of site per page. The results are summarised in Table 6.2. The links in the comments on the Facebook pages connected the comments to a range of sites, including online archives, blogs, other Facebook pages, news reports, Wikipedia articles and audio-visual resources such as music and videos on YouTube. However, the two memorial pages differed in what kinds of sites were most often promoted through the intertextual links. The links in the Mandela Memorial page comments were most often to other Facebook community pages and photographs. The photographs reproduced many of the iconic images of Mandela that also occurred in the posts made by the community page owner and which appeared in many other mainstream media contexts. In contrast to this, within the comments that responded to posts on the Thatcher memorial page there were far fewer images, no links to photographs on other Facebook timelines and no examples of tribute art. Instead, in the absence of iconic visual representations of Thatcher, there were many links to resources where competing stories were told about her leadership and its outcomes, including news reports (28 percent of links), blogs (11 percent) and Wikipedia articles (2 percent). However, most frequently the intertextual links were to YouTube clips of music videos (32 percent). The affordance of music as a resource for interaction between co-tellers is examined in the following section.

Collectivised Consumption: Multimodal Engagement

The differences in the intertextual source material connected to the Facebook comments are important because their multimodal affordances can individualise or assimilate the tellers who interact with them. Different modes can open up opportunities for engagement that emphasise individual or collective consumption of the text in question. In the two sets of Facebook comments, the differences between the use of image and music opened up contrasting options, where the images used in the comments posted to the Mandela memorial page did not represent the commenters at all, but reproduced individualised representations of Mandela as an elite figure (that is, he was represented alone rather than as one of many people in each image). The group identity of the commenters was excluded, and only inferable from their repeated reproduction of Mandela's image. In contrast to this, the musical intertextuality in the YouTube music videos drew on collectivised representation. Music videos were embedded via intertextual links in the comments to the Thatcher memorial page, such as the following examples:

Love Billy Bragg and his music. http://youtu.be/IlkXQm7tSCY

Here's a good ode to her legacy http://www.youtube.com/watch?v=oAga3ZQ0BxU

Other artists known for their political activism, such as the British reggae artist Macka B and his performance of the song 'Get Rid of Margaret Thatcher', and more recent artists such as John McCullagh and his song 'I'll Dance on your Grave Margaret Thatcher', also featured in the Facebook comments. The lyrics of these songs criticised privatisation, the decline of the trade unions and the military interventions initiated under Thatcher's leadership. The lyrics used collectivisation to represent the opponents and supporters of Thatcher. For example, Bragg's song was entitled 'Thatcherites', who were addressed generically in lyrics such as, 'you privatize away what is ours'. As McKerrell (2015) argues, music videos draw on a combination of semiotic resources to create interpersonal and ideological positioning. This is true of the music videos in these examples, where the songs were played over a montage of still images that were recontextualised from the mainstream media. These images individualised Margaret Thatcher, but collectivised other groups, such as striking miners, protestors and military personnel, all of whom were represented en masse in crowds.

More generally, the collectivising potential of music as a form of discourse lies in part in the simultaneity of musical interaction, which invokes its capacity to 'unite people and create group feelings' (van Leeuwen, 2012, p. 323). There are many different kinds of musical genres, and many different kinds of 'group feelings' which can result, carrying various ideological implications. Amongst these, popular protest songs (Way, 2016) combine the 'group feelings' invoked through music with the ideological meanings that counter mainstream or institutional forms of representation. The social meanings of music as a collectivising form of intertextuality are particularly evident in the comments made on the memorial page for Thatcher, where the music videos were all protest songs, drawing on the folk and punk genres associated with political dissent during the time that Thatcher was in power.

Collectivised Consumers

The second aspect of intertextuality that collectivised tellers was derived from the way in which the co-tellers were positioned within groups that might interact with the material. Examples of intertextuality that invited collective interactions included texts such as a petition (signed by many people), a Wikipedia page (constructed by many editors) and another Facebook community group page (which connected tellers within a network). Typically, the hyperlinks to these collectivising examples of intertextuality were accompanied by imperatives in the comments, which invited further interaction on the part of the addressee. The types of collective identity created by the intertextuality could vary, and included the fans of particular artists, as in the following illustrative example:

In honor of black history month, this artist releases an art work of people that have influenced black history. Today's feature is Madiba. Please see attached. Visit the artist facebook page – https://www.facebook.com/pages/Truartist83/115449675220673 Thanks.

In other cases, the collective intertextuality positioned the tellers as campaigners, as in the following example:

http://epetitions.direct.gov.uk/petitions/45966. Instead of spouting shit sign this petition to stop taxpayers money paying for her funeral.

Other examples of collective consumption were specifically economic, with opportunities to purchase commemorative memorabilia. These intertextual links were to online stores where items such as the Mandela Rand note or sweaters bearing recontextualised images of Mandela were for sale:

Was Nelson a Hero? Collector's Edition: The Nelson Mandela Rand Note – http://t.co/AJqLPdiXnr

Collective Co-construction

In contrast to the intertextual references that encouraged collective consumption of other content, other kinds of collectivised interactions allowed the tellers not only to consume but also to co-construct the intertextual material. One of the important distinctions in the mediated forms of co-tellership found in the shared story is the extent to which the tellers' creative contributions were included in the processes of telling and redistribution. In the Facebook comments from these memorial pages, one important genre which demonstrated collectivised interaction was found in music videos posted to the video-sharing site YouTube. These videos included remixes which creatively recontextualised protest songs that circulated in the aftermath of Thatcher's death. Several such protest songs circulated after Thatcher's death, which indexed stance towards her as a political leader. One was taken from 'Ding-Dong! The Witch is Dead', created by Arlen and Harburg as part of the 1939 film adaptation of *The Wizard of Oz*. Following the news of Thatcher's death, her opponents created a remix of the 1939 song which circulated through YouTube in a video that juxtaposed the overlaid soundtrack (derived from the film) against images and video footage of Margaret Thatcher taken from the mainstream news during her leadership. The inferred parallels between the lyrics in the film and the characterisation in the images were obvious, casting Thatcher in the role of the villainous witch, whose long-anticipated demise had finally been confirmed and was considered the cause for celebration. The use of the song in this campaign was highly controversial, with British mainstream media channels debating whether or not to ban its play, on the grounds of the well-rehearsed tension between freedom of speech and respect for the dead (in relation to Thatcher).

As a remix, the intertextuality of the 'Ding-Dong!' protest song opened up further collective co-construction by the tellers. There were many versions of the remix that were linked to the Facebook comments, which illustrated the various ways in which the tellers co-constructed protest songs. The variation is evident in the different types of image that were combined with the song. Some remixes altered the visual content recontextualised from the film to include images of Thatcher. Others combined the soundtrack with images of news events from during Thatcher's time in power (such as the poll tax riots and the sinking of the *Belgrano*). In yet other examples, the soundtrack was played over a montage of images that showed anti-Thatcher street parties which celebrated her death.

Aggregated Identities-in-Interaction

In his framework for assimilation, van Leeuwen (2008, p. 37) distinguished between collectivisation and aggregation. Aggregation presents the assimilated or group identity for social actors in quantified terms. The options for tellers to interact with the intertextual material in the shared stories found in online contexts are mediated. As a result, the tellers' interactions become tractable, and therefore quantified and represented in forms of aggregation. Examples of aggregation include the numerical totals provided on sites such as online petitions, or the numerical figures that quantify the number of times a video has been viewed or ranked. In these data, the number of times a protest song was downloaded was interpreted as a form of stance-taking, which could be used to collectivise those who consumed the song into an aggregated figure that was compared with other kinds of online interaction. For example, in the following comments, the quantification of downloads was compared with the quantification of 'likes' or with the rival protest song promoted by Thatcher's supporters:

Interesting fact. Apparently 28000 people (idiots) have downloaded Ding Dong the witch is dead. There are nearly more people liking this pic. More likes required!!!!

[name] ding dong reaching No.2 nearly 94,000 likes haha FAIL!!

Down load the rival song from iTunes I'm in love with Margaret Thatcher was 191 this morning now 11. Lets knock ding dong off no 1. RIP Maggie

The aggregated consumption of the intertextual content linked to the Facebook comments exploited the affordances of online interaction where the quantified consumption of online content could serve the interests of one group at the expense of another. As van Leeuwen (1996, p. 49) pointed out, aggregation is ideologically powerful, as 'in our society the majority rules'. Within the context of social media, the majority also seems to 'rule': the greater the number of interactions, the more success is ascribed to the group. These comparisons need to be treated with caution; an aggregated total of interactions need not be interpreted as a single shared expression of endorsement, nor are the interactions which are compared with one another necessarily of the same value or status, even if comments that compare 'likes' and 'downloads' suggest they are perceived as equivalent. The ideological interpretation of the interaction varies according to a number of factors, including the assumed social meanings of the intertextual object. Purchasing commemorative memorabilia is quite different from purchasing a protest song. Joining a petition is quite different from joining a fan page for an artist. Being able to recreate your own version of an intertextual reference is quite different to reproducing an institutionalised, authoritative version of events. We should be careful, therefore, not to 'read off' a single, ideological interpretation of the different kinds of collectivised and aggregated identities that resulted from the intertextual interactions with

Table 6.3 *Comparison of the collective identities construed through the intertextuality in the comments posted to the Facebook memorial pages for Margaret Thatcher and Nelson Mandela*

	Multimodal engagement	Collective consumption	Collective co-construction	Aggregated interactions
Facebook community pages for tribute artists	Images individuated Mandela as a bonding icon, tellers not represented	Positions tellers as fans within the networked context of the Facebook page	None	Number of 'likes' for the page aggregates tellers around a shared interest
Protest songs	Music carries group meaning, tellers are collectivised in the song lyrics and images	Positions tellers as opponents or supporters who downloaded the song	Remixes allow for participatory co-construction	Number of downloads aggregates tellers into competing groups

the shared story. Instead, the different types of collectivised consumption, co-construction and aggregated interactions provide parameters against which the mediated interactions with the shared story can be compared and contrasted. This applies to the Facebook comments considered in this chapter, but is also relevant to the intertextuality found in other mediated contexts for storytelling. As an illustrative example, I close by showing how these parameters help illuminate the different collectivising potentials of the most frequently occurring types of intertextuality in the Facebook comments to the two memorial pages.

As the summary in Table 6.3 suggests, the types of collective and aggregated identities that are enabled through the intertextual interactions in the shared story open up qualitative comparisons of social actors across different mediated contexts. The importance of these differences expands the range of collective identities beyond that of the 'us' and 'them' construed through lexico-grammatical choices alone. Instead, collective identities need also to be understood in relation to the interactions in which people are positioned. These interactions are mediatised and multimodal, illustrated here in relation to the social network site Facebook, but with relevance to many other online contexts.

Conclusion

In this chapter, I have argued that co-tellers use collective identities as a way of aligning with one another relative to a particular social category. On the one hand, this is an important resource for creating common ground between tellers, in line with the emphases of the shared story. On the other, collective identities also allow tellers to differentiate themselves from others who are not within that same group, by creating either distancing effects of stance such as an 'us' versus 'them' polarity, or a contrast based on individualisation as compared with a group identity. The analysis of the comments made on the Facebook community page confirm earlier patterns documented in Critical Discourse Analysis, where collective identities are used to promote positive attributes when the teller is positioned within that social category as an in-group member, but are used negatively when the teller is instead positioned in the out-group. In the case of shared stories, these collective identities are particularly important as entitlements to tell the story. Where a collective identity positioned a teller who did not share the same socio-historical experiences as the other tellers within an out-group, their stories were delegitimised.

Shared stories do not rely on representation alone to attribute collective identities to their tellers. Intertextuality is also an important means by which the co-tellers are positioned within social identities. The analysis of the intertextuality in the comments extends our knowledge of how assimilation (van Leeuwen, 1996, 2008) can be realised through interactions that either collectivise or aggregate tellers. The intertextual forms of assimilation were differentiated on the basis of how far the multimodal affordances of the source material enabled collective engagement. In the examples considered here, music videos enabled greater possibilities for collective engagement than did the use of images. Intertextual collectivisation also varied according to how far tellers could consume or co-construct the intertextual material, where co-construction of the intertextual material is considered to endow the tellers with greater collective expression than purchasing online goods (such as commemorative memorabilia). The tellers' interactions with intertextual material were mediated, in that for all of the examples considered in this chapter even clicking on a hyperlink would leave traceable evidence. As mediated interactions, the collective identities that are construed for these tellers are ultimately open to aggregation, where tellers are positioned within competing groups. This reinforces a rhetorical strategy, where the quantification of the interaction becomes more important than the nature of the interaction itself. The power of aggregation as a form of collective identity reminds us that the sites in which stories are shared are not neutral but are driven by algorithms that promote frequency of interaction over the quality of the interaction, and where the quantifiable forms of sharing can be co-opted for multiple purposes. In this chapter, the purposes of sharing were put to political uses. In the next two chapters, I turn to the socio-economic implications of sharing in a different social media context: Twitter.

7 Shared Stories and Social Television Practices in Twitter

Introduction

In this book, I have argued that shared stories are multidimensional, mediated forms of narration that can serve multiple purposes for different tellers. In Chapter 6, I explored how sharing on Facebook community pages could simultaneously bring some tellers together whilst creating disagreement between others. In this chapter, I continue to explore the mediated ways in which stories are used to create common ground between tellers, turning to the context of the micro-blogging site Twitter. The discussion focuses on hashtags as a key resource within Twitter. I argue that hashtags are a form of mediated tellability which derives from, but is now in part independent of, their affordances as a search term. I use the narrative analysis of hashtags to extend and refine the concept of ambient affiliation (Zappavigna, 2011), setting out three types of affiliation: referential, contextual and evaluative. This framework is important, first, because it identifies contextual affiliation as a hitherto undocumented use of hashtags, and second, because it avoids a simplistic interpretation of affiliation as producing homophily. Instead, distinguishing between referential and evaluative types of affiliation explains how tellers can talk about the same topic but adopt very different stances towards it. Distinguishing between the three types of ambient affiliation opens up questions about how hashtags might serve different purposes for the people who use them. I address this question by examining a particular use of hashtags within Twitter as a form of social television practice, thereby bringing into focus the socio-economic value of shared stories. The chapter builds on the critical evaluation of social media practices as solely democratic or emancipatory and argues that the different types of affiliation can be exploited for commercial ends within the virtual market of Twitter. The analysis is important given the use of Twitter to bridge the gap between mainstream and social media forms of narrative production and reception, especially in relation to social television practices.

Social Television and Shared Stories

Since its inception in 2006, Twitter has become part of the social media landscape, with many millions of members using the site for diverse purposes. One aspect of Twitter which has begun to gain particular critical attention is its role as an environment for social television practices. Social television is the quasi-simultaneous interaction with other viewers via social media sites during the broadcast of a television programme (Buschow et al., 2014, p. 103). Although various social media sites can be used to engage audiences whilst viewing a television programme in real time (such as Facebook fan pages or YouTube channels), the fast-paced, public interactions of Twitter mean it has led the way in developing social television practices, where it is considered the primary site for measuring social media engagement with television viewing (Huddleston, 2016).

Social television practices are important as a context for shared stories, for they bring into focus the commercialised politics of sharing. Within the emerging research literature on social television, key questions have been raised about the social and economic outcomes of participation, asking who might benefit from the act of sharing responses to a television series. On the one hand, the ability for the audience to move beyond passive consumption to active, public expression of their opinions has been seen as a positive recognition of their contributions (Deller, 2011). This has built on the concept of audiencing developed within cultural studies; that is, the public performance of belonging to an audience for a particular mediated event or programme (Fiske, 1992). At the same time, the potential of this audience interaction through the 'second screens' (Bury et al., 2013, p. 308) of social network sites is valued by television producers as a means of encouraging real-time consumption of particular shows, thus boosting show ratings and developing a tractable fan base (Bober, 2014). Other studies have begun to explore whether social television practices unite the viewing audience into a single group with a common interest, or whether audiences might be more complex, and contain many diverse groups with competing interests. Whilst the benefits of audiencing might lead to an enhanced collective experience of 'live' television which might defragment the public sphere (Harrington, 2013, p. 244), the audiences of social television can vary according to the type of programme (Doughty et al., 2012) and national context (Highfield et al., 2013). One way in which this diversity is expressed is through the collective identities that can emerge from the interaction, where participants are positioned within particular in-groups or out-groups, such as fans, anti-fans (Gray, 2005) and snark fans (Harman and Jones, 2013). As with the other shared stories analysed in this book, these collective identities are predicated on the stance that the tellers take towards a particular object, which in this chapter include the programme and its performers. Analysing social television practices as a context for shared stories is an important step in teasing out the various ways in which the potential of sharing is embedded in these wider, ideological contexts where sharing can be valued or disrupted for different socio-economic ends.

Social television practices are also important as a distinctive, mediated context in which new narrative practices emerge. Not all the interactions which are incorporated within social television practices are necessarily narratives: they can include a heterogeneous mixture of communicative genres, including advertising, asking questions and taking part in competitions. However, the nature of commenting on a programme as it is consumed in real time, especially where the programme has a narrative structure, lends itself to the production of stories in social media contexts, and to the production of shared stories in particular. One reason for this is that social television practices incorporate the four characteristics of shared stories. Like shared stories, Twitter-based social television practices have distributed linearity, for they consist of many posts that unfold during the course of the televised broadcast. Social television practices are necessarily co-constructed by multiple participants from the audiences and participants in the television programme. Social television is also richly intertextual, for the tweets reference the programme to which they respond, often in creative ways that exploit the shared meanings that particular fans or critics recognise. In this way, the wider socio-cultural contexts of social television are presupposed in the enactment of the shared interactional norms, and so contribute to the discursive construction of shared knowledge presumed by these tellers and their audiences.

The X Factor

The shared stories analysed in this chapter relate to the social television practices which took place in Twitter in relation to the international franchise *The X Factor*, focusing on the responses to the series screened in the United Kingdom (series 10) and the United States of America (as *The X Factor USA* series 3), both in 2013. *The X Factor* is a hybrid format that combines a singing competition with reality television. It was launched in the United Kingdom in 2004, and during the following decade it ran series on an annual basis, with many franchised variations in other countries, including three series in the United States of America (2010–13). The narrative structure of *The X Factor* is akin to that of many other reality television formats. The over-arching progression of the series follows a goal-achievement pattern (Hoey, 2001), where the desired outcome for the contestants is to win the competition, with the prize of a recording contract and the promise of a successful career within the music industry. The structure of the series derives momentum from the suspense-driven results of each episode, as both contestants and audience await the evaluation from the judges and the results of voting polls to discover which contestants will or will not progress to the next round. The selection process in the series follows a generic format. Contestants must first audition for the judges, then proceed to 'boot camp'. A selected shortlist of contestants proceeds to the 'judges' houses', where the mentors for each category in the competition (solo boys, solo girls, 'over 25s' and groups) select the contestants who will perform on the live shows. Once the live shows commence, the outcomes no longer lie in the hands of the judges alone, but are in part determined by audience votes, where those contestants with the least votes are at risk of leaving the competition. As Keating (2013) points out, these competitions are characterised by hybrid narrative formats which derive from episodic serials (in the reliance on suspense, which must be sustained across the series as a whole) and film documentary (in the representation of the contestants' experiences, which in turn includes the background narratives of their personal history).

The macro-narrative offered by *The X Factor* exemplifies the demotic turn (Turner, 2010) in entertainment, which proposes that ordinary people can be transformed into celebrities. Like other examples of reality television, *The X Factor* depends on revealing the very constructedness of this transformation from 'ordinary' to 'celebrity' status, commoditised in the narration of a mediated self. The use of personal narrative is overtly exploited in the many confessional excerpts from contestants integrated within episodes of *The X Factor*. The excerpts document each contestant's transformation from their previous, 'ordinary life' by providing the backstory which contextualises their progression within the series and their aspirations for future success. These excerpts are highly selective in support of the programme's mythic structure, where the greater a contestant's potential transformation, the more tellable their experience and the more likely their story is to be included in each episode. The personal narratives which contain elements of a contestant's hardship or personal difficulty are often foregrounded as melodramatic 'sob stories' which function as examples of 'mediated voyeurism' (Stefanone et al., 2010, p. 510) to be consumed by the viewing public. The voyeuristic constructions of the mediated self also circulate outside the programme in personal stories about the contestants in the tabloid press, which exploit and collude with the series as a source of infotainment (Peters, 2011). The selection of the backstories and confessionals outside the genre-sanctioned boundaries of the show is driven by their news value of negativity, especially where a contestant's behaviour is unsanctioned in some way (for example, committing criminal offenses or being involved in inappropriate sexual activity). The various stories of the mediated self can therefore be commercialised in different ways by different tellers, which in this case include the television series and the tabloid press.

The real commodity from which the show profits is not the celebrities it claims to produce, but the audiences who engage with it (Wall, 2013). *The X*

Factor is a highly commercial form of reality television. Like other shows, it is a source of direct and indirect advertising for its sponsors, and it appeals to its contestants not in order to empower them but to draw in viewers and revenue for the series' producers. The audience's participation is integral both to the narrative design of the series in the form of telephone voting, which allows the viewer co-constructive power in determining the outcome of the competition, and to the economic success of the franchise as a means of generating revenue for its producers. In order to maintain the motivation for the audience's economic participation in the franchise (their votes), the programme also offers a wider set of invitations which encourages the audience's engagement through a range of discursive activities. For example, the UK series' companion programme, *The Xtra Factor*, which screens immediately after the results show, has always included opportunities for the viewing audience to phone in and discuss the outcomes of the results with the programme's judges. The series has also had a social media presence for many years, including the British Twitter account @TheXFactor (created in 2008) and the American series account @TheXFactorUSA (launched in 2010). Both accounts are still maintained at the time of writing, although the American television series was cancelled at the end of 2013. Like many other examples of convergence culture (Jenkins, 2006), the audience responses enabled through these social media accounts are interwoven with the televised episodes, for example with hashtags displayed during performances. In return, selected posts are read or shown during the televised episodes, offering the opportunity for the audience to have its messages redisplayed.

Like the audience's interaction with the series through viewing of the episodes and voting for the contestants, the social television practices encouraged by *The X Factor* are open to commercial exploitation. For example, the hashtag thread for the programme operates as an overspill (Deery, 2014) where advertisers related and unrelated to the franchise can place additional promotional content and where the audience can be invited to engage further with the programme's producers and performers. More generally, the social media interaction by the audience serves the interests of the series' producers, for as Wood and Baughman (2012) suggest, Twitter offers forms of participation that can be put to commercial ends as indirect, fan-generated forms of advertising. By enhancing the visibility of the series through sharing its responses in social television, the audience commentary has been considered as a form of unpaid publicity work. Finally, there are commercially driven sharing practices 'behind the scenes' which operate in relation to the Twitter-based interactions of social television. As entextualised responses, the audience's reactions to the series via Twitter form a tractable commodity of value to the producers and advertisers, which can be mined as a source of data about the viewing public and its sentiment towards the franchise.

Table 7.1 *Sampled episodes and data sample of tweets from* The X Factor *(2013)*

Series	UK Series 10	US Series 3	Total English-language tweets
Date and title of episodes	12–13 October, (Live Show 1	10 October, Four Chair Challenge	25 825
	2–3 November, Live Show 3	29–30 October, Live Show 1	42 375
	23–24 November, Live Show 7	27–28 November, Live Show 5	46 179
	14–15 December, Finale	18–19 December, Finale	45 301
Total			159 680

Data

The data for this study were gathered during October–December 2013 in relation to *The X Factor's* UK series 10 and US series 3. Tweets were collected using the analytic tool Tweet Archivist (www.tweetarchivist.com), which gathered tweets containing the topical hashtag #xfactor. This was the official hashtag for the franchise as a whole, and so gathered tweets relating to both the UK and the US series, which ran concurrently. The total number of tweets archived in this period was 1.6 million. There are a number of limitations to this method of data collection. Although using the official hashtag for the franchise allowed those posts marked as related to the television show to be archived, it could not capture posts about the series which did not use the hashtag or which used alternative hashtags such as #xfactoravoidance. The data inevitably provide a partial picture of the Twitter responses to the series during this period. Nonetheless, they still yield a sizeable sample which is suitable for discourse analytic scrutiny.

This chapter concentrates on a specific subset of the data: the English-language tweets that circulated in response to selected episodes from the series. These episodes were selected at three-weekly intervals in order to capture the commencement and finale of the live shows from the UK and US series. Because the live shows commenced later in the latter case than in the former, the data include two mid-point episodes from the British series and one episode from prior to the US series' live shows (the last 'Four Chair Challenge'). A detailed summary of the data is given in Table 7.1. The selected English-language tweets were then analysed using quantitative and qualitative methods of corpus-assisted discourse analysis in order to examine the resources used for sharing stories, beginning with the hashtags present in the data.

A quantitative analysis of the hashtags in the social television datasets gathered for *The X Factor* series in 2013 showed that they occurred extensively. In the 159 680 English-language tweets collected in relation to the four selected episodes which form the basis for analysis, 273 593 hashtags were present. A large number of the tweets (43 percent) contained multiple hashtags, and many of the hashtags appeared repeatedly throughout the dataset. For example, the hashtag #happythanksgiving occurred over 10 000 times. When the list of all hashtags was counted using Antconc, a word list of 10 843 unique hashtags was identified. I then downsampled from this list to compare the most frequently occurring hashtags and 1000 of the hashtags which occurred only once each in the data, so as to avoid skewing the qualitative analysis in favour of the most frequently occurring hashtags whilst retaining a dataset that was manageable for qualitative analysis. Each hashtag was considered in its immediate co-text; that is, the tweet in which it occurred.

Hashtags as a Resource for Shared Stories

Hashtags are one of the resources that Twitter members have developed in order to manage the fast-paced, 'noisy' interactions in this social media environment. Hashtags are similar to other kinds of tags that occur in the metadata of online content, in that they provide 'information about information'. However, the affordances of hashtags in Twitter are distinctive and make them a particularly important resource for shared stories. Unlike metadata, which is embedded as code, or is separated from the textual content as appended 'tags' (for example, added to blog posts or to images in Flickr, Instagram or Tumblr), the hashtags in Twitter posts are included within the verbal content of the message itself, and as such they can be part of the narration in a form of 'sharing as telling'. The hashtag symbol, #, can be added as a prefix to any lexical item, and the resulting hashtag integrated flexibly within the lexico-grammatical patterns of the tweet without restriction. As lexical items, hashtags serve a referential function, in that they convey content and can categorise a tweet as being about a particular topic. In social television practices, this includes the use of the hashtag that associates a tweet with the programme in question (such as #xfactor), but it can also include other, more specific categorisation of content, such as the use of #80s in the following tweet to position it as belonging to a particular episode in the series ('80s Night'), and the artists it names as associated with a specific decade of musical production:

Some amazing Louis Walsh song choices tonight. Sting. Spandau. Bryan Adams. #XFactor #80s

The referential function of the hashtag is important, as in the early development of Twitter, adding a hashtag influenced the distributive nature of the lexical item by turning it into a search term. Within Twitter, users could seek out hashtags using the 'search function', which at the time the data in this chapter were

Figure 7.1 Screenshot showing a sample of the hashtag #XFactor search results (4 November 2014)

collected (in 2013) was clearly associated with hashtags as a '#Discover' tab. Searching for a hashtag produced a timeline of results that aggregated all posts containing that hashtag, known as the 'hashtag thread' (see Figure 7.1).

As a search term, hashtags enhance the visibility of the post in which they are embedded by increasing its contexts of publication and so operating as a form of 'sharing as distribution'. In this way, hashtags increase the portability of the tweet. Instead of only appearing in the post author's timeline and the timelines of their followers, once the post is published in the context of the hashtag thread, the potential audience who might engage with it is increased to all those who might find the thread. The increased visibility can be considered as a form of emphasis, by drawing greater attention to the tweet in question for the audiences within Twitter. The searchability of hashtags renders them inherently interpersonal; they mark an item as searchable and emphasised for a particular audience. The emphatic meanings of hashtags have become more pronounced over time. In 2014, Twitter improved its 'discover' function so that it would search for any word published in a tweet, with or without a prefix of a hashtag. The use of a hashtag to demarcate a search term was non-essential from this point onward. Nonetheless, the use of hashtags has continued, although it now needs to be understood as a rhetorical strategy rather than merely an affordance-based function. As a result, hashtags have become a 'highlighting device' (Scott, 2015) that fulfils both referential and interpersonal functions.

From a narrative perspective, the highlighting function of the hashtag has much in common with the concept of tellability, whereby the narrator marks their story as particularly relevant for the audiences whom they address. As such, I propose that in a narrative context, hashtags are a mediated form of tellability that highlights content as searchable or emphatic for particular audiences.

The dual referential and interpersonal uses of the hashtags in Twitter have been explored in earlier research, where they have been analysed as a means of creating topical threads within the site (Papacharissi and de Fatima Oliveira, 2012) and for their different linguistic functions (Zappavigna, 2015). The differing uses of hashtags have been interpreted as variously projecting identities for different site members (Page, 2012b; Zappavigna, 2014b) and their stance towards particular objects (Evans, 2016). However, the connection between the hashtag's referential and interpersonal functions is most prominent in the concept of ambient affiliation. Ambient affiliation is comparable to the notion of bonding (see Chapter 5). This is seen most clearly in Zappavigna's (2014b, p. 210) description of ambient affiliation as the means by which 'social bonds are configured in order to commune with a mass online audience'. Based on the principles of Systemic Functional Linguistics, ambient affiliation presumes the separable but interrelated ideational and interpersonal functions of language (Zappavigna, 2011, p. 8) where the imagined audience who might use the same hashtags would be like-minded, posting messages about the same topic, to an imagined audience who shared the same interest. Ambient affiliation has much in common with the shared story, in that both examine how shared ground between multiple participants is constructed. However, the homophily presumed by 'affiliation' is somewhat fuzzy and needs further clarification.

As an interpersonal resource, affiliation has multiple dimensions. First, it can indicate referential connection insofar as tweets are marked as about the same topic. However, within pragmatics, affiliation carries an additional, affective dimension, implying a pro-social aspect and a shared evaluative stance between participants (Stivers et al., 2011, p. 21). It is this second dimension that I will extend in relation to the shared stories. I do this by showing that whilst the referential and affective aspects of hashtag use often overlap, they are also separable. The distinction between the two aspects is evident in the different narrative elements that are highlighted as tellable by the use of a hashtag. Hashtags can highlight narrative events and contexts or contribute to stance as a form of evaluation. It is therefore quite possible for participants to tweet about the same topic and use the referential function of the hashtag to connect one tweet to another within the networks of Twitter, but not share the same affective stance towards the topic with the other members using the same hashtag thread. As the analysis in Chapter 6 showed, it is possible for different people to take a stance towards the same object but to evaluate that object in quite different ways. Drawing on Du Bois' (2007) analogy of the stance triangle once again, the axes towards the stance object are separable. Similarly, to assume that all hashtags enable ambient affiliation in the same way ignores this important distinction between the types of affiliation that are possible. In the following sections, I will show how a narrative analysis of the hashtag helps refine the concept of ambient affiliation and use this analysis to question whose interests the ambient affiliation might serve.

Referential Affiliation: Hashtags and Tellable Events

The use of hashtags to create ambient affiliation by drawing together tweets about a particular topic relies on their original function of making content searchable and thereby connecting posts that are marked as being about a shared interest. This principle is used within social television to promote the interests of the programme itself, for example by creating a hashtag for that programme (here, *The X Factor*) and related hashtags for individual aspects of the content broadcast within it. In the following examples, the referential focus of the hashtags places the events and participants in the performance of *The X Factor* at the centre of the tweets' tellability. Some used hashtags to categorise and give emphasis to particular events within the macro-narrative of *The X Factor* series, such as the theme of an episode (including #xffinale, #disco, #motown, #liveshows, #judgeshouses):

So this week on #xfactor is #bigband wonder what song Gary will choose for the boys personally I want Mr. Bojangles #lovethesong <3

Others marked the outcomes of episodes as tellable:

They've left the show for their abode. The disco fails for Kingsland Road #xfactor #resultsshow #home #kingslandroad #departure #shocker

The worthy winner, well done Sam #xfactor #xfactorwinner2013 #sambailey http://t.co/jnL9hHVIkf

A subset of the referential hashtags included multiword compounds that narrated notable moments in the series as breaking news. Like the tellability identified in personal narratives more generally, some of the 'breaking news' marked with a hashtag was considered noteworthy as a breach from the norm (see Norrick, 2007). An example of this can be seen in the hashtag #kellyandsimonkiss, which occurred in a tweet capturing a moment from *The X Factor USA* when the judge Kelly Rowland kissed the judge Simon Cowell after a contestant's performance:

Probably the best part of the night! Hahaha @KELLYROWLAND @SimonCowell @TheXFactorUSA #xfactor #KellyandSimonKiss http://t.co/cWL6mBQebF

However, the referential focus for the hashtags containing stories of breaking news also went beyond the tellability associated with personal storytelling and constructed the commercial value of the shared stories in this context. The tellable events which occurred in the hashtags promoted the performances and merchandise associated with *The X Factor* franchise. These included announcements of the particular episodes or events in the series, such as #tonightwegolive and #votinglinesnowopen, as well as news about singles released by performers who appeared on the show, such as the announcements for the British bands Little Mix (#Littlemixmoveoutnow) and One Direction (#Storyofmylifevideowillbreaktherecordonvevo). Rather than a participatory resource used by fans to reach out to performers or reimagine the programmes' outcomes, the mediatised tellability in these examples strongly suggests that social television practices were co-opted in the socio-economic interests of the programme's producers, who used the hashtag to broadcast their content to the Twitter-based audience.

The referential function of hashtags to promote the content of the television programme was also used to highlight the names of the participants in the broadcast episodes, such as the judges, contestants and guest performers. The hashtags were not a form of addressivity in the way that using the participants' Twitter usernames would be. Instead, the hashtags positioned the participants' names as a topic to be talked about, not talked to, as in the following examples:

RT @its_emi98: Say something performed by #AlexandSierra on #xfactor was so fcking beautiful ! ❤

Check it out #nicholesherzinger and #xfactor contestants having fun at the @Roller_Disco on our skates! http://t.co/wSVokmpXUL.

Like the hashtags which highlighted events within the broadcast episodes as tellable, the referential hashtags used for performers' names seem to have promoted the interests of the programme and its personnel. However, the use of hashtags to mark a person's identity as tellable was not limited to those who appeared on the series. Using a hashtag as a prefix to a name was a key practice of the fandoms which emerged around contestants or established artists who performed on the series. Each fandom built its own shared identity, which it promoted through hashtag-marked fan group names. Examples of fan identities included plural forms derived from the name of their idols, such as #callafans (fans of British contestant, Sam Callahan) or #friendies (fans of British contestant, Luke Friend):

@samcallahan94 doesn't deserve the negative comments! think you did amazing! you have your #callafans so youll be here next week!#XFactor

RT @MXPhoebe: omg x factor final tonight, everyone vote for @LukeFriendMusic #friendies #xfactor #XFactorFinal #voteluke

Other names of fandoms emphasised their shared interest through the use of collective metaphors, such as 'armies', 'families' and 'teams', compounded with the names of the idols. Examples included #GBarmy (fans of singer, Gary Barlow) and #TeamTim (fans of American contestant, Tim Olstad):

#GBarmy what is your fave moment of Gary during these 3 years of #xfactor???...comment below pls:)

I almost passed out when they sent home @TimOlstadMusic. Thank god it was just like a horrible nightmare. Phew! #TeamTim #XFactor #US.

The referential use of the hashtag for collective fan-based identities supports the central meaning of affiliation as belonging to the same group. However, the use of hashtags to emphasise the names of the performers and the fans does not mean that these participants were represented as equally tellable in the context of social television. The lexico-grammatical differences in the hashtags also point to the socio-economic hierarchies at work in the shared story. The performers were individualised through the use of their personal names, whilst the identity of individual fans was subsumed within collective labels of the fandoms as whole. A quantitative comparison of the frequency of the hashtags used for participant names reinforces the different values of these hashtags within the economy of Twitter, where the names of fandoms constituted only 6 percent of the hashtags: proportionately, three times smaller than the names of performers (18 percent of the hashtags). The interpersonal emphasis of the hashtags in this dataset thus illustrates the ways in which the double logic of mediated empowerment and exploitation in social media operated (Van Dijck, 2013). Both fans and performers could make their identities visible by using a hashtag, but in quantitative terms, this favoured the interests of the mainstream media producers rather than those of the audience.

This is not to say that the fans' use of the hashtags was without value. The fans used the visibility afforded by the hashtag to create calls for action in the form of imperatives prefixed with a hashtag, either directed to other fans, as in the formulaic command to '#vote[contestant's name]':

Ahh my love for @RoughCopyUK is getting out of hand. If they 'rough copy' any song they can make it sound so good. #VoteRoughCopy #XFactor

or directed to the performers and producers of the show, as in campaigns to reinstate ('#bringback[contestant's name]') or remove performers from the competition:

RT @ukpoynter: @SimonCowell hey I want @IamJamesKenney back!!!! #bringbackjames #XFactor

I love #XFactor but if they go ahead and put that vile homophobe on their show I won't be watching #dropjamesarthur

These imperatives projected the co-constructive involvement of the audience within the meta-narrative of the television series. For example, the calls to action encouraged viewers to participate in ways that might change the outcome of events, either by voting (and so helping particular contestants remain in the competition) or by putting pressure on the series' producers to alter the content of programmes. Of course, the extent to which these calls to action actually influenced the narrative line of the series remains open to question. In the examples given here, the contestants Rough Copy did not make it to the final of the UK series, James Kenney was not reinstated to appear in the live shows and former winner James Arthur was not dropped, but went on to perform in the seventh live show of UK series 10. Whilst the interpersonal affordances of the hashtag seemed to endow the audience with greater visibility and direct access to the producers of the franchise, this interpersonal potential also served the interest of the mainstream media producers by building a tractable fan base, whose use of the #xfactor hashtags meant that their interactions operated as a form of indirect publicity by attempting to increase further engagement from the programme's audience.

Contextual Affiliation: Hashtags and Narrative Orientation

Affiliation was achieved not only through the referential nature of the hashtags but also through contextual information contained in the hashtags, in the form of narrative orientation. This included hashtags which gave the details of when and where the reported events in the tweet took place. Affiliation was not projected via a shared interest signalled through the topic of the hashtag. Instead, contextualising hashtags emphasised shared temporal, geographical and affective proximity between the participants.

The contextual hashtags included references to the time at which the author was viewing the televised episodes, such as #weekend, #night, #now or days of the week. Like the referential hashtags, the contextual hashtags were used to anticipate key turning points or performances in the series, as in the following examples:

It is ABOUT to go down. #xfactor #clutch #tonight

I am so excited that @cher is going to be on #xfactor tonight. The only thing that could make it more exciting is if she dueted with Meatloaf #XFactor #tonight

The immediacy of this temporal orientation in the hashtags projected a shared sense of 'nowness' (Fiske, 1987) that is associated with the live broadcast of television, recaptured in the social television practices of watching and commenting on the television series in real time. More generally, the emphasis on the present moment is also typical of social network sites like Twitter, which tend to privilege recency over retrospection in the construction of temporality (Page, 2012a, p. 192). The contextual affiliation arises from the 'nowness' of the hashtags, which created an illusion of temporal co-presence, even whilst the tellers posting the tweets may have been geographically remote from one another.

Given the potential geographical remoteness between the tellers who posted tweets about *The X Factor* franchise, it is all the more intriguing that the contextualising hashtags also gave details of where the reported events in the tweets took place. Unlike the hashtags which contextualised the viewing in relation to the immediate temporal proximity of the teller, there were no uses of generalised deictic references in the location hashtags, such as the adverbs 'here' and 'there'. Instead, these hashtags located the audience of the reported events as co-present in particular places, such as countries (#uk, #italy, #australia), cities and towns (#london, #daytonabeach) and venues (#wembley), as shown in these examples:

@AandSFans PLEASE #RETWEET #RT Be at the live taping of #XFactor @ #DaytonaBeach Band Shell 7pm Wed to support #AlexAndSierra!#XFactor2013

Got our tickets! #xfactor #live #finals #tickets # tonight #excited #happy #london #wembly #arena

The affiliation in these cases arises from co-locating the participants in geographical places relevant to the series, along with other members of the audience. In other cases, the hashtags were used to emphasise the place identity of the contestants who were performing in the series, where the hashtag emphasised their home location, appealing to their local fan base:

better late than never but nice 1 on getting thru again tonight Sam #shamazing as always #XFactor #leicester

So #Croydon has three acts in the #XFactor lives. Good luck to all of them (@lornasimpsonx @HannahBMusic and @RoughCopyUK) this evening

Alongside the geographical locations associated with the contexts of tweets, the hashtags also highlighted the affective relationships constructed as part of the audience participation. These hashtags occurred in the stories which highlighted the collective nature of the offline experience of watching the show with friends. The hashtags in these tweets were used to give emphasis to affectionate terms, such as #bestfriendsforever and #cuddles:

Fantastic night with my girls last night now to catch up with my @manjowithane this evening! #beer #xfactor #bestfriendsforever

Tonight is deffo another chill night with the family! #xfactor #chinese #cuddles ❤

Other hashtags positioned watching the television series in relation to the narrator's participation in communal events, with hashtags like #party, #fiesta and #snight:

Its my birthday yaaaaaaaaaaaaay....#party #drinks # bigscreen #xfactor #xfCarlito

Finally, contextualising hashtags were used to emphasise other programmes that the viewers were watching alongside *The X Factor*:

Gonna have a lazy day + night, catch up on tv! #breakingbad #homeland #towie #xfactor #corrie

These hashtags positioned *The X Factor* alongside comparable examples of singing competitions (#thevoice, #idol), reality television (#towie, #madeinchelsea, #americasgottalent, #dwts and so on) or programmes that were screened at the same time as it (#spoty (*Sports Personality of the Year*) #downton, #strictly). Unlike the narrative orientation that emphasised the participants in the programme and promoted the value of the individual celebrity figures, the social television practices were used by the audience to make visible, emphasise and share a collective experience of consumption. These contexts of consumption clearly emphasised the affective dimension of viewing as pleasurable and to be celebrated. As such, these hashtags might seem to promote the interests of the audience, rather than the producers of the television series. However, the visibility of the audience and its experiences should not be interpreted as solely for its own benefit. Instead, the double logic of empowerment and exploitation continued to operate. Whilst the contextualising hashtags seem to make tellable the audience's experience (and hence their value), the use of the programme's hashtag alongside the tweets about the audience means that ultimately, even the audience's celebration of its own viewing served to reinforce the visibility and value of the programme.

Hashtags and Evaluation: From Affiliation to Disaffiliation

The affective nature of the audience's viewing experiences contextualised through the hashtags brings to the fore the interpersonal potential of hashtags as a rhetorical resource in narrating shared stories. The potential for hashtags to combine affective and interpersonal meaning is most fully realised in their use to express evaluation. Evaluative hashtags were used to indicate the stance of a tweet's author, positioning them as a fan or critic of the performers or the programme. They were not unified in their affect. Instead, a range of different evaluative expressions occurred in the hashtags, which could express either approval or criticism of a performer. This included their appearance, which could be positive (#cute, #beautiful, #sexy), and their performance, which could be negative (#shite, #fail). Likewise, hashtags were used to emphasise the emotional responses of the audience to the programme and its outcomes, which could be either positive (#excited, #loveit, #happy) or negative (#gutted, #cringe, #wtf). Illustrative examples which show the variation in the kinds of stance that were expressed in the hashtags include the following tweets:

Tonight I lost all hope in America.....tonight @JoshLeviWorld and @LillieNicoleMc went home #XFactor #insanity #sadface

Ahhh can't wait to see @LittleMixOffic perform on @TheXFactor this evening! #excited #XFactor #Move:-D

The diversity of the affective potential of the evaluative hashtags is important, as it leads to a re-evaluation of the interpersonal potential of hashtags generally, especially the assumption that they might promote a single shared attitude as a form of 'affiliation'. As these examples suggest, hashtags do not just emphasise referential content: they can also emphasise stance, and that stance need not be shared. Relying on the ideational aspect of hashtags to establish referential affiliation cannot also ensure that additional kinds of pro-social affiliation will necessarily follow. As a result, it is unlikely that a single shared story will emerge from a hashtag thread. Rather, a hashtag thread can be co-opted for other purposes, such as advertising goods or services unrelated to the programme in question as a form of 'spam'. Other tweets at odds with a shared affiliation came from anti-fans who sought to criticise those collectively consuming the programme. The stance expressed in the main body of a tweet need not be shared with other viewers of the programme at all, as the following examples illustrate:

How egoistical can #XFactor finalists be? Floggin' their own tacky merch. Talk about believing one's own hype. Glad I don't watch the crap!

RT @EmmaMooreCoUk: No #xfactor for me. National Theatre Anniversary Show on BBC 2. Perfect. #nationaltheatre #proud.

The potential for the shared stories of social media to incorporate both ambient affiliation and disaffiliation might seem at odds with the aspirations of social television to defragment the viewing audience. However, the increased visibility of the hashtag and the collective consumption of a television programme do not rest on all viewers sharing the same sentiment. Indeed, the confrontainment that characterises reality television genres like *The X Factor* capitalises on disagreements as the very means of generating attention. Likewise, even if a member tweets about their experiences of not watching the series as a means of critiquing the franchise, the presence of the #xfactor hashtag means that the visibility of the programme is still increased within Twitter. If the goal of social television is ultimately to benefit the television producers, rather than the audience, then disaffiliation and affiliation may well be welcomed alike.

Conclusion

In this chapter, I presented an analysis of hashtags within Twitter as a highly valued resource for shared stories as they emerge in the context of social television practices. I argued that hashtags function as a mediatised form of tellability. Like the tellability found in other forms of narratives, the hashtag highlights selected referential content for the imagined audiences, and as such is an inherently interpersonal form of searchable talk. The interrelated but separable dimensions of tellability are used to expand and refine the concept of ambient affiliation. I proposed that ambient affiliation can be created in three ways: as referential affiliation, where the hashtag highlights a shared interest, such as a topic; as evaluative affiliation, where the hashtag highlights a shared stance; and in an as yet undocumented form of affiliation, as contextual affiliation. Unlike referential affiliation, the hashtags used for contextual affiliation do not emphasise the main topic of the tweet, and therefore would not be a logical choice for a search term. Instead, contextual affiliation draws attention to the role of narrative orientation (such as time and place) in creating common ground or social bonds between participants. In the data used in this chapter, the contextual affiliation confirmed the ongoing importance of temporal immediacy as a means of bridging the physically remote contexts in which the participants were situated. In addition, hashtags emphasised the places in which the audience was situated (such as towns, venues and countries) and so co-located the tellers within shared contexts based upon where they were, or where they were from. Finally, contextual affiliation constructed shared social encounters, where the tellers were positioned in affective proximity to other participants.

The three aspects of ambient affiliation are important because they expand and refine the ways in which hashtags can create common ground between tellers. The distinction between referential, contextual and evaluative affiliation also avoids a simplistic interpretation of shared ground and points to the complex ways in which stance, positioning and visibility are interrelated. Using a hashtag to talk about the same topic does not mean that all tellers will share the same evaluative stance. The visibility which endows the hashtag with its highlighting potential can be co-opted for multiple purposes, not just to draw together tellers who might be interested in the topic, but also to criticise or reject the interests of the group altogether.

The framework for ambient affiliation I have set out in this chapter is derived from data taken from social television practices. The importance of the distinction between referential, contextual and evaluative affiliation allows us to question and differentiate the ends to which these kinds of affiliation are put in this growing form of social media storytelling. Sharing via a hashtag serves multiple purposes for different tellers. Referential hashtags gave emphasis to the programme and its performers, whilst contextual hashtags increased the visibility of the viewers in public displays of audiencing and evaluative hashtags were used by both the programme's producers and the audience to express endorsement and criticism of the series. However, given that in these data, all the tweets were accompanied by the referential hashtag used to aggregate tweets about the franchise (#xfactor), the additional contextual and referential hashtags ultimately served the affordance-based purpose of promoting the visibility of the programme within the context of Twitter. The hashtags therefore give further substance to the claim that social television practices both empower and exploit the audience, whose interactions might make visible its collective consumption and evaluations of the programme (thereby granting it expressive power), but simultaneously exploit those interactions as one means to increase the visibility of the programme as a whole.

Although this chapter has focused on hashtags used in Twitter in relation to social television practices, the framework for ambient affiliation is relevant to other kinds of hashtags, such as those used for campaigns, protests and mediated events that take place across distributed contexts. It also opens up further lines of inquiry regarding the use of hashtags in other social media contexts beyond Twitter, such as Instagram, Tumblr and Pinterest, where the mediated affordances and social meanings of hashtags continue to evolve in various directions. The narrative perspective on ambient affiliation is therefore important not only to narrative scholars as a means of extending our understanding of the mediated forms in which tellability is achieved and the functions it might serve, but also to media scholars as a way of explaining how the double logic of exploitation and empowerment present in many kinds of social media interactions might operate.

8 Co-tellership in Retweets

Introduction

In Chapter 7, I examined the shared stories that were found in social television practices, focusing on the Twitter-based responses to the international franchise *The X Factor*. I argued that the different types of affiliation that were constructed by the hashtags in the tweets could have the potential to promote the interests of one group of tellers rather than another, so that tellers were caught in a double logic of exploitation and empowerment associated with social television practices. In this chapter, I continue to explore how the co-tellers involved in social television practices were positioned relative to one another, focusing on retweets. As a form of 'sharing prior talk' (Draucker and Collister, 2015), retweets are an important phenomenon, found within Twitter, which allow tellers to take up various participation roles and which may give rise to further interactions that can generate rapport-enhancing or rapport-threatening outcomes. These participation roles and the subsequent interactions prompted by retweets are important as a means of exploring how far sharing might be evenly distributed between co-tellers and used for various socio-economic purposes.

There are two types of hierarchy that are created between tellers who interact with one another via retweets. First, the participation roles available through the practice of retweeting create communicative hierarchies, where some tellers create content whilst others redistribute that content. Second, the potential for retweets to draw on shared knowledge between the participants can result in rapport-enhancing, in-group interactions, or in rapport-threatening responses that create an out-group. These hierarchies can benefit the different groups of tellers involved in social television practices, such as the producers and performers related to the programme, and the audience, which includes both fans and critics. The mediated narrative analysis of the retweets builds on the critical evaluation of social media interactions, especially in social television practices, where the apparent 'empowerment' of the audience to respond to the series via retweets is also understood to serve the interests of the series (and its producers) by promoting its visibility within the context of Twitter.

Figure 8.1 Screenshot showing a sample retweet

Retweets as a Resource for Shared Stories

Retweets are a form of quotation, in which one Twitter member reposts a message originally created by another. Since 2009, it has been possible to retweet a message using a semi-automated 'retweet' button which prefixes the reposted message with the abbreviation 'RT'. More recently, within Twitter's interface, retweets are indicated by a caption above the post, which states '[Username] retweeted' (see Figure 8.1).

Within the context of Twitter, retweets are important because of the ways in which the action of retweeting redistributes publicly available content within the site. When a Twitter member reposts a tweet, it is distributed to their follower list and thereby is opened up to a wider audience. The original author is also notified that the retweet has been sent, thus enhancing the visibility of the original tweet, the retweet, the original author and the retweeter. Given that visibility is prized within Twitter, retweeting can be considered as a symbolic interaction whose meanings extend beyond information sharing to incorporate other pragmatic outcomes for the persons involved in this communicative practice (Puschmann, 2015, p. 30). In the existing research, the pragmatic outcomes associated with retweets have been interpreted for their interpersonal potential, such as 'conversational' interactions (Boyd et al., 2010) that can signal affiliation between the person reposting the tweet, the original author and their audience. However, as Boyd et al. (2010) point out, this relational work is often ambiguous in nature. The potential to use retweets to display connection with others can be embedded in socio-economic hierarchies, where the 'conversational' characteristics of the interaction are closer to one-to-many broadcasts rather than dyadic exchanges (Page, 2012a, p. 115), and therefore can be co-opted for various socio-political purposes, such as activism (Potts et al., 2014), or to manage a fan base as a form of celebrity practice (Page, 2012b). The emerging research also suggests that the practices of retweeting may vary according to the particular community (Mahrt et al., 2013), so that affiliation may not be the only pragmatic outcome available.

Retweets are a powerful resource for shared stories, in that they combine intertextuality (as a form of quotation) with co-tellership (as they are co-constructed by the original author of the tweet and the person who retweeted it) in practices that can result in shared meanings that are reinforced or contested between participants. In this chapter, the narrative potential of retweeting is explored through the analysis of the Twitter-based social television practices that responded to the international franchise of *The X Factor* (see Chapter 7). The analysis focuses on how co-tellership and intertextuality are used to position the performers and the audience as narrative participants relative to each other, both within localised interactions and within the broader socio-economic context of the social television practices.

Data and Methods

The data analysed in this chapter are a subset of the larger corpus of 159 680 tweets gathered for the hashtag #xfactor between October and December 2013, posted in response to UK series 10 and US series 3 of *The X Factor* franchise. As discussed in more detail in Chapter 7, the corpus was sampled diachronically, with four episodes selected for closer scrutiny at the start, end and mid-points of the live shows from the two series. In these data, retweets constituted over half of the tweets posted in response to each episode, and 60 percent on average of the posts in the data from the selected episodes combined. The total number of 95 672 retweets generated in responses to the selected episodes of *The X Factor* was nearly equally divided between the two series, with 51 percent relating to the US version (47 828 tweets) and 49 percent to the UK version (46 960 tweets). The proportion of retweets in this dataset is important, for it is markedly higher than that found in earlier research. For example, the random sample of tweets gathered for Boyd et al.'s (2010) study reported that 5 percent of posts were retweets. In my earlier studies of Twitter-based interaction, retweets similarly occurred as only 5 and 10 percent of the sample (Page, 2012a, p. 99). In studies of datasets of tweets containing a hashtag, retweeting was more prominent, although not to the extent found in the data of the present study. For example, Larsson and Moe's (2011, p. 736) analysis of an election-based hashtag (#val2010) reported retweets at a frequency of 32 percent. Puschmann's (2015) analysis of hashtags noted variation in the frequency of retweets dependent on the topic of the hashtag, with the highest proportion of retweets (39 percent) associated with news streams that disseminated information on technology topics (#bigdata). The unusually high proportion of the retweets in the data collected with the #xfactor hashtag suggests that retweeting is a distinctive function in social television, and therefore offers a particularly rich and extensive opportunity to explore further the language of retweeting and its narrative potential.

The methods used to analyse the retweets examine their content and interactional context from quantitative and qualitative perspectives. A quantitative approach was used in two ways. First, the frequency of the different participants in the retweeting process was analysed, distinguishing the different roles that tellers could take according to Goffman's (1981) participation framework. Second, using corpus approaches, a keyword analysis of the retweets was used to identify the lexical items that were most frequently overused in the retweets for the data selected from the episodes in the #xfactor tweets. The results of the quantitative analyses are used inductively in a qualitative analysis of how particular tellers used the retweets in different kinds of stories that projected affiliation and disaffiliation between the participants.

In the second part of the chapter, mixed methods are used to explore the intertextuality of the retweets. A quantitative analysis of the retweets identified linked content as a particularly important feature of these interactions. The intertextuality in the linked content in the retweets is then analysed using multimodal discourse analysis to question the ways in which visual and verbal content was recontextualised in interactions that projected different kinds of rapport-enhancing and rapport-threatening outcomes for the audiences of this television series.

Co-tellership and the Politics of Participation

Like shared stories, retweets necessarily involve more than one teller. The communicative roles in a retweet comprise at least the author of the original tweet and the Twitter member who retweeted it. As Draucker and Collister (2015) propose, Goffman's (1981) framework for analysing the process of narrative production brings to light the different communicative functions of these roles. Goffman makes a key distinction between authors, who produce the original content of a message, and animators, who reproduce that content as a form of quotation. For any given retweet, the author is the Twitter member who posted the original content and the animator is the retweeter who reposted the content. The difference in these two roles can be seen in the following example, where the author is the Twitter member @TimOlstadMusic and the animator is the Twitter member @BlondieSF19:

> RT @TimOlstadMusic: Hanging with my amazing mentor, @paurubio, after our session tonight! @TheXFactorUSA #XFactor http://t.co/u4UM3dhS2o
>
> Retweeted by @BlondieSF19

In the model of shared stories, Goffman's distinction between the author and the animator aligns with the different meanings of sharing, where the author's function emphasises sharing as telling, whilst the animator's role emphasises the types of sharing involved in distribution. These sharing functions might be understood within a hierarchy, whereby the author who generates content is privileged and the animator's labour of reproduction serves a subordinate function which may not involve the additional creation of content.

The bold distinction between the communicative roles of authors and animators as co-tellers is most readily applicable to tweets which are reproduced using Twitter's semi-automated retweet button, which preserve and do not alter or add to the original tweet in any way (which Draucker and Collister call 'preserving tweets'). However, more complex co-tellership patterns emerge when retweets are also edited by the person who reposts them, which Draucker and Collister call an 'adapting retweet', and which I have referred to in my earlier work as a 'modified retweet' (Page 2012a, 2012b). In an adapted retweet, the animator also takes up the role of author by contributing content to the message, for example by adding an evaluative comment or paraphrasing the original tweet in some way. The more complex participation roles in an adapting retweet are illustrated in the following example (where bold text is added for ease of reference):

RT @jileysoreos: "@Flawlescyrus: **"Miley is said to replace Demi on the next season of #xfactor" is this true ?"** OMG that would be amazing

In this example of an adapting retweet, the Twitter member @jileysoreous has retweeted a post originally authored by @Flawlescyrus. The original post authored by @Flawlescyrus is marked by the quotation marks (and reproduced in bold here, for clarity). @Jileysoreous has animated this portion of the earlier tweet but also taken up a role of second author by adding a further, evaluative comment after the final quotation marks: 'OMG that would be amazing'. Examining who takes up these co-tellership roles allows us to see how the communicative hierarchy between telling and distribution operates in the social television practices within Twitter. As a first step, I compared the number of Twitter accounts that had reposted content with those whose content had been reposted. In this initial comparison, I did not count the authorship of animators who also added further content to a post as secondary authors, as I was most concerned with the practices of redistribution as compared with primary content creation. Interaction with original tweets, including adding further content to a retweet, is discussed in the second half of this chapter.

Theoretically, it would be possible for there to be an equal number of authors and animators who contribute to the co-tellership of retweeted stories. However, in the data analysed in this chapter, this was not the case. The 95 672 retweets that were posted in response to the eight selected episodes of *The X Factor* were generated by 71 517 unique animators, who reposted content originally created by 6527 authors: a ratio of more than ten animators to each author. There are also differences in the statuses of the members who took up these roles. Some posts were retweeted many more times than others. At one end of the scale, Twitter members like @ddlovato (the account maintained on behalf of the American celebrity, Demi Lovato) created posts that were retweeted repeatedly. For example, one of her posts was retweeted 20 251 times. At the other end

Table 8.1 *Mean size of the follower list for the authors of the 100 most frequently and 100 least frequently retweeted posts on US series 3 and UK series 10 of* The X Factor *(2013)*

	The X Factor USA series 3	*The X Factor UK* series 10
Authors of the 100 most frequently retweeted posts	2 293 932 followers	1 129 373 followers
Authors of the 100 least frequently retweeted posts	1050 followers	3226 followers

of the scale, there were Twitter members whose posts were retweeted only once. One difference between the authors of these retweets is the size of their follower list. I calculated and compared the mean total of the follower lists for the authors of the 100 most retweeted posts and the 100 least retweeted posts. The results of this comparison are summarised in Table 8.1. They suggest a quantitative difference, where the Twitter members with larger follower lists were more often retweeted than those with smaller lists. This disparity was much more marked for the audiences responding to the US rather than the UK series of *The X Factor*. The differences in the identities of the accounts contrasted in terms of the size of their Follower list (and hence number of retweets), which confirms a pattern that is well documented in other studies of Twitter interaction (Suh et al., 2010). The accounts with large Follower lists were primarily those maintained by celebrities and news agencies, as summarised in Tables 8.2 and 8.3.

The contrast between celebrity identities associated with the production of mainstream televised content and the audiences that reproduced that content is apparent in a comparison of the Twitter members who functioned as authors of primary content and those who functioned as animators. I compared the account names of the authors of the 100 most frequently retweeted posts with the account names of the animators for the dataset of 95 672 retweets. There was very little overlap between the two. The fifty-three authors of the most

Table 8.2 *Twitter members who authored the 100 most frequently reposted tweets for US series 3 of* The X Factor *(2013)*

X Factor personnel	Series account (@TheXFactorUSA), judges (Demi Lovato), series 3 contestants (Carlito Olivero, Al Calderon, Colton Pack, Andrew Scholz, Ellona Santiago, Sierra Deaton)
Entertainment industry	Producers (Alfredo Flores), supporting artists (Josh Devine, Alexander Gold), artists (Jasmine Villegas)
Fan news accounts	@demetriaaalove, @Demilovabr, @LatestAbout1D
Entertainment news	@eonline, @enews, @JustJared
Fans	@EricaSLP

Table 8.3 *Twitter members who authored the 100 most frequently reposted tweets for UK series 10 of* The X Factor *(2013)*

X Factor personnel	Series account (@TheXFactor), Judges (Sharon Osbourne, Gary Barlow, Nichole Scherzinger), series 10 contestants (Kingsland Road, Matt Kingsland, Sam Callahan, Luke Friend), performers (James Arthur, Little Mix), former contestants (George Shelley, Rylan Clark)
Fan news accounts	@taylornation13, @1DFAMILY
Entertainment news	@HolyMoly, @itvthismorning, @HylandIan
Commercial accounts	@KFC_Choir, @BeautyLabLondon, @BOHEMnails
Parody accounts	@KatieWeasel, @Charles_HRH, @JCartwrightN0T
Entertainment industry	Comedians (Frankie Boyle), footballers (Rio Ferdinand), reality TV stars (Lucy Watson, Kirk Norcross), fashion designers (Julien McDonald)
Fans	@MrsAnneTwist, @GbArmy, @BieberAnnual, @fatherteebird, @celebritain
Humorous accounts	@BritishLogic

reduplicated retweets acted as animators of retweets (that is, they reposted a tweet originally authored by someone else) on only 161 occasions (0.3 percent of the retweets), and twenty-nine of the authors (over half) never retweeted at all in response to the four episodes considered in this dataset. The participation roles found in the retweeting practices in this dataset are strongly asymmetrical, where the authors (emerging and established celebrity figures) very rarely redistributed other people's material. Retweeting thus seems to be typical behaviour of the series' audiences rather than characterising the discursive behaviour of the celebrity figures that performed on *The X Factor*. If the value of the animators is understood to boost the value of the content created by authors, then it would seem that social television practices exploit the work of the audience to promote the content produced by the celebrity figures. However, the value of the animators cannot be fully assessed without considering what kind of content was retweeted. In order to explore the relationship between the co-tellers and the social television practices, I turn next to an analysis of the retweets and their content.

The Language of Audiencing in Retweets

In line with the methods of mediated narrative analysis, I began by using corpus approaches to examine the verbal content of the retweets. As with the other case studies in this book, keyword analysis was used to identify the lexical items which were most frequently overused. Keyword searches are helpful insofar as the overused items might be considered as particularly prominent within a specialised corpus as compared with a reference corpus. The kinds of items that are overused might then yield insight about the content that was most distinctively valued within the retweets that circulated within social television practices. However, the numerical thresholds for the keyness values need to be considered carefully, especially with data such as the retweets that are scrutinised here. As stated earlier, some of the retweets in this dataset were repeatedly reposted. Some were reposted without any modification, whilst others had material added to the post. Even if the specialised and reference corpuses were adjusted so that exact duplicates of a retweet were removed (for example, duplicates of preserving retweets), this still means that keyword searches might be skewed by adapting retweets. A second challenge for carrying out keyword analysis of data gathered from Twitter is to find a suitable reference corpus for comparison. The topical focus within Twitter can change quickly given the rapidity with which the quasi-real-time posting occurs. A generalised corpus of tweets taken from a different timespan may well be too different in terms of topic to make a reference corpus suitably comparable. In order to mitigate these two factors, the keyword analysis was carried out by treating the retweets on the eight selected episodes as a specialised corpus (256 113 words) and comparing this with a reference corpus of the entire set of tweets gathered for all twenty episodes of the UK and the US series of *The X Factor* (a total of 2 528 300 words). In order to retain comparability, duplicate tweets were left in both corpora.

The top thirty most frequent keywords in the retweets are summarised in Table 8.4. Twelve of the items on this list include the names of contestants, performers and judges from the series (*The X Factor*, *Sam*, *Tamera*, *Luke*, *Sam Bailey*, *Nicole*, *Rough Copy*, *Gary Barlow*, *Kingsland Road*, *James Arthur*, *Abi*, *Hannah*). This is an unsurprising outcome, where the keywords seem to reflect the central content of the programme in their overuse of words relating to the performers from the series. As Toolan (2016) points out, deciding upon a threshold at which to distinguish the degree of overuse that is distinctive for a particular dataset is complex, and further thresholds should be applied in order to remove the distorting effects of particular genres (such as the overuse of personal names that is evident here). In his study, Toolan suggests that in addition to the keyness, the absolute frequency of the lexical items should also be taken into account, where the keyword list should be further filtered for lexical items with a raw frequency of >0.1 or >0.2 percent for personal names. Toolan applied this additional threshold to his data on the grounds of the small sample sizes with which he was working. Whilst the prominence of the personal names in the keyword list from the *X Factor* retweets suggests that there may be similar imbalances in the social television tweets to those found in narratives more generally, the datasets considered here are considerably larger, with the corpus of all tweets totalling 2 528 300 words and the specialised corpus of retweets 256 113. The additional thresholds of absolute frequency

Table 8.4 *Top thirty keywords for the retweets on selected episodes as compared with all tweets from US series 3 and UK series 10 of* The X Factor *(2013)*

Rank	Raw frequency	Keyness	Lexical item
1	1795	673.808	thexfactor
2	660	331.302	sam
3	670	322.341	remember
4	600	305.003	staircase
5	606	303.441	directioners
6	418	273.435	tamera
7	1020	272.318	do
8	478	269.797	luke
9	369	214.144	sambaileyreal
10	290	189.704	lukefriendmusic
11	291	179.561	copy
12	282	173.736	rough
13	230	140.127	roughcopyuk
14	267	137.554	nicole
15	233	134.475	nicolescherzy
16	205	116.669	nicholas
17	178	116.439	arthur
18	172	112.514	gary
19	179	107.266	abi
20	200	107.247	james
21	275	107.132	bailey
22	163	106.627	samcallahan
23	157	102.702	hannah
24	182	102.097	nickymcdonald
25	165	91.366	garybarlow
26	137	89.619	kingsland
27	132	86.348	kingslandrd
28	5442	84.038	x
29	126	82.423	yahooomguk
30	209	77.457	friend

appropriate for a small dataset may not be appropriate here, and therefore they were tested and reassessed for use in this case. Applying a threshold of >0.1 percent in absolute frequency for lexical items and >0.2 percent for personal names to the keyword list reduced the lexical items which would appear most prominent to the following list:

remember, Sam, directioners, staircase, Tamera, should

The high prominence of *Sam* is explained by the names of the contestants of the UK series, which included two participants with the same first name

(Sam Callahan and Sam Bailey), one of whom won the series. However, the high prominence of the name *Tamera* and the other lexical items that appeared above the threshold are explained by other factors, namely the repeated reposting of the same message within the data. For example, one of Tamera's fans repeatedly requested acknowledgement from her by reposting the following message:

@TheXFactor please I want a #txfsign from Tamera. I do need it and deserve it.

Likewise, the overuse of the items *remember*, *directioners* and *staircase* resulted from the repeated recirculation of a tweet from the @TheXFactor account addressing fans of the former British boy band, One Direction:

#Directioners . . . do you remember this staircase?

In order to identify the overused lexical items that were not a result of the repeated reposting of retweets, further thresholds were applied to the keyword list. The personal names and lexical items which appeared in reduplicated retweets were removed from this list. When the threshold of >0.1 percent for absolute frequency was then applied, no keywords remained. The threshold was then adjusted to >0.05 percent, given that the size of the subcorpus of retweets was 200 times greater than the small datasets considered in Toolan's analysis. The following list of ten keywords for the corpus of retweets resulted, presented here in order of keyness:

looks, ever, should, well, performing, fuck, yes, omg, know, most

Each of these keywords was then analysed in context. Unlike the keywords that appeared in the duplicated retweets, these appeared in many different retweets, rather than in exactly repeated posts. Two of the items on this list, *performing* and *well*, continue to reflect the thematic content of the series, where *well* occurred most frequently in the two-word cluster *well done* (eighty-three instances). However, for all the other keywords in this list, the clusters in which they occurred showed that in this dataset, retweets were typically used to express evaluation. Some keywords functioned as what Labov (1972) called 'comparators'. For example, the most frequent keyword, *looks*, occurred in clusters (with a minimum range of three and a minimum frequency of five) where it was used in comparisons, as in the following illustrative examples:

RT @NatalieWizzle #Xfactor catch up . . . . Poor Sam Callahan! Shoot the make up artist -he looks like a bloody Ken doll

RT @SimplyBeth_: Demi looks like a clown with blue hair and red lipstick, and she sounds terrible live #xfactor

Other comparators, which used modal auxiliaries (such as *should*) or superlative forms (*most* and *ever*), were used to evaluate contestants either explicitly or implicitly against others in the series:

RT @Leah131998: Luke was so much better, Nicolas should have gone home

RT @lionhatted: Sam Bailey is just the most talented, beautiful, and cutest woman ever to grace #xfactor

The clusters in which the keyword *know* occurred showed the verb in comparative forms of negation that prefaced evaluative statements, with the most frequent cluster (fourteen occurrences) using it in the phrase *I don't know*, as in the following example:

RT @ShivJephtha: I don't know why but I seriously dislike Hannah:/ #XFactor

Other keywords functioned as intensifiers to boost the sentiment expressed in the tweet:

RT @Brit_Probs: Cringeworthy as fuck when they all sing together on #XFactor

RT @AndersonNatalie: Yes Luke Friend!!! Amazing again!!!

RT @syn246gates: FUCK YES GET IN THERE SAM!!!!!! OMG LUKE IS GONE!!!!!

These keywords suggest that the distinctive nature of the retweets over and above that of the duplicated posts is their overuse of evaluative language. In part, this is explained by the purpose of social television practices, which is to capture the audience's response to a programme and so might be likely to be rich in evaluation. However, when the keywords are considered in context, they also show that the sentiment that was expressed by the audience varied and was by no means simply a positive affective response. Instead, the reactions that were intensified or comparatively enhanced in the retweets could also include disappointment with an outcome, or criticism of the series as a whole. This serves as an important reminder that social television practices can be used to promote the expressive empowerment of the audience, and that the audience may either endorse or criticise the performers and the series itself.

In summary, the keyword analysis of the retweets suggests that these posts were characterised in two ways. First, the over-use of items above the threshold of >0.1 percent for absolute frequency in addition to keyness confirmed the patterns observable from the quantitative comparisons of the co-tellership, namely that certain posts were repeatedly retweeted. Notably, the posts which were repeatedly reposted and distinctive for their use of keywords were not exclusively retweets that had originally been authored by an account with a high follower list. One post was authored by the UK series account, @TheXFactor, whilst another was authored by a fan of one of the contestants. This shows that the repeated use of retweets to gain visibility is open to the programme's producers and members of the audience alike. Contrary to the quantitative analysis of the participation roles, which suggested that within social television practices the audience (as animators) serves the interests of the series' producers and performers (as authors), the keyword analysis showed that the content retweeted by the audience need not create a hierarchy whereby it is the producers of the programme alone whose interests are promoted. Instead, the evaluative language found in the keywords of the retweets provides an important alternative perspective to the assumption that retweets are simply the work of an audience animating the contents of posts authored by the celebrities who perform in a series. The keyword analysis is therefore an important contribution that points to the more widespread use of retweets: namely, to redistribute evaluative comments made about performers and thus promote the opinions of the audience.

Intertextuality: Images as a Resource for Sharing and Interaction

The co-tellers in the retweets were positioned not only in relation to their participation roles, but also within interactions with one another which emerged in response to the retweets. To carry out analysis of every reply thread that responded to a retweet in this dataset would be unmanageable, given the size of the set and the separate sampling process that would be needed to collect the replies to a retweet (as the Tweetarchivist tool did not automatically do this). In order to narrow the focus for the analysis of the co-tellers' interactions found on reply threads, I focused on a specific part of the dataset that was notable for its use of intertextuality. The reason for this focus is twofold. First, intertextuality is a key characteristic of the shared story. As I have argued in Chapters 4 and 6, intertextual references in the shared story often appear as stance objects around which the tellers can align (or fail to align) and create common ground. Retweets with increased intertextuality might therefore be particularly likely to prompt further interaction between the tellers. Second, in the previous research, retweets which contained links were more likely to be reposted than those which did not (Suh et al., 2010), and therefore were valued more highly within the social television practices observed here. In the next section, I consider how the co-tellers were positioned relative to one another, in two ways. First, I show how the performers in the series were visually positioned relative to the viewing audience through their representation in the intertextual material. Second, I show how audience members aligned with one another vis-à-vis the intertextual material as a stance object. I then use the interaction between the tellers who replied to the retweets to show how rapport-threatening mockery was used to create in-groups and out-groups within the audience. I begin by providing a quantitative overview of the intertextuality in the retweets, before going on to discuss the retweets which were authored by the performers and those which were authored by the members of the audience.

Mediated Intertextuality: Linked Content in the Retweets

The shared stories found in Twitter-based social television practices were not just verbal messages, but were embedded within the intertextual context of the World Wide Web. The tweets and retweets that responded to the UK and US series of *The X Factor* also contained links to additional content beyond the 140-character limit of the post. Using Antconc, the frequency of links within tweets (as evidenced by a URL) was calculated for all the English-language posts from the four selected episodes of each series and then compared with the frequency of links in tweets that were redistributed as retweets. In this comparison, I made a further distinction between the retweets that were duplicated once and the 100 most frequently duplicated retweets from each series. I calculated the proportion of posts in each subset of the data which contained a link to further intertextual content.

The results showed that tweets with linked content occurred more often in the 100 most frequently reposted retweets (of which, 54 percent contained a link) as compared with retweets which were only posted once (of which, 27 percent contained a link) and with the dataset of all English-language tweets that responded to the ten episodes of each series (of which, 29 percent contained a link). The frequency of linked content in all the tweets and single retweets was broadly similar to that observed in the celebrity use of Twitter I analysed in my earlier work on stories in social media (Page, 2012a), where links occurred in 23 percent of the data. This suggests that links are particularly associated with retweets (at least in relation to social television practice), and therefore that this kind of intertextuality is of particular value as content to be redistributed. In order to explore why this might be so, I cross-referenced every URL in the 100 most frequently distributed retweets from the UK and US series' episodes against its content. Within this subset of the retweets, over half (54 percent) of the links were to images, either embedded in the tweet via platforms like Twitpic or located on other photo-sharing sites like Instagram. The frequency of the images within the linked content is again noteworthy compared to the results of earlier work. In my previous study of celebrity practice in Twitter, celebrities linked to images more frequently than did 'ordinary' members of Twitter, but images constituted only 23 percent of the links in 2010 (Page, 2012a, p. 112): half the frequency seen here. In order to explore this pattern further, a qualitative analysis of the images was carried out, beginning with the co-tellership of the retweets. As for retweets more generally, the use of images in the retweets considered here can be further categorised according to the author of the original post. This might be a performer from or a producer of the series, or it might be a member of the viewing audience. I begin by considering the first of these: the retweeted images produced by the performers and producers of the show.

Images and Stories of Celebrity Practice

The retweets that were authored by the performers and producers of the show included multimodal narratives which illustrate two forms of celebrity practice. First, the breaking news in these retweets typically featured remediated content from particularly tellable moments of the televised episodes, such as the outcomes of a vote or a performances by well-known artists:

RT @TheXFactor: They couldn't have given their #SaveMeSong more. RT to give @KingslandRd a deserved round of applause. #XFactor http://t.co

RT @TheXFactor: #Gratuitous1DPix @OneDirection sing #MidnightMemories on the #XFactorFinal. #xfactor http://t.co/sfYqJZeMwI

These reproductions of televised content recontextualised the 'frontstage' performances, where the representation of the participants positioned the performers as the main focus of the image, shown situated on the stage where the televised performances took place. Whilst the studio audience was also represented in these pictures, it was backgrounded (van Leeuwen, 2008) in the composition. The audience was shown much smaller in size and out of focus as a generic collectivised mass in the darkened background behind the stage and the celebrities. In terms of the interpersonal positioning implied by the images, the celebrity figures were not represented as gazing at the camera or an implied viewer. There was no interpersonal invitation projected by the image that suggests the Twitter audience was being directly addressed by eye contact from the celebrities.

A second type of celebrity practice included breaking news stories that were situated in a backstage context, which were composed so as to imply interpersonal intimacy between the performer and the imagined audience. The settings shown in the images which accompanied the backstage stories included the televised sets and the spaces within the studio used during rehearsals, as in the following examples:

RT @TheXFactorUSA: Look who @KELLYROWLAND ran into backstage during #xfactor rehearsals... http://t.co/Tv21gfEXui

RT @LittleMixOffic: In the trailer feeling good in my #LittleMixMakeUp but getting nervous for the #XFactor performance... http://t.co/vAyPxz...

Two aspects of visual representation are important for the positioning of the performer and the audience: the social distance implied by the actor and the modality with which the image is reproduced (van Leeuwen, 2008). Some backstage images were composed in ways that reduced social distance between the figure (a performer) and the imagined audience. The celebrity figure was presented in the centre of the image, occupying most of the visual frame (certainly more than their representation in the reproduction of the frontstage performances in televised stills). In terms of proximity, the camera – and, by implication, the viewer – was afforded closer proximity to the celebrity figure; social distance was reduced. Performers were often shown facing the camera directly and appeared to be making eye contact with the person behind the camera, and by implication with the viewer of the image, reinforcing the reduced social distance with a visual form of synthetic personalisation. The visual modality of these images also suggested authenticity. The images were slightly grainy, as if they had been taken with a smartphone camera and without the staged lighting and high colour saturation typical of the franchise's official branding, as used in the televised stills and the official website. These visual resources reinforced the projection of co-presence afforded by the assumed immediacy of the breaking news, and invited responses from the imagined audience that reproduced and consumed this content.

The interactional context of the retweets in the form of the replies posted to them suggests that the celebrity practice of sharing images along with breaking news of their front- and backstage performances prompted responses that signalled rapport-enhancing affiliation from the audience directed towards the performer. This included evaluation of the celebrity figures as 'cute', 'sexy', 'perfect' and 'gorgeous', and the use of terms of endearment such as 'baby'. Responses to the retweets also included affective exclamations, such as 'aww', 'ILY' (I love you) and exclamations also found in the retweets: 'OMG'. Other responses included rapport-enhancing messages, directly addressed to the performers, such as 'Good luck', 'never give up', 'you should have won', 'going to miss you', 'Have a safe flight' and 'Good night cutie'. These responses reproduce the parasocial relationships associated with fandoms both in Twitter and in other contexts (Stever and Lawson, 2013). The interactional context of the reply threads suggests that the socio-economic hierarchies that promoted the interests of the performers as the authors of the posts exploited this parasocial form of affiliation as a means by which the illusory rapport between performer and fan might be maintained. Given that interaction also promotes visibility within Twitter (so that the greater the number of replies, the more visible the (re)tweet becomes), these responses from the audience clearly served the interest of the performer as a means of promoting their representation within the site.

However, the parasocial responses to the images were not the only responses possible. The interactional context of the reply threads enabled the audience to express affiliation and disaffiliation directed towards the performers. The polylogal context of Twitter meant that the replies posted in responses to images tended not to be structured as turn-by-turn exchanges, where the replies generated interaction between the different participants who posted their responses. I counted all the replies to the images in the 100 most frequently redistributed retweets and then analysed whether they were a response to the retweet or a response to another reply within the thread. Of the 1113 replies, only 1 percent (twelve comments) were positioned as responses to another post in the same thread through 'format-tying' resources (Bolander, 2012) such as names, pronouns, quotations or technological affordances like 'replies'. There were no instances where the original author of a post including an image replied to a response. The lack of conversational coherence between the replies to a retweet meant that the thread could include responses from members of Twitter who did not align with the positive evaluation of the celebrity figure represented in the visual content of the image. The reply threads were liable to disruption by the reactions of anti-fans who did not comply with Grice's (1975) maxims to be polite and relevant, but instead posted evaluative expressions of distaste and dislike for the performer in question. Examples of these rapport-threatening criticisms include statements like, 'I just vomited in my mouth' and 'Oh my god, I feel sick', as well as seemingly irrelevant responses such as rejections, refusals and farewells, including, 'I'm so done', 'Bye Friends' and 'No thanks!' The potential for social television practices to empower the audience in terms of their expressive freedom thus also allowed the audience to critique the series, in similar fashion to anti-fans (Gray, 2005, p. 847) who express 'active or vocal dislike or hate of a given text, personality or genre'.

The alignment between the stance taken by the members of the audience and the original author of the post can also be seen in the ways in which retweets were modified. As discussed earlier, when retweets are reposted, they can be adapted so that the animator of the retweet edits the original tweet by removing or adding content. These modifications show how animators can increase their communicative contribution by adding their voice to the reposted message. Unlike replies to retweets which are not redistributed along with the original post, an adapting retweet will broadcast the animator's additional response to all those viewing the retweet.

The increased visibility afforded by the functions of the retweet could then be harnessed by the power of the fans. In this dataset, modification of a retweet occurred most often in relation to a retweet authored by the @TheXFactor account, which posted a message with an image that was repeatedly reposted. The verbal content of the tweet – and, in slightly modified form, the caption overlaid on the image – was a question addressed to the fandom associated with former British boy band, One Direction:

#Directioners . . . do you remember this staircase?

As discussed earlier, the repeated reposting of this message throughout the series of *The X Factor* in 2013 meant that the language of this tweet appeared in the keyword list for the retweets. However, it would be misleading to assume that the fandom and the band in question were simply promoting a form of celebrity practice that projected affiliation between the performers and the audience. The original tweet from @TheXFactor presumed shared knowledge from One Direction's fan base, which would recognise the allusion to the former boy band's video diaries in which the band members were filmed sitting on a staircase. However, the image in the original tweet from @TheXFactor was criticised by the fans as showing the incorrect setting: simply a generic staircase, not the staircase that appeared in the video diaries. The high frequency of reposting of this retweet seems to have resulted from the audience's negative reactions to the post. In the modifications made to the post as it was redistributed, the reactions of the audience used rapport-threatening forms of conventionalised impoliteness, such as threats and taboo language, as in the following illustrative examples (where bold text is added for clarity):

RT @_fancynarry: "@TheXFactor: #Directioners... do you remember this staircase? #XFactor http://t.co/TW57tADLHn" **nO WTF DID YOU DO TO THEM**

RT @1DAnna_Sheeran: "@TheXFactor: #Directioners... do you remember this staircase? #XFactor http://t.co/8lIHnGA2SF" **don't you fcuking dare**

The adapted retweets show how the potential visibility enabled by the sharing resources of images and retweets could be used by the fandom of 'Directioners' against *The X Factor* franchise, by redistributing the content to new audiences which might in turn join the discontented fans by adding further complaint. This example is important, for it shows the range of evaluative responses that may be present in social television practices and the ways in which these are embedded in the double logic of empowerment and exploitation. On the one hand, the fans' criticism of the @TheXFactor account seemed to offer them greater expressive power, and one which allowed them to criticise the franchise in ways that could damage the series' reputation. On the other, the repeated recirculation of the retweet still served the underlying function of promoting the hashtag, which contained the name of the series. If visibility alone is prized, then criticism as well as praise can equally serve the function of promoting the series.

Images and Audience Response

The potential for the practices of retweeting to promote the interests of the audience by allowing people to express a negative stance towards the series is evidenced most clearly in the retweets with images that were authored by audience members. Amongst the 100 most frequently redistributed retweets from the selected episodes of *The X Factor* UK series 10 and US series 3, three of the retweets with images were posted by accounts other than those associated with the programme (that is, the official accounts for each series or for the performers who appeared on the show). These three examples appeared in the top retweets that were posted in response to the UK series. The intertextuality and the interaction in these examples demonstrated how the audience's expressive power was used in ways that critiqued the series and its performers, rather than engaging in affiliative acts of parasocial rapport.

The images that occurred in the audience-authored top retweets were qualitatively different from those posted by the celebrity figures and producers of the series. In terms of the intertextuality, they recontextualised content originally created by the series producers in ways that further removed the visual content from its original source. In so doing, the additional layers of recontextualisation opened up new interpretations of the images. Specifically, the recontextualisation reframed the televised content as material viewed by the audience. Two of the three top audience-authored retweets that contained images were photographs of moments in the screened episodes that were taken during the process of watching television. The two retweets were:

RT @kirk_official: When Gary pulls this face you know you've f*cked up! #XFactor http://t.co/mjkFx6DrLI

RT @MoreMon3yPlease: The way Hannah tensed like she was in Gym tho #Xfactor http://t.co/S5mTIZq1oK

The tellability of the narrative moments that were selectively represented in the images linked to these tweets also differed from those in the images reproduced by the series account. The tweets created by the audience recontextualised scenes from the series that depicted the performers in an unflattering light, not necessarily at a teleologically significant moment. In their visual representation of a non-present third party, the authors and animators of this content created satirical forms of mockery that amplified and extended the series' use of confrontainment. However, unlike the sanctioned forms of impoliteness used in the screened episodes of the series, where the judges made rapport-threatening criticisms of the performers (Blitvich et al., 2013), the socially mediated critiques of the contestants from the viewing audience used conventionalised impoliteness to intensify the reactions, as in the semi-censored use of taboo language by @kirk_official. The responses to these critiques in the data suggested that the impoliteness was not considered inappropriate and that it generated rapport between the author and those who responded to the post. Evidence for this rapport-enhancing interaction between the members of the viewing audience is found in the modifications to the retweet as it circulated and the replies that were posted to it. The audience's responses included expressions of humour ('Haha', 'funny stuff', 'Loool'), emojis showing positive sentiment ('tears of joy' face) and explicit statements of alignment, such as:

Watching the exact same thing #classic

Lol I just watched that too! Thought the same!

Same opinion as you!!

Other responses extended the critique of the performer with creative comparisons. For example, @Moremon3yplease's critique of the contestant's physique ('like she was in Gym') was further modified by other retweeters who continued the unflattering allusions with intertextual word play, such as 'the incredible bulk' (alluding to the Marvel character, the Incredible Hulk). The indirectness of the impoliteness and the intertextual references relied on the audience's shared knowledge of these cultural figures, which led to a shared stance of mockery towards the contestants. However, the indirectness also meant that the in-group nature of the affiliation between the audience members was itself open to disruption. As with all forms of implied rather than stated shared knowledge, in-group humour can be used simultaneously to position an out-group: those without the relevant knowledge to interpret the referents adequately. The vulnerability of shared group knowledge was exploited in the third image-based retweet authored by a member of the audience.

This third retweet illustrates the participatory potential and risks taken by the audience when using multimodal intertextuality to express criticism within social television practices. The type of image, the intertextual references and the resulting interaction all differed from those discussed so far. The retweet reposted content originally authored by the parody account @KatieWeasel. This account parodied former contestant, Katie Waissel, who was a source of controversy when she appeared in the UK series 7. The following tweet was posted at the start of the live shows, and retweeted several hundred times:

RT @KatieWeasel: The final 12 #XFactor http://t.co/0lT07Bd6eH

The image created by @katieweasel is a 'macro'; that is, a humorous multimodal genre which circulates in social media contexts. The generic format of a macro includes an image with a caption superimposed, where the humour results from the cultural dissonance between the messages conveyed in the visual and verbal semiotic streams. As a form of participatory practice, macros illustrate neatly the ways in which fans can move beyond a traditional broadcast model that positions them as passive consumers. Typically, this participatory practice is associated with 'lolfans': those who engage with a media product with the purpose of mocking it in forms of satirical humour (Klink, 2010, p. 23). Macros are often highly contextualised, and require extensive knowledge of the referents in order to understand the ways in which they offer subversive critique. The image within the macro created by @KatieWeasel replicated the layout and content of the official *The X Factor* website, which displayed images of each of the finalists who appeared in the live shows and linked through to the biographical accounts of each contestant. However, whilst the visual representation of each contestant in @KatieWeasel's macro reproduced official images from the series, the captions given in place of each contestant's name provided alternative identities that made unflattering comparisons between the contestant and other media figures. Whilst neither the images nor the verbal content of the tweet was a narrative in itself, the captions embedded in the visual content were intertextual references to other shared stories that undercut any myth of celebrity transformation. For example, the UK series 10 contestants Kingsland Road, who were similar to former contestants One Direction, were labelled 'No Direction', while Hannah Barrett, a black British contestant, was given the name 'Gamu': another former contestant who infamously was eliminated from the series 7 before reaching the live shows. Other intertextual references in the captions included films and other TV programmes, positioning *The X Factor* in relation to other singing competitions (*The Voice*), comedy (*Little Britain*), horror films (*Deliverance*) and soap operas (*Prisoner Cell Block H*). The macro also evoked knowledge of the intertextual world of *The X Factor*, referring not only to former unsuccessful contestants from three previous series but also to tabloid speculations about the personal narratives of the series 10 contestants and judges.

Retweeting this macro might then be interpreted as a subversive practice which critiqued the series and disrupted the viewing pleasure of the fandoms emerging around particular contestants. However, the reactions in the replies to the 'Final 12' macro suggest that it was a source of humour and solidarity only for those who recognised the joke, as evidenced by endorsements ('that just about sums it up'), laughter ('loool', 'ahahahaha') and emojis (such as the 'tears of joy' face). Other reactions indicated the limits of the macro's humour. These replies to the retweet failed to identify the author as a parody account, instead interpreting the comment as if it had been authored by the former contestant, Katie Waissel, and making rapport-threatening evaluation of her as 'bitter' or 'sad'. The misinterpretation of the macro as face-threatening revenge by the former contestant on the programme's producers was quickly corrected by other members of Twitter (although not by the account owner, @KatieWeasel), as shown in the following examples:

Reply 1: Someone's bitter I thought you were good on X Factor but obv your attitude stinks xx

Response to Reply 1: [@username1] This is a parody account not Katie Waissel

Reply 2: Just because you didn't win the x factor. . . .sad

Response to Reply 2: [@username2] This is a parody account, not Katie Waissel the contestant.

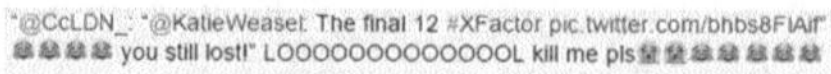

Figure 8.2 Screenshot showing a retweet with responses

The interactions within the reply thread to the retweet show how the failure to interpret the humour could be used to position the members of the audience within a hierarchy. Other respondents mocked the audience that had not interpreted the humour of the parody, turning this out-group into the object of ridicule. This kind of interactional positioning between the co-tellers was embedded in complex, iterative responses where one member of Twitter would adapt the retweet by reproducing it and adding their own response. The mixture of the co-tellers' voices within a single, adapted retweet is illustrated in Figure 8.2.

In this example, the original post created by the parody account @KatieWeasel appears within the second set of quotation marks. The account @CcLDN retweeted the post and adapted it by adding four 'tears of joy' emojis and the rapport-threatening criticism, 'you still lost!', apparently misinterpreting the identity of the parody account for the genuine contestant, Katie Waissel. In turn, a third Twitter account retweeted the adapted retweet and adapted it once again, by added the response, 'LOOOOOOOOOOOOOL kill me pls' along with a string of emojis that represented 'crying loudly' and 'tears of joy'. This response suggests that the misinterpretation of the macro as genuine and thus face-threatening between audience and programme producers was a source of humour. The followers of the parody account (who experienced in-group solidarity by mocking *The X Factor*) positioned the fans (who interpreted this critique as face-threatening) as a source of humour to be mocked along with the programme. The out-group of fans who took the account at face value thus became an object of ridicule, positioned as participants who lacked the media literacy to read the parody account, the macro and indeed *The X Factor* itself correctly.

Conclusion

In this chapter, I have shown how the analysis of the co-tellership and the intertextuality of retweets provides contrasting perspectives on the double logic of exploitation and empowerment in Twitter-based social television practices. Analysing the co-tellership in terms of the participation roles suggested a communicative hierarchy, where authors created content and animators redistributed that content. In this dataset, the quantitative analysis of the Twitter accounts showed that these participation roles were taken up in an asymmetrical pattern. Retweets were authored by celebrity figures with large numbers of followers and animated by fans who redistributed that content. However, to assume that the retweets entirely or uniformly exploited the practices of fans in the service of celebrity figures is not to understand the whole story. The analysis of the keywords in all of the retweets and of the images in the retweets authored by members of the viewing audience suggests that the audience also had at least some measure of expressive empowerment. Fans could petition their favoured celebrity for attention, or evaluate the series in ways that both endorsed and criticised the performers and the franchise itself. Fans also modified retweets, including appending their disagreements with the franchise in ways that could damage as well as boost the reputation of *The X Factor*. Finally, the images that the audience recontextualised in its retweets mocked the performers and the franchise itself. The additional layers of intertextuality and shared knowledge required to interpret the mockery correctly meant that a hierarchy within the audience was constructed, where those who understood the shared knowledge correctly and found this humorous were positioned as a superior in-group compared to those who interpreted the mockery as impolite.

9 Citizen Journalism and Shared Stories in YouTube

Introduction

In this chapter, I return to the question of whether shared stories exploit or empower their tellers by examining the citizen journalism practices found in YouTube. The chapter develops the nucleus^satellite model for print news (White, 1997) to account for the multimodal linearity of the televised news rebroadcast in YouTube. This aspect of the shared story is important, because it shows how the structure and values associated with news stories are shaped through the affordances of YouTube as a site for narration. The expanded model of the nucleus^satellite news narrative can be used to compare different forms of journalism, including mainstream, independent and citizen-based practices. This contributes to narrative theory by expanding the analytical tools needed to explore the increasingly multimodal forms of news narrative. It builds on the critical evaluation of sharing in social media contexts by showing how the tellers contribute to the different aspects of the news narratives in ways that promote the interests of some participants rather than others.

YouTube and Shared Stories: Television News and Citizen Journalism

YouTube is a video-sharing site that was founded in 2005 by Chad Hurley, Steve Chen and Jawed Karim. Since its inception, YouTube has grown exponentially in size and interaction, and it is now regarded as a part of the contemporary media landscape. In 2015, the most popular videos on YouTube had been viewed over a billion times, and the site stated that it had more than a billion members. As a video-sharing site, YouTube is important for its multimodal characteristics and for the ways in which these can be used in practices that can be understood as more or less participatory. YouTube enables its users to upload video-files, but it is more than an archive, as videos are linked to 'community functions' (Burgess and Green, 2009, p. 1) found in other social network sites, such as the option for members to create an online profile on the site and to build a networked audience in the form of subscriptions to a member's channel. The uploaded video is embedded in the visual layout of the YouTube templates, which allow the site members to add a title and description and to enable options for other site members to respond to it. These resources include options to rank the video (with 'likes' and 'dislikes'), to redistribute the video on other social media sites (through a share button) and to add written comments.

This chapter focuses on a particular use of YouTube as a site for shared stories: citizen journalism. Citizen journalism is sometimes seen in opposition to mainstream news production. However, as I discussed in Chapter 1, citizen journalism is a form of participatory culture that can incorporate a range of practices that bridge and blur mainstream and 'lay' forms of journalism. YouTube has been described as a 'change agent' in relation to citizen journalism (Soukup, 2014, p. 16), exemplified by the ability to upload lay persons' eyewitness footage of noteworthy events. In the emerging scholarship, studies have tended to focus on the eyewitness footage posted to YouTube that has presented civil authorities in a negative light, such as unwarranted attacks on civilians (Antony and Thomas, 2010), or that has been interpreted as a critique of surveillance practices (Reilly, 2015). In some cases, such eyewitness footage marked YouTube as an alternative to highly censored mainstream news reporting, such as during the Arab Spring uprisings in 2011 (Wall and El Zahed, 2011). At the other end of the participatory spectrum, citizen journalism also includes mainstream media's use of YouTube to rebroadcast content already produced in traditional or institutional formats. For example, some television companies maintain YouTube channels as a means of archiving traditional broadcast materials. In other cases, online news may include YouTube clips embedded in its reports. In between these two extremes, YouTube is home to a variety of other citizen journalist practices, where independent news companies, such as The Young Turks, use their channels to commentate on events without the restrictions and censorship of the mainstream news. Some YouTube channels specialise in curating clips of specific kinds of news. For example, The Lady Justice is a channel that aggregates live-streamed criminal trials. Other channels remediate or remix the news, such as Tomonews, which present animations of 'the most entertaining news on the Internet'.

The relationship between mainstream and social media is particularly important given the commercial development of YouTube. When YouTube was first founded, its slogan, 'Broadcast Yourself', emphasised the possibilities for lay persons with relatively little technical expertise to upload their own video content that documented their personal everyday experiences. The amateur endeavours that were shared within YouTube were simultaneously celebrated and derided as examples of vernacular creativity and participatory culture. A key turning point in YouTube's history occurred relatively early on, when the site was sold to Google in 2006. Since then, YouTube's relationship with mainstream media has become increasingly complex. After the purchase by Google, the potential for its members to benefit commercially from the site increased, as demonstrated by the advertising that can now be added to videos and the sale of keywords that monetise the searchable talk embedded in the YouTube template. The interactivity that YouTube templates offer to audiences, which can add their evaluations of and comments on the content, is by no means a democratic gesture, but rather the means by which advertisers and the Google can generate revenue. As with the social television practices that have begun to emerge within Twitter, citizen journalism within YouTube is shaped by the dual logic of empowerment and exploitation. On the one hand, the site members' freedom to rebroadcast or comment on news opens up greater expressive opportunities. On the other, these opportunities are placed in a context where interaction is a means of generating socio-economic value, often for the mainstream producers of the news.

YouTube Coverage of Oscar Pistorius

The case study in this chapter considers the YouTube coverage of the South African Paralympian, Oscar Pistorius. As a high-profile, mediated figure, Pistorius has attracted critical attention as an icon whose personal narrative brought together debates about race, disability, celebrity status and masculinity. He rose to international prominence in the first decade of the twenty-first century as a sporting hero, winning three gold medals in the 2008 Beijing Paralympics. His success developed towards international celebrity status, with commercial sponsorship from major companies, and his story of overcoming adversity to achieve sporting excellence led to his mainstream global adoption as an inspirational figure. This trajectory reached a high point when he represented South Africa in the 2012 London Paralympics and Olympics, a move which positioned him alongside Caster Semenya to represent symbolically South Africa as a 'rainbow nation' (de Robillard, 2014).

Even within this macro-social narrative, Pistorius attracted controversy, specifically in relation to his demands to compete alongside able-bodied athletes and in relation to whether technology gave him unfair advantage, so that he was more-than-able-bodied (Harvey, 2015). However, it was in 2013 that Pistorius' news value shifted, when he was arrested for shooting and killing his girlfriend, model and television presenter Reeva Steenkamp. In the verdict of his trial (*The State* vs *Oscar Pistorius*), Pistorius was found not guilty of murder and sentenced to five years' imprisonment for culpable homicide. The verdict was strongly criticised for its leniency in both the mainstream and social media responses to the trial. In December 2015, this ruling was overturned and a second verdict convicted him of murder. However, a similarly lenient sentence of six years' imprisonment was made, in July 2016. The online responses to the media coverage of Pistorius both prior to and after the death of Steenkamp took place in a number of contexts, including Twitter, Facebook, blogs, websites and online news coverage. To date, the YouTube coverage of Pistorius and his trial has not been considered in an academic context. This is perhaps all the more surprising given that the 2014 trial was the first criminal trial in South Africa to be broadcast live through television channels and instantly streamed online (Chibba, 2014). The coverage of Pistorius and his trial within YouTube is of national and international importance as a landmark trial, and more generally as a counter-balance to the analysis of citizen journalism in YouTube, which has thus far focused on the participatory practices of lay persons as 'eyewitness' narrators to newsworthy events.

Data

The dataset of YouTube videos that forms the basis of the analysis in this chapter was collected using ContextMiner (Shah, 2009). The collection consisted of 635 videos containing the search term 'Oscar Pistorius' in their title, description or tags. The videos had been uploaded to YouTube between the years 2008 and 2015, and were accompanied by 161 361 comments. YouTube allows its members to categorise their videos. In this dataset, the categories assigned to the videos reflected the various aspects of Pistorius' iconic and newsworthy identity, including coverage of sports events ('sports'), documentaries about the technology involved in his prosthetics ('technology'), the commercials in which he featured ('entertainment') and the live trial and its news coverage ('news', 'people' and 'films'). The data contained videos which responded to Pistorius' arrest, trial and sentencing in the form of parody ('music'), satire ('comedy'), rants ('entertainment') and expert commentary that discussed legal issues ('education'). YouTube members also used the categories to make meta-discursive evaluation of Pistorius, including one example which positioned the video under the category of 'animals'. The quantity of videos in each category varied, as shown in Table 9.1. Over 500 of the videos (79 percent of the data) were categorised as news, reflecting the importance of the stories told about Pistorius in relation to Steenkamp's death and the later trial. Unsurprisingly, the times at which these videos were uploaded also reflect Pistorius' changing news value, where the sports videos were published in 2008–12, whilst the news videos began to be uploaded in 2013 and were mostly concentrated in 2014, during the period of the trial. There were no music parodies or satires of Pistorius relating to him as a sports personality. These appeared only once he became subject to critique as a fallen elite figure after his arrest in 2013 and during the trial in 2014.

Given the predominance of the news videos in this dataset, the following analysis concentrates on the videos relating to the news coverage of Pistorius, both from the mainstream news and in citizen journalists' responses. The

Table 9.1 *YouTube videos including the search term 'Oscar Pistorius' (2008–15), by category*

Categories of video	Raw count
Animals	1
Comedy	12
Education	4
Entertainment	23
Film	7
Music	2
News	501
Non-profit	2
People	44
Shows	5
Sports	31
Technology	3
Total	635

videos categorised as 'news' included televised coverage reported by national and international news outlets and responses from independent online news channels and video-loggers. However, the majority of such videos consisted of the live-streamed recordings of events from the Gauteng High Court in Pretoria. The decision to live-stream the trial was granted by institutional authorities (Gauteng Judge President Mlambo), allowing a wider audience immediate access to the audio-visual coverage of the court proceedings. The live-streamed court trial was not a global precedent, for live-streamed trials became permissible in the United Kingdom in 2013 and were part of the North American pilot led by the Ad Hoc Committee on Cameras in the Courtroom between 2011 and 2015. However, Pistorius' case was the first live-streamed trial to feature a national and international figure and to be disseminated through multiple news channels via YouTube, thereby illustrating most clearly the 'fault line' (Goode et al., 2011) between mainstream and citizen news practices in YouTube.

Television News and Narrative Structure

In order to explore the different kinds of citizen journalism found in YouTube, we need a model that accounts for the distinctive, multimodal nature of television news. Previous research that examined the narrative potential of news reports suggested that although there were points of similarity with the elements found in canonical narrative genres (such as Bell's (1991) early attempt to map Labov's (1972) framework on to the headline and body text of print news), the organisation of the verbal elements in news reports was distinct from narratives of personal experience. Unlike the linearity of narratives of personal experience, where the order of the reported events matched the order in which those events were deemed to have occurred, the structural characteristics of news reports are driven by news values. In particular, the headline and the lead (the first summarising sentence of the body text) are ascribed with particular priority, as attention-grabbing resources around which the later text revolves. As I argued in Chapter 1, the retellings found in news narratives are offline analogues for the shared stories found in sites like YouTube, for in print news, the body text which follows the headline and lead does not simply recount the events in a plot-like sequence of complicating action followed by resolution, but instead recycles events, background information and evaluation (Hoey, 2001) in textual segments that White (1997) describes as 'satellites' which are dependent on the 'nucleus' of the headline and lead.

In White's (1997) description of the nucleus^satellite model, he suggested that the textual satellites could include narrative functions such as:

Elaboration: a more detailed retelling of the nucleus.

Contexualisation: content which places the nucleus in a temporal, spatial and social context.

Concession: content which provides information counter to the headline and lead.

Appraisal: evaluation or commentary, typically by an eyewitness or expert.

The 'orbital' relationship between the segmented content in the report and the headline means that these 'satellites' are not tied to a fixed place in the linear organisation of the verbal text. In turn, as Caple (2017, p. 212) argues, the model allows 'a great deal of flexibility in both the function and ordering of the satellites'. In the context of print news, this flexibility is understood as an interpretive felicity. Although readers of print news might choose to read some satellites and not others, they do not (usually) dismantle and rearrange the textual content of the report to create new versions of events. However, in the context of social media, there is potential for the flexibility of the nucleus^satellite arrangement to account for the practices of citizen journalism, where content from one report can be recontextualised in other reports, in many different textual arrangements. The flexibility of the satellite's position relative to the headline and lead means that as news narratives are reconfigured in social media sites like YouTube, the different elements of the news report (the headline, lead and various satellites) can be spatially redistributed between the multimodal content of the video, the different elements of the YouTube template (the title, description and comments) and the architectural features of the site (such as search terms), rather than ordered within a fixed textual sequence of printed words in a single printed or digital report. In order to account for these multimodal arrangements, the nucleus^satellite model needs to be updated so that it can address the semiotic complexity of narratives that are conveyed in more than words alone.

A multimodal approach to narrative means that the nucleus^satellite model should take account of the narrative contributions made by the full range of semiotic resources used in storytelling. This is important, given that news reports are multimodal compositions, and that increasingly the role of images in discursively constructing news value has begun to be considered (discussed most extensively in Bednarek and Caple, 2017). However, the weaker affordances of images to convey a sequence of temporally ordered actions have prompted debate about the narrative potential of television news. Whilst some critics have argued for the importance of storytelling as a way of shaping content within the televised report (Ekström, 2000), Montgomery (2005) argued that in its reliance on visual elements, the coherence of television news is fundamentally at odds with narrative structure. Montgomery's critique draws on models of narrative coherence rooted in canonical narrative studies such as Labov's framework. The features of television news that Montgomery suggests run counter to narrative coherence – such as the use of present-tense verbs and the co-reference between visual and verbal content, which constructs a sense of proximity to the reporter's location – are indeed at odds with the typical past-tense, primarily verbal characteristics found in canonical narratives of personal experience. Whilst this is true, more recent approaches which recognise the variation in narrative dimensions would not dismiss the narrative potential of television news so readily. In its multiple co-tellership, present-tense, unfolding linearity, and with its moral stance that shifts in line with news values, television news seems to contrast with canonical personal narratives, but it can be accounted for effectively within the framework of shared stories.

An updated model of the nucleus^satellite pattern recognises that the function of the 'nucleus' and 'satellites' can be achieved through various semiotic resources, not just the words produced in a news report. The analysis of visual content as satellites builds on existing work in social semiotics. This earlier research, led by van Leeuwen (1991) and summarised more recently by Martinec and Salway (2005), proposed systematic frameworks for image–text relationships derived from Halliday's (1994) logico-semantic categories of extension, enhancement and elaboration. The trans-generic application of these earlier models is useful, but they do not have a specific narrative focus. As Caple (2013, p. 145) argues, the sense relations between an image and text in the case of news narratives can be much more difficult to pin down. The narrative functions suggested by White (1997) provide an alternative framework for analysing the image–text relationships in television news. Here, the nucleus is carried by the verbal content of the report, and the visual content can function as different types of satellites. Following White's categories, images can *contextualise* the nucleus by providing orientation (such as showing the persons in the reported event or the places where the reported event took place). The selection of the visual content can also be highly evaluative and so can *appraise* the nucleus, for example by showing a person undergoing particular emotional reactions that index affect, or by using a lighting or focus to draw attention to particular features or to obscure others. The visual content may show particular events or actions taking place and hence *elaborate* the nucleus. Finally, where the events or actions in the image are at odds with the reported events, the visual content can function as a form of *concession*. This multimodal approach to the satellites recognises that the boundaries between one satellite and another are fuzzy, and that the functions of one satellite can be embedded within those of another. The nucleus^satellite model thus does not lend itself well to strictly quantitative methods of analysis. However, some types of satellite may be found more often in one type of news report as compared with another, and comparison of these satellites can prove useful as a means of mapping out the practices of citizen journalism that take place in YouTube. This is important, for it allows me to question how far the opportunities for extending news-making practices extend beyond the (re)production of mainstream news and might open up opportunities for other people outside the mainstream news to elaborate, appraise or counter the content of the news.

Analysing Citizen Journalism: Rebroadcasts of Mainstream News

One use of YouTube by mainstream news companies is to replicate the broadcast of their televised reports through social media in order to reach new audiences. Of the 500 videos about Oscar Pistorius in this dataset that were categorised as 'news', 412 (82 percent) were uploaded by a mainstream news company. Excluding the videos of the live-streamed trial, which were broadcast through SABC and the ENCA channels, the mainstream news company that uploaded the most videos reporting the events of the trial was Sky News (fifty-six of those videos categorised as 'news'). Sky News' use of YouTube might be regarded as the least participatory practice associated with citizen journalism. The Sky News videos in this dataset were recontextualised footage that had been broadcast also through Sky's other outlets. There was little opportunity for the YouTube audience to respond, as the comments on all the Sky News videos in this dataset were disabled. However, these videos are useful as they provide an example of how the nucleus^satellite patterns occurred in the mainstream television news, against which citizen journalism can be compared.

The most viewed report uploaded to YouTube on the Sky News channel during Pistorius' trial was 'Pistorius Sick in Court', from 13 April 2014. The analysis of the nucleus and satellites in the verbal and visual content of this report sets out the typical structure of televised news. A transcription of the opening minute of the report is provided in Table 9.2. This follows the classic pattern of a headline and lead, and functions as a nucleus for the body of the report that follows. The nucleus is given prominence as the first material to be presented, and, like its print analogues, uses grammatically distinctive patterns in the headline, summarising the content that is considered the most tellable aspect of the report. The selection of the headline's focus on the 'most tellable' events in this case is clearly driven by the news values of recency (reporting the events of the trial that had taken place that day), negativity ('the bloody scene' and 'extreme physical distress') and focus on the elite person (Pistorius). The headline is set apart from the rest of the report by the accompanying visual content, which uses still images from the recorded events in the courtroom to illustrate those events, first contextualising 'the bloody scene' by showing remediated images of police photographs of the crime scene as reproduced within the courtroom, and then appraising Pistorius' distress by showing two images of him in postures indicating negative emotional responses. The use of editing effects to zoom out and zoom in on the close-up images of Pistorius clearly emphasises the appraisal of Pistorius, signalling the focus on his elite status and negativity as the most attention-grabbing aspect of the report.

The multimodal content of the headline (still images) contrasts with the audio-visual content used in the lead, which showed the reporter walking in the corridors of the High Court as she narrated lines 3–7. At this point, the function of the visual content contextualised the narration of the report (the telling world), rather than the reported events (the tale world of the trial itself). In line with this, the framing focus of the lead is demarcated by the direct address to the audience, 'Good evening', and provides orientation to contextualise the report with details of where the events have taken place, 'from Gauteng High Court in Pretoria', and the persons involved: in this case, a specific witness, Colonel Schoombie van Rensburg. The lead also repeats the events in the headline, where sentence 1 is elaborated with more detail in sentences 3 and 4, and sentence 2 is later expanded in sentence 5 with specific detail of Pistorius' distress.

Following the headline and lead, the remainder of the Sky News report was structured as a series of verbal and audio-visual satellites that elaborated, contextualised and appraised the events in the opening seven sentences. For example, the report continued with the voice-over of a second reporter, who appraised and elaborated the lead as he retold the events of Pistorius' reaction in more detail, and quoted from the police officer's testimony. The report went on to reproduce excerpts from the trial (the police officer's testimony), before returning to the first reporter, shown outside the courtroom, who elaborated again the recorded testimony used in the trial. Finally, the report concluded with two instances of appraisal in the form of interviews with two

Table 9.2 *Multimodal transcription of the verbal and visual content in the first minute of the Sky News report, 'Pistorius Sick in Court'*

Structure and time	Audio narration	Description of the visual content	Image–text relationship
Title sequence 00:00–00:10	Instrumental music in a minor key plays	Series of images shown of Pistorius in side profile, fading in and out against a dark backdrop. The caption 'The Pistorius Trial' and the Sky News logo appear on the left-hand side of the screen	
Headline 00:10–00:17	1. Tonight, the bloody scene which greeted police officers when they arrived at Oscar Pistorius' house	Footage of the courtroom from the recorded trial, showing images of a blood-stained room on a computer screen	Visual content *elaborates* the verbal content by providing more details of the 'scene'
00:17–00:22 00:23–00:27	2. And the Olympian is again left in extreme physical distress after graphic images of his shot girlfriend are accidentally shown during the hearing	Still image of Pistorius from the live trial in distress with camera panning out Still image of Pistorius, seated but doubled over with the camera panning in	Selection of images *appraises* Pistorius by showing his emotional reactions
Lead 00:28–1:00	3. Good evening from North Gauteng High Court in Pretoria, where a senior police officer has told how he followed a trail of blood through the home of Oscar Pistorious to the bathroom where Reeva Steenkamp was shot 4. Colonel Schoombie van Rensburg described how he had arrived at the scene in the early hours of Valentine's Day last year 5. So graphic were the scenes shown to the court that an emotional Pistorius broke down and vomited 6. He denies the premeditated murder of his 29-year-old girlfriend 7. A warning that Paul Crawford's report contains images that some viewers may find distressing	Reporter Alex Crawford is shown standing and then walking in the corridor outside the courtroom, talking directly to the camera A caption as a footer appears onscreen, giving her name	Visual content *contextualises* narration and the narrator

expert witnesses (one a lawyer and one a former police officer), both of whom gave their evaluation of the events of the trial. Notably, the lawyer's appraisal critiqued the actions taken by Pistorius' defence lawyer, incorporating an element of concession.

The Structure of Independent News Commentary

One of the key functions of citizen journalism is to open up contexts for commentary on the mainstream news. In the YouTube coverage of the Pistorius trial, there are several examples of this practice, two of which I present for analysis. One was uploaded by the channel for the independent news channel, The Young Turks. The second was uploaded by the YouTube channel for the Paralympian Josh Sundquist. In both cases, as with the mainstream news coverage, the video began with an opening statement, which functioned like the nucleus, summarising the tellable aspects of the report. For example, The Young Turks' programme began with the statement:

> The latest update to the Oscar Pistorius story is that he did not know that he was shooting at his girlfriend.

Josh Sundquist's video began:

> So, earlier today, the judge in the Oscar Pistorius case offered her initial finding about the case, and today I want to tell you why that judgement is a giant step back, yes, pun intended, for amputees.

In both cases, the temporal orientation in the nucleus foregrounded the recency of the events in question; for example, by locating them relative to 'today' or as 'the latest' news. As with the mainstream television news, the verbal content of the nucleus in these videos was accompanied by still images, but rather than elaborating the specific events of the report (as did the mainstream news), the images that contextualised Pistorius in these examples used stock photos (for example, from the Getty archives) that reflected his former status as an iconic figure. The contextualising relationship between the verbal nucleus and the visual satellite here suggests that the news commentary generated outside the mainstream channels was not driven by the same event-based news values as the breaking news, but instead was more personalised and driven by the news value of Pistorius as a celebrity figure.

The satellites that follow the nucleus suggest similarly that this practice of citizen journalism is less concerned with reporting events and more with generating evaluative commentary about the events. In both The Young Turks' and Josh Sundquist's videos, the nucleus is followed by a single satellite of elaboration, where the speaker recounts a summary of Pistorius' testimony (see Table 9.3). In contrast to the mainstream news reports, in which these events

Table 9.3 *Multimodal transcription of the verbal and visual content in The Young Turks' report, 'Pistorius "Didn't Know" he Shot Girlfriend in Bathroom'*

Verbal content	Visual content	Image–text relations
The latest update to the Oscar Pistorius story	Ana Kasparian sitting at desk, talking to camera	
is that he did not know that he was shooting at his girlfriend Now he alleges that she was in the bathroom	Still image of Oscar Pistorius running on race track in SA colours, superimposed on The Young Turks' branded background	Image *contextualises* the person in the report
and that he thought she was an intruder Therefore he shot uh through the door And he uh shot four times	Still image of Oscar Pistorius and Reeva Steenkamp posed on their first date	Image *contextualises* the persons in the report
Three of the bullets struck her and uh obviously she died as a result of those gun wounds	Still image of Reeva Steenkamp in a publicity shot for the reality television show, *Tropika Island of Treasure*	Image *contextualises* the persons in the report
And um uh he's been basically saying, you know, it was self-defence, well, not self-defence, but it was an accident – he didn't know what was happening, he didn't realise his girlfriend wasn't in bed, that she was in the bathroom	AK (Host) shown at desk talking to camera, with banner displaying her name superimposed on the screen	Visual content (captions) *contextualise* the narration

were repeatedly retold in further satellites of elaboration, in the independent news channels, the satellites that followed contained repeated instances of concession and appraisal. In these satellites, unlike the single instance of concession found in the mainstream news, which was voiced by an 'expert figure' interviewed by the reporter, in the videos by online news programmes and v-loggers, the concession was voiced by the reporter him- or herself. For example, The Young Turks host declared:

> Now, there's a couple of elements to this which makes me think [3.0] not buying, I mean if I were an investigator I would think BS, not buying this for a single second.

Likewise, Sundquist follows the elaboration with his evaluation, 'Now, there's a lot of problems with his story', and concludes that the Judge's verdict is 'a huge step back for the perception of people with disability and amputees'. In this way, the satellites typically found in the video-based citizen journalists' commentary reconfigured mainstream news production, reproducing the opening narrative pattern of nucleus^elaboration, but then adding multiple satellites of concession and appraisal instead of further elaboration. The choice of generic, stock images derived from the mainstream news in these reports again suggests the reliance of citizen journalism on mainstream news production, but also a move away from the specific to a more generalised multimodal recontextualisation. Both points of transformation show how this form of citizen journalism opens up spaces for criticism of the institutional discourse, for speculation and for personalised response from those outside mainstream news production.

The YouTube Template and News Structure: Description as a Satellite

Most discourse analytic and sociolinguistic research on YouTube to date has focused on the analysis of the content of videos and their appended comments. Little research, as yet, has considered the contribution of the Description as a textual resource within YouTube (in this book, 'Description' is capitalised hereafter to distinguish the element of the YouTube template from the everyday use of the term). However, advice to YouTube members on effective use of the site suggests that the Description is a crucial paratextual element that supports the audience's engagement with the video content. Unlike the title (which is constrained in length to 100 typed characters), the Description provides site members with a template of up to 5000 characters in which to provide a synopsis of the video, which should contain search terms as metadata that help the viewing audience locate the content within YouTube's archive. Descriptions are authored by the channel owner who has uploaded the video content. As such, they are part of the multimodal ensemble of the news as (re)produced in YouTube and can contribute to the narration of the reported events. The Descriptions which accompanied the videos in the YouTube coverage of Pistorius varied considerably. The length of the text contained in the Descriptions ranged between seven and 130 words, with an average length of sixty-eight words. More importantly, the Descriptions varied in the ways in which they related to the narrative content in the title or the video itself, containing a range of satellites that fulfilled different narrative functions. The Descriptions also varied in how often these types of satellites occurred.

Contextualising Orientation

One use of the Description was to contextualise the information in the title and the content of a video. As contextualisation, Descriptions might provide more details to orient the viewer about the narrative in the video, such as the people and places involved in the reported events. This accounted for 19 percent of the Descriptions in the data. An illustrative example follows:

Title: Oscar Pistorius Trial: Tuesday 4 March 2014, Session 1

Description: Day Two of the Oscar Pistorius murder trial begins with the Paralympian's lawyer resuming his cross examination of the first State witness. Michelle Burger lives close to the blade runner's home in a security complex east of Pretoria, where he shot and killed his model girlfriend, Reeva Steenkamp, on the early hours of Valentine's Day last year.

SABC Digital: http://www.youtube.com/watch?v=0bFDaTnyvuE

Elaborative Retellings

Other Descriptions elaborated the information in a video's title by providing a more detailed retelling of particular events. The Descriptions which retold events reported in the videos were the most frequently occurring type of satellite, accounting for 63 percent of the examples in this dataset. Within this category, the length of any given Description varied, as did the type of narrative. Some of the retellings in the Descriptions which elaborated a title or video were quite brief and used present-tense, breaking-news announcements to help viewers identify what events were being reported, like this example:

Title: Oscar Pistorius Trial: Friday 14 March 2014, Session 1

The North Gauteng High Court in Pretoria continue to hear how the prosecution's 13th witness describes the crime scene at Oscar Pistorius' Pretoria East home.

SABC Digital: http://www.youtube.com/watch?v=Fa7VBVeJ9LQ

In other cases, the stories told in the Description included past-tense summaries of particular aspects of the events, as illustrated here:

Title: Graphic testimony rattles Oscar Pistorius

Description: Graphic testimony about Reeva Steenkamp's gunshot wounds led to a judge-ordered media blackout, and a breakdown from the defendant, at the Oscar Pistorius murder trial on Monday. Pathologist Gert Saayman testified that Steenkamp died from multiple gunshots, with three shots fired through a locked toilet door apparently striking her in the head, arm and hip. For more information please visit http://www.hlntv.com/video/2014/03/10/oscar-pistorius-reeva-steenkamp-trial-autopsy

HLN: http://www.youtube.com/watch?v=OBl2XMbXtOY

Alternatively, other narratives which elaborated the title were lengthy (up to 130 words) and exactly repeated the transcription of the video itself.

Evaluative Appraisal

Finally, 10 percent of the Descriptions appraised the narrative events by providing evaluation from expert commentators. A typical example of a Description that functioned as appraisal follows:

Title: Oscar Pistorius contradicts himself – law expert

Description: Criminal law expert William Booth says Oscar Pistorius crumbled under Gerrie Nel's cross examination by presenting different versions of what happened on February 14. Subscribe to News24: https://www.youtube.com/user/News24Video

News24: http://www.youtube.com/watch?v=rIkhiFpo5Dg

The functions of the Description in the YouTube template to contextualise, elaborate and appraise the video coverage of Oscar Pistorius and his trial can be explained in part by the narrative nature of the trial, which unfolded sequentially in YouTube as it was live-streamed, reported and commented on over time. The frequent use of the elaboration satellites in the Description suggests the ongoing importance of eventhood in the news as the content which needs to be most searchable, even in contexts where citizen journalism opens up opportunities for conversation and commentary. However, these satellites were included in the Description alongside content which promoted the identity and interests of the news producers. The Descriptions also included 'boiler-plate' content, through which the news producers invited the viewing audience to engage with them, providing links to the channel owner's other accounts, other social media outlets (such as Facebook pages, Twitter accounts) or apps available on iTunes. As such, these Descriptions exploited their affordances as the section of the YouTube template where the most tellable content from the video was coupled with commercial imperatives to drive the audience towards consuming other online content associated the channel owner, which here was most often the mainstream news.

Satellites in YouTube Comments

As the analysis of the videos posted about Oscar Pistorius showed, a key function of citizen journalism is to open up conversation about reported news. Within YouTube, conversation about the reported news takes place in the comments that can be added to the videos. Comments are necessarily a response to the video (they can only be added after a video has been uploaded), and each comment can generate its own reply thread. Like the polylogal context of Facebook pages, the resulting interactional coherence of a YouTube commenting section can be complex, including comments that respond directly to the video content and comments that respond to other comments, both on an individual and on a collective basis (Bou Franch and Blitvich, 2012). The asynchronous nature of YouTube means that comments can be added over an indefinite period, so that they diachronically extend the telling world beyond the timescales of the events narrated in the YouTube video itself.

In this dataset, there were 161 361 comments added across all videos. In order to examine how far commenting took place in response to news videos, rather than in response to other kinds of videos in the dataset, a thinned sample of ten examples from each of the different categories in the set, along with the comments from each video (N = 16 678), was analysed for the frequency of each participant's contribution. When the comments were disaggregated according to their category, the news videos had the highest average number of comments per contributor. In every category apart from the news videos, commenters on average posted once or twice to each thread. In contrast, the commenters to the video of the verdict uploaded by the news channel AFP posted on average sixteen times each, and the video of the sentencing uploaded by the SABC news channel was characterised by commenters who posted on average eight times each. This seems to suggest that the creation of video content related to news remains in the hands of the mainstream news producers, and that the main expansion of citizen journalism is to enable viewers to respond to rather than create the news.

Like the Descriptions, the YouTube comments provide a context for narration where the individual comments contain satellites which extend the narrative content found in the video, title or Description of the news report. In principle, it would be possible for the comments to serve any of the narrative functions suggested by White's satellites. However, in contrast to the Descriptions, which most often elaborated the titles with retellings of the breaking news that foregrounded the newsworthy nature of the videos, in this dataset the comments served the primary function of evaluating the events shown or reported in the videos. The various affective responses of the audience appraised the personnel involved in the events. This included evaluation of Pistorius:

I do want to believe he didn't intend to kill her... Poor guy cried in the court... so sad...

Oscar you lying little whinge.

and of the other legal personnel involved in the trial:

Gerrie Nel is awesome love this guy

my Lady is in total control of this trial her verdict will be well thought out

This Translator from Afrikaans to English is Terrible! She even got the stopwatch explanation completely completely wrong!

The evaluative language in the comments was characterised by comparators, which, as Labov (1972) noted, function by comparing one state of affairs with another that might have happened, but did not. This included small stories that projected future outcomes related to the trial, such as speculation on the verdict and sentencings:

he wont serve a full jail sentence i bet

Other comparators included rhetorical questions that implied the account given in the live-streamed trial was implausible:

Did this couple sleep together?..did they share the same bed?..if he was so concerned about their safety, why didn't he check to see if she was still laying next to him before he went to the bathroom?. . . .holes and more holes.

Other comparisons were used to highlight contradictions in Pistorius' account:

Wednesday April 9 session 4 at 22–10 Oscar said he held on to the door handle when he placed the fans in the room, now look at where he said he placed them in this session at 1–13–42. He must have very long arms.

The comparative nature of the comments suggests that they function as concessions, satellites which provide an account of events that runs counter to that given in the nucleus. Like the concessions found in the videos that commented on the news reports, these alternative accounts were speculative and critical of the trial. However, in contrast to the video-based commentary, where participation was limited to those involved in producing the video (such as the v-logger or the online news channel), in the concessions found in the comments, these evaluations were embedded in an interactional context where other participants could agree, disagree or add further examples to extend further the discussion of the case.

Conclusion

In this chapter, I developed the nucleus^satellite model of news narrative to account for the television news that was broadcast through YouTube. The expanded nucleus^satellite model is an important analytic tool, for it allows narrative scholars to account for the multimodal complexity of audio-visual forms of the news and the mediated contexts in which they are (re)produced and consumed. Crucially, the nucleus^satellite model explains how textual hierarchies between the nucleus and the satellites can be reinforced through the affordances of mediated contexts such as YouTube. The textual priority of the nucleus as the initial content of a news report is mapped on to the centrality of the video and its searchable title within YouTube. In this dataset, the nucleus, as the privileged centre of video content in YouTube, remains produced for the most part by mainstream news companies. These tellers replicated the satellites typical of the mainstream news in the Descriptions that accompanied the videos and coupled this narrative content with invitations that promoted the news producers' online presence. In this respect, the affordances of YouTube continue to empower the existing mainstream news producers, who can promote their content through the most searchable and visible spaces of the site (the video and the Description).

In comparison, satellites are textually subordinate in their dependency on the nucleus of the news report. The type of satellites found in the contributions made by tellers outside the mainstream news companies, such as independent news channels, v-loggers and members of YouTube who commented on the video, contrast with those found in mainstream news. In both the independent news videos and the comments to the mainstream news, the increasing use of appraisal and concession suggests that in prominent media cases like Pistorius' trial, the contribution of citizen journalism is not to create the news but to comment on or create conversation about the events reported by the mainstream media. On the one hand, in terms of frequency, the numbers of participants involved in creating the satellites of appraisal and concession in the comments suggest that citizen journalism in YouTube opened up conversations for many thousands of people to evaluate and debate the mainstream news. On the other, the satellites of appraisal and concession are not only subordinate to the ideological and textual primacy of the nucleus, but also serve to increase the nucleus' value. In YouTube, comments increase the visibility of a video, and thereby promote the identity and interests of the site member who produced it, rather than those of the commenters. The citizen journalism practices in this dataset suggest that in cases like the Pistorius trial, the hierarchies between producers and consumers of content remain intact. The 'fault line' between the mainstream and amateur news narration in YouTube further amplifies the differences between the participants, where sharing promotes the commercial interests of those in the mainstream news, rather than those who consume it.

10 Creative Sharing and Laughter in YouTube Comments

Introduction

As a context for shared stories, citizen journalism presents the opportunity for many tellers to co-construct news narratives as they retell and respond to reported events. In the case of large-scale, international news stories such as Pistorius' trial in 2014 (*The State* vs *Oscar Pistorius*), the key contribution of citizen journalism lay primarily in the ways that conversation about the events via social media sites opened up possibilities for narrative co-construction as a commentary on the events. In Chapter 9, I examined how the televised coverage of the trial, live-broadcast through YouTube, functioned as a shared story, showing how the YouTube template reconfigured the distributed linearity of the news narrative. I argued that the mediated affordances of the template gave value to certain parts of the narrative (those found in the video, title and Description), whilst other parts (which were found in the comments) were textually subordinate. If we only examine the distributed linearity of the shared story, it seems that from a mediated perspective, forms of citizen journalism in the YouTube coverage of Oscar Pistorius reinforced the socio-economic interests of the mainstream media which produced the videos, titles and Descriptions. This fails to take into account the content of the comments, and the role that the commenters as co-tellers might have played in opening up critique of the stories that were narrated in the audio-visual content of the YouTube coverage. The comments that responded to the video coverage of Oscar Pistorius were characterised by subjective, personalised responses about the reported events or people in a way that is typical of affective news (Papacharissi, 2014). I focus on a particular kind of affective response, laughter, and the ways in which laughter as a resource for shared stories can accomplish a range of relational outcomes.

The analysis in this chapter is important for two reasons. First, for researchers interested in citizen journalism, it draws attention to the importance of responding to the news, rather than assuming that the value of citizen journalism lies only in the production of news content. In particular, the focus on laughter as an ambivalent, creative form of affective news has not yet been explored. The mediated narrative analysis of laughter provides a robust and linguistically informed explanation of how the 'discordant' aspects of affect (Papacharissi, 2014, p. 7) are exploited. Second, the analysis of laughter as a form of affect develops the model of shared stories, showing how the tellers used laughter as a contextualisation cue (Gumperz, 1982) to indicate how their comments and the interactions should be interpreted. These contextualised interpretations relied on various kinds of shared, interactional norms that were implied rather than explicitly stated and which could result in different kinds of relational work that was characterised by ambiguity and ambivalence, such as mockery.

I interpret the importance of laughter as a form of affect in the light of the Russian philosopher Bakhtin's (1984) concepts of carnival. Bakhtin's thinking about carnival emerged from his reading of Rabelais' work, where Bakhtin interpreted the traditions, practices and meanings of renaissance carnival as a counter-cultural space that was excessive, intentionally transgressive and in which the institutional orders were (temporarily) overturned. It is a space characterised by plurality and, above all, laughter. There is resonance between Bakhtin's view of carnival and the description of YouTube as an 'unruly public' space (Goode et al., 2011). Likewise, the ideological interpretation of affect has drawn attention to its provocative and plural nature (McCosker, 2014, 2015), which finds expression readily (although not exclusively) in the debates that take place in YouTube (Van Zoonen et al., 2010). Within computer-mediated discourse analysis, Bakhtin's ideas have been applied to examples of interaction within YouTube, most notably by Androutsopoulos (2010) and Deumert (2014), both of whom explored parody videos. In their work, these scholars illustrated how the nonlinguistic concepts in Bakhtin's have powerful interpretive value when they are combined with empirical linguistic analysis. In Deumert's (2014) study, she focused on the carnivalesque forms of laughter acronyms, whilst Androutsopoulos (2010, 2011) examined the linguistic forms in which vernacular creativity occurred. My analysis builds on this earlier work in sociolinguistics. Following Deumert, I take the laughter acronyms as a point of departure for the linguistic analysis. Following Androutsopoulos, I explore how the laughter co-occurred with forms of creativity. Discourse analytic approaches to creativity point to the contextual knowledge that tellers bring to their interactions with the shared story. Jones (2012, p. 6) puts it like this:

> Implicit in this analytical stance towards creativity is also the notion that underpinning the creative process is our ability to recognise and exploit our experience of the world and in the semiotic systems within which we work... On the one hand, creativity involves understanding and being able to exploit old patterns, structures and rules, and on the other it involves breaking out of old patterns and coming up with new ones.

Similarly, within the shared story, tellers recognise and exploit their experience of their contexts, which in the case of this citizen journalism, centres on their shared knowledge of the live-streamed trial of Oscar Pistorius and its socio-cultural context. In their creative recontextualisations of the trial as it co-occurred with the use of laughter, the tellers also exploited multiple patterns and structures relating to their interactions. In order to analyse the ways in which they broke out of these patterns and came up with new ones, I draw on the combined methods of mediated narrative analysis, bringing together corpus approaches and interactional pragmatics. This allows me to scale up the analysis of laughter acronyms and creativity emerging from previous research in sociolinguistics and discourse analysis, with a specific interest in how these function as resources within the narrative genre of the shared story.

Data and Methodology

The YouTube comments that are scrutinised in this chapter are a subset of the 161 361 comments appended to the 635 videos containing the search term 'Oscar Pistorius' identified within YouTube using the data-mining tool ContextMiner (Shah, 2009). As ContextMiner does not extract the comments that are posted in response to individual videos, Klostermann's YouTube Comment scraper (http://ytcomments.klostermann.ca/) was used to extract the comments from a smaller number of selected videos. Forty videos were selected in order to represent each of the categories in the dataset (see Chapter 9), and so reflect the various representations of and responses to Pistorius as an iconic and a fallen elite figure. I further selected a range of videos in the categories of news, sport and comedy, in order to include the responses to a range of mainstream and more participatory forms of video production. Together, the subset of comments responded to representations of Pistorius as an iconic sporting hero (in the sports videos), in his live-streamed trial and the related news coverage, and in the comedic responses which mocked his demise (both in mainstream television programmes and in parody videos). The total size of the comments corpus as counted using Antconc (Anthony, 2014) was 784 543 words.

The importance of laughter as a verbal phenomenon in the YouTube comments was evident from the corpus-driven (Tognini-Bonelli, 2001) exploration of the data. The high-frequency items as they appeared in the word list for the comments ranked the acronym *lol* forty-seventh, the first of the nongrammatical items within the list other than the names of Oscar Pistorius and his prosecutor, Gerrie Nel. However, raw frequency alone is insufficient as an indication that laughter was a distinctive feature of the YouTube comments. Given the ubiquitous nature of the acronym *lol*, I generated a keyword list, using the YouTube comments as a specialised corpus in relation to a reference corpus compiled of all the data gathered for this book that could be considered as responses: namely, the comments posted to the Facebook memorial pages for Margaret Thatcher and Nelson Mandela, the tweets containing the #xfactor

Table 10.1 *Top twenty keywords for the specialised corpus of YouTube comments about Oscar Pistorius*

Rank	Raw frequency	Keyness	Lexical item
1	16 703	33 547.43	he
2	4080	14 713.22	oscar
3	3085	10 765.77	op
4	2885	10 220.77	nel
5	2529	9211.957	reeva
6	6281	8778.4	his
7	1684	6134.02	roux
8	3558	5413.427	him
9	1434	5223.387	pistorius
10	1438	4032.327	door
11	15 927	3856.613	is
12	2647	3300.988	lol
13	995	3246.171	gun
14	1838	2972.423	judge
15	986	2907.574	Shot
16	928	2883.227	toilet
17	940	2831.629	bathroom
19	1781	2312.952	guilty
20	572	1993.829	intruder

hashtag and the talk pages for the Wikipedia article on the 'Murder of Meredith Kercher'. As an illustrative indication of the keywords, the first twenty items on list are presented in Table 10.1. Inevitably, the variety in the subject matter in the data would influence the keywords that emerged (such as the names of the figures mentioned in each dataset). Nonetheless, given that the forms of impoliteness present in the interactions within the data had some similarities (for example, in containing disagreements), it was likely that verbal representations of laughter might occur in each of the datasets and therefore provide an appropriate reference corpus in this case. The keyword list for the YouTube comments is surprising then, not for the grammatical items (*he*, *his*, *him*, *is*, *not*), nor for the subject specific names and references to the key figures in the trial (*Oscar Pistorius*, *Nel*, *Reeva*, *judge*), nor the lexical items related to the crime scene and trial (*door*, *gun*, *shot*, *toilet*, *bathroom*, *guilty*, *jail*), but rather for the presence of the acronym *lol*.

The overuse of *lol* in the YouTube comments suggests that the forms of laughter in this dataset merit further exploration. Although *lol* was the only laughter initialism to appear as a keyword, it is not the only way to represent laughter in a lexical form. Alternative laughter initialisms include *rofl* and *rotfl*, *lmao* and *lmfao*, and expressive respellings of *lol* (such as repeating the vowel

Table 10.2 *Laughter initialisms according to the type of YouTube video in the Oscar Pistorius dataset (calculated to a relative frequency per million words)*

YouTube channel	lol	rofl	rotfl	lmao	lmfao	lolol	lool
AFP	5060	193	0	1062	116	39	39
ENCA	5085	0	0	378	29	12	83
SABC	26448	248	41	1055	248	83	414
The Young Turks	0	17	0	34	17	0	0
Sports	1471	40	0	199	99	0	0
Comedy	0	0	0	276	276	0	0
Rant	3562	0	0	3166	0	0	0
Vlog	791	0	0	0	0	0	0
Total	42417	498	41	6170	785	134	536

or the final syllable; for example, *loool* or *lolol*). Other options include verbal laughter, such as *hahaha* or *hehehe* (and respelled variants). In order to capture as full a picture of the verbal representations of laughter in the YouTube comments as possible, I went on to use Antconc to search for and quantify each of these terms. The laughter forms *hahaha* and *hehehe* occurred infrequently in the data (a combined total of nineteen times, as compared with 2647 occurrences of *lol*). The remaining discussion of the verbal forms of laughter in the YouTube comments therefore focuses on the initialisms alone.

I quantified the occurrences of the laughter initialisms according to the type of video to which the comments containing them had been posted. I then normalised the results of this analysis to a relative frequency per million words. The results of the quantitative comparison of laughter intialisms are summarised in Table 10.2. As the numbers in Table 10.2 show, *lol* was by far the most frequently occurring laughter acronym in this dataset, occurring over six times more often than did the next most frequent acronym, *lmao*. More importantly, the distribution of the laughter initialisms varied according to the category of the video to which the comments responded in a surprising way. They occurred least frequently in response to videos categorised as comedy, and most often in response to videos posted by the mainstream news outlets AFP, ENCA and SABC (appearing most frequently of all in relation to the latter). In order to explore why this might be so, I examined the frequency of the laughter abbreviations according to each individual video, using the Concordance Plot function within Antconc. The laughter acronym *lol* did not occur with equal frequency in relation to all videos posted to these channels. Instead, it occurred particularly often in relation to three events, where its frequency accounted for over 0.1 percent of the file size (as calculated as a percentage of the characters per file). For the SABC news, the video with the most laughter acronyms was the live-streamed trial on Friday, 11 April 2015, when Pistorius testified. For the AFP news, the most frequent use of laughter acronyms was in response to the live-streamed verdict of the trial. For the ENCA news, the most frequent use occurred in relation to the sentencing of Pistorius. The laughter acronyms are important for their overuse in the YouTube comments as compared with other kinds of comparable social media interactions, even more so in the light of their use responding to the news in particular as a form of citizen journalism.

Having identified the laughter acronyms (N = 2647) using Antconc, I next manually extracted all the comments and the exchanges in which they were embedded from the YouTube threads for qualitative analysis. Following Partington's (2006) approach to analysing laughter in a large-scale corpus, I analysed the occurrences of the laughter abbreviations for the three news videos in question in relation to the interactional co-text. This included the content of the comment in which the laughter acronym occurred and, where the comment was 'format-tied' to a preceding comment, the content of the preceding comment, too. As YouTube is a polylogal context, the comments that were format-tied were not necessarily adjacent to each other within the thread but could be traced by using the forms of addressivity in the comments (such as another commenter's name). In the examples given for illustrative purposes in the discussion that follows, the format-tied interactions are presented consecutively, with any intervening comments removed. This is to avoid lengthy quotation of irrelevant content and so improve the readability of the examples.

Laughter as a Resource for Shared Stories: The Multiple Meanings of Lol

As an affective response to the serious events broadcast through the news channels in the YouTube coverage of Oscar Pistorius, the laughter acronyms are important as a carnivalesque form of critique. Bakhtin's description of the mediaeval folk carnival stressed the ambivalence of laughter, which pushes aside the serious forms of authority and introduces multiple perspectives through its heteroglossic potential. One way to articulate the ambivalent meanings of laughter is to draw on linguistic research, where laughter is found to fulfil many different functions. Within pragmatics, laughter has been studied in relation to the multiple forms and functions of verbal humour (see Dynel, 2009 for a useful overview). More specifically, within conversation analysis, laughter has been analysed as an interactional paralinguistic phenomenon (most notably in response to the seminal work of Jefferson, 2004), which occurs in humorous exchanges and in examples of trouble talk. As these researchers point out, laughter need not map on to a straightforward meaning that it marks a stretch of speech as 'funny'. Partington (2006) offers an extensive survey of the different kinds of supportive and distancing functions that laughter might serve in conversation as a form of evaluation, joking or meta-linguistic resource. One outcome of the multifunctionality of laughter means that its interpretation is highly context-sensitive and by no means straightforward. Distinguishing the target of the laughter, its meaning and its potential for rapport-enhancing, threatening and saving behaviour amongst different sets of participants can be highly complex.

The analysis of the laughter acronym *lol* is similarly complex and context-dependent. Uygur-Distexhe (2014) points out that the semantic denotation of *lol* as an acronym for 'laughing out loud' has now bleached so that the function of the term now is phatic, rather than referential. She argues that *lol* is best thought of as a discourse marker that serves to organise an interaction and to signal the ways in which stretches of writing might be interpreted. In other studies, the pragmatic interpretation of *lol* has focused on its rapport-enhancing potential. For example, Baron and Ling (2011, p. 54) suggest that *lol* could be used to express personal sentiment. Tagliamonte and Denis (2008) focus more on the interpersonal potential of the marker, and interpret *lol* within a corpus of IRC and SMS messages as a signal of interlocutor involvement. Similarly, West and Trester (2013) suggest that in Facebook exchanges, *lol* serves mitigating functions, such as self-deprecation. As McSweeney (2016) points out, the range of pragmatic outcomes that result from the use of *lol* vary according to context, and therefore cannot be limited to a single meaning. Instead, she suggests that in her corpus of SMS messages, *lol* was a signal to the receiver that the illocutionary force and the locutionary force of a message did not match. Although she does not say so explicitly, McSweeney's conclusion suggests that *lol* signals additional implicatures to be derived from the utterance containing the acronym (see Chapter 2). My analysis of the examples of *lol* that occur in the YouTube comments considered in this dataset extends the pragmatic exploration of the acronym in several ways. First, the data considered here are quite distinct from those considered in these earlier studies. The interactions in the YouTube comments are publicly available (rather than gathered from private or semi-private interactions between known participants) and focus on a public, large-scale event (the trial of Pistorius). Second, the data are not dyadic, but rather part of a many-to-many interactional context that takes place in a polylogal setting where the participants can be responding to an adjacent comment, a non-adjacent comment or the video to which the comment was appended. Finally, the sentiment towards Pistorius and the criticism of the trial and its outcome present an opportunity to analyse the use of *lol* in interactions that might be expected to be face-threatening and replete with disagreements, rather than ones that seek harmony.

The varying interpretations of *lol* in the research to date suggest that it is an important resource for signalling affect (following Baron and Ling, 2011), but that it is also ambiguous in its referential range and pragmatic function. In part, this explains why laughter has the potential to generate the ambivalence that Bakhtin associated with carnival. In the discussion that follows, I argue that the affective meanings of *lol* are constrained contextually and that it does not always signal a mismatch between the illocutionary and locutionary force of the message. Instead, drawing on work from interactional pragmatics, I argue that the types of rapport effects and affective meanings that can be signalled by laughter acronyms can be contrasted in terms of the type of contextual match or mismatch that accompanies the acronym. In so doing, I conceptualise *lol* as a contexutalisation cue (Gumperz, 1982, p. 131) which 'contributes to the signalling of contextual presuppositions'. This recognises the interactionally produced nature of the meanings of *lol*, but does not limit these to a single pragmatic or affective outcome.

Lol as an Affective Signal of Humour

The first step in determining whether *lol* might signal an implicature is to assess whether there was a contextual mismatch that accompanied the acronym. Where there is no mismatch, then the opportunity for interpreting implicatures in relation to the comment is greatly reduced, and the referential meaning of *lol* as 'laughing out loud' and its pragmatic function of marking a stretch of text as 'funny' can be sustained. In the YouTube comments examined in this chapter, *lol* occurred occasionally in comments where the commenter evaluated the video content in positive terms. These examples occurred exclusively in the responses to the videos categorised as comedy, including the parody videos that satirised the persons involved in the criminal trial. Responses to the parody videos included comments such as the following:

LOL cool rap

Brilliant for SA, supporting SA talent lol

LOL ! Excellent

This is brilliant – 25 times lol

In these examples, the affective meaning of the acronym seems to be closest to the earlier referential meanings of *lol* as 'laughing out loud', evaluating the comedic video as 'funny'. This interpretation is contextually congruent. In terms of the genre, laughter is an expected and preferred response to comedy. The verbal content of the comment as praise or positive evaluation is in line with a sentiment that suggests laughter as a response to humour. The comments did not contain any face-threatening criticism or mockery that targeted a third person. There is no mismatch here between the prompt for the laughter (comedy), the content of the comment (praise for the comedy) and the meaning of *lol* as 'laughing out loud'. This suggests that *lol* does not always generate a mismatch between the locutionary and illocutionary force of a message. Instead, the potential for *lol* to signal implicatures rests not only on the presence of the acronym, but also on its use in context.

Lol as a Signal for Implicatures

The possibility for *lol* to signal implicatures occurs when the interpretation of the surrounding co-text no longer matches with the surface meaning of 'funny'. The mismatches can be generated at a number of levels. At the level of the discourse, there may be a mismatch between the generic norms for response and the use of laughter. This is evident in the data, where the most frequent use of *lol* occurred in response to the key events in the live-streamed trial that were broadcast through mainstream news channels. In these cases, the generic context (as the broadcast of a legal proceeding) did not generate an expectation of laughter as a preferred response. The most frequent occurrences of the laughter acronyms were found at the most serious points in the trial, namely, when Pistorius was on the stand, when the verdict was announced and when the sentence was passed. These events were highly troubling, and brought into sharpest focus the failure of Pistorius as a credible witness and the discontent with the outcome of the trial. In these cases, the interpretation of the serious legal events cannot be that these were 'funny'. Instead, additional implicatures must be interpreted.

The use of *lol* as an affective response in these instances generated an implicature that a play frame should be used to interpret the interaction. In a comedic context, *lol* can be considered as keying a play frame (Goffman, 1974, pp. 40–41) where the activity is not expected to be taken seriously. Similarly, the use of *lol* in response to the key events in the trial might then be interpreted as a way of recontextualising the troubling moments in the trial as impossible to take seriously. In line with this, many of the comments used the metaphor of a joke to make a serious point about the perceived inadequacy of the legal proceedings and their outcome. Indeed, laughter acronyms collocated with *joke* on sixteen occasions, including specific comments which clearly criticised the trial, such as the following illustrative example from a comment that responded to the verdict broadcast through the ENCA YouTube channel:

Can't believe this is a real murder trial. What a joke PMSL lol

The potential for *lol* to generate implicatures thus rests on the disruption of the interactional norms at a generic level, which here can be interpreted as recontextualising the serious content of the trial within a play frame as a metaphorical joke that cannot be taken seriously.

Lol and Playful Recontextualisation

More specific mismatches occur where particular scenes, events or persons from the trial were recontextualised by the commenters. In these examples, the recontextualisation inverted the institutional order, akin to Bakhtin's description of the carnival. The mismatch in these comments was generated by the intertextuality, where the scenarios narrated in the comments reframed the events that had been shown in the trial scenes in the courtroom. The incongruity of these comparisons (such as a temporary break in the legal proceedings that was compared to a trip 'to China', or a lawyer checking a cell phone as compared with playing a game) contained indirect criticism of a third party, in that they 'poked fun' at the legal personnel. However, the analogies were light-hearted and the resulting play frame of a non-serious interpretation built rapport between the commenters on the thread. Evidence for this appears in the format-tying and co-constructed narration that occurred between the comments using the laughter acronyms, as in the following examples:

lol [name] they've gone to china

lolol I also think they have been kidnapped

and:

Nel is playing candy crush on his phone

lol at [name]. nel is probly at level 40

Or he is playing Hangman lol

or Ruzzle lol

Lol, you guys are crazy. Nel is doing what? Wena Nthabi o mosadi wa mang mara? *dies*

The potential for the laughter acronyms to signal a shift into a play frame was present in the intertextual examples where *lol* co-occurred with examples of puns and other forms of verbal creativity. These cases of word play recontextualised voices from the trial, quoting instances where communicative disfluency on the part of the legal personnel occurred. Faux pas or mispronounced words, especially from authority figures, were mocked, such as in Masipa's strongly accented pronunciation, where the fronted South African English vowels (relative to British English) were reproduced in eye dialect in the comments:

lmao . . . cricket bed

Ealy Delight or LED light? LOOOOOOOL

Other examples of verbal creativity used Pistorius' name as inspiration for puns. The following comments show how his surname (Pistorius) and his former moniker (The Blade Runner) were lexically recontextualised with the insertion of gun-related lexis (such as *pistol*, *gunner*):

they will resume when lol-car pisstol – ius stop crying

Lmao blade gunner

These puns were then repeated, spreading in meme-like fashion as a shared joke amongst the commenters. Similarly, laughter acronyms functioned as contextualisation cues that signalled intertextual references as jokes that relied on shared knowledge of popular culture. In the following example, the reference to the television series *Orange is the New Black* was used to predict Pistorius' punishment:

ORANGE IS THE NEW BLACK... MALE PRISON lol

lol [name of commenter] he will look good in orange

In each of these cases, the recontextualisation of the narrative content from the courtroom relied on creative forms of humour in recognisable forms of word play, such as puns and shared intertextual references. The target of the joke in each case was a non-present third party (that is, a person who was part of the courtroom proceedings, not a member of YouTube). The co-constructed nature of these examples of word play, shared across multiple comments and multiple tellers, suggests that although face-threatening in their mockery towards the persons in the court-room, these examples of humour produced a shared alignment between at least some of the commenters.

Implicatures of Disbelief

In other cases, the laughter abbreviations were used to preface comments where the implicature of a non-serious interpretation was rather less playful. Instead of signalling a 'joke', the non-serious meanings suggested that the events broadcast through the live-streamed trial were interpreted with incredulity. These examples did not include recognised forms of humour which might have mitigated the non-serious meaning as playful. Instead, an implicature of 'non-serious meaning' was directed to the institutional discourse (such as Pistorius' testimony or Masipa's ruling). In some cases, the implicature of disbelief was strengthened through the metalinguistic adverb, which explicitly questioned whether the courtroom discourse could be taken 'seriously':

lol seriously? he intended to hurt whoever was behind it, i dont just shoot at a door for fun

lol Judge Masipa like seriously Masipa

The criticism of the trial that accompanied the laughter acronyms often co-occurred with comparators that juxtaposed content from Pistorius' testimony with the commenter's interpretation of the testimony. The contextual mismatches were structured by the syntactic forms of the comparators, which used questions and negation to evaluate Pistorius' testimony. Typical examples included:

LOL i've heard him saying that so many times he can answer the easy questions but when they becoming difficult he suddenly doesn't remember.

lol his tired??? lol from lying yes

why would that light bother him, was he intending to watch it while trying to sleep, lol

All of these positioned Pistorius as a figure whose testimony could not be taken seriously. Instead, he was recast in a negative light as an inauthentic and untrustworthy narrator. In these cases, there was no mitigation of the non-serious meanings signalled by the use of *lol*, but rather the face-threatening criticism was intensified through the use of comparators as evaluation.

Impoliteness and Laughter

The potential for the play frame cued by the use of *lol* to generate face-threatening criticism occurred when there was a mismatch between the content of the comment and the norms for politeness that were contextually appropriate. In a further set of comments, laughter acronyms occurred alongside forms of implicational impoliteness (Culpeper, 2011) such as innuendo. Like the examples seen previously, these comments recontextualised quoted content from the live-streamed trial, and used it as a source material for puns and word play. However, the sexualised nature of the puns could be regarded as a form of nonconventionalised impoliteness, such as the innuendo present in the following examples:

totally want black judge lady to "render verdict" on me ollolololol

But she would JUDGE you in bed LOLOLOLOL

In carnivalesque fashion, the innuendo in the comments reframed the judge's institutional power as sexual power, which ambivalently inverted heteronormative scripts of dominance as a source of hyper-masculine pleasure. The carnivalesque excess was intensified in the expressive punctuation in the extended *lol* sequences and capitalisation. The paralinguistic cues such as the expressive punctuation in the laughter in these examples might seem to scale up the potential for the offence.

In other cases, the laughter abbreviations co-occurred with conventionally impolite formulae such as insults. The targets of these insults included figures from the trial, such as Pistorius:

What a pussy this oscar is lol

In other cases, the target of the insults was another commenter:

[commenter name] lmao u are a faggot

lol, what a racist fool you must be to bring racism into a murder trial

Whether these insults were supposed to be taken as face-threatening or not is a moot point. The ambivalence of carnivalesque laughter relies on the interpretation of the insults to be at once offensive and playful, and therefore allows the commenter to deflect any charge of the intention to offend others. Indeed, the laughter acronyms were used by some commenters to key the comment thread as a place for play, not for serious conversation. For example, when one commenter complained that the commenters were 'seriously wrong', another responded with a comment including the laughter acronym:

lol [name] nobody is perfect...

Play and Provocation: Disruptions to the Comment Thread

Within the comment thread, there were two further uses of *lol* which reframed the interactions between the co-tellers as both playful and provocative: trolling and copy pasta spam. The communicative mismatches were distinctive from those covered earlier, in that the intertextual point of reference was no longer drawn from the video content (and so from within the co-textual or generic context), but rather was from the wider online culture shared by the YouTube commenters. The interpretation of the comments within a play frame thereby required a greater amount of inferential work than did those comments that recontextualised content from the trial. The targets of the laughter in these comments also differed from those considered thus far, in that they were no longer figures from the trial but instead always fellow commenters. The rapport-threatening potential of this laughter could disrupt the interactions between the co-tellers, and therefore brought into question the value of the comment thread as a space for citizen journalistic commentary.

The first type of disruptive commenting behaviour marked as 'non-serious' was trolling. The communicative characteristics of trolling have begun to attract scholarly interest and attention from the mainstream media in recent years. Hardaker (2015, p. 202) defines 'trolling' as a term used to describe online antagonism undertaken for amusement's sake. The association between play, amusement and trolling is evident in the comments that responded to the live-streamed trial of Pistorius, where the laughter acronym prefaced the evaluation of a comment or a commenter as *trolling* or a *troll*:

loll this is trolling

lol hes a troll

crazy Trolololo

The commenters' description of the comments or commenters as trolls allows us to observe exactly what kinds of interactional behaviour prompted these responses and so shed further light on trolling as a form of disrupting the shared story. The kinds of behaviour that the YouTube commenters labelled as 'trolling' are important more generally, because the examples in this dataset are quite different from the communicative behaviours associated with trolling in previous research on the topic. In Hardaker's (2013) study of Usenet posts, she identified a range of trolling strategies that included digression, (hypo)criticism, antipathy, endangerment, shock and aggression. Other researchers have examined particularly sensitive environments in which trolling breached social norms, such as memorial pages on Facebook (Marwick and Ellison, 2012; Phillips, 2011). Many of the communicative behaviours that fall under the heading of 'trolling' appear overtly provocative in their antagonistic nature. However, in the YouTube comments that responded to the coverage of Oscar Pistorius, the interactions labelled by the participants as 'trolling' that co-occurred with a laughter acronym were not aggressive, uncivil or critical.

In the comments responding to the live trial, the comments that were labelled as 'trolling' typically expressed positive sentiment towards Pistorius. The comments did not contain examples of conventionalised impoliteness, such as threats, profanity or insults. In the SABC channel's and ENCA's comment sections, a particular account called 'Gladwrap Channel' was the source of many pro-Pistorius comments. Gladwrap's comments represented Pistorius in eulogistic terms, often in connection with his former iconic status as a sporting hero:

OP a great guy and I think no one really can imagine how it feels to loose a partner in such a tragedy.

Free the gold medalist with no legs!

Oscar you made SA proud in the world by your courage. Please forgive OP!

On the surface, there is little that appears provocative about 'Gladwrap's' comments. They are similar to the positive evaluation of Pistorius found responding to the sporting videos that pre-dated the death of Reeva Steenkamp in 2013. However, other commenters clearly found the comments inappropriate:

Gladwrap you are acting weirdly. I think you forgot you are representing your company and not yourself

Gladwrap was interpreted as an unwanted intrusion in the comment thread:

No please don't mention gladrap. Just now you jinx it and he comes on.

Others categorised the commenter as a troll:

Gladrap is a troll DUH wake up

Gladrap is being a troll and making it obvious

Trolling relies on a contextual mismatch between the troll's contribution and what is discursively constructed as normative within the particular comment thread. In earlier studies of trolling, these mismatches typically relied on flouting the Gricean (1975) maxims for co-operation, for example by introducing irrelevant comments, or breaching norms of politeness. In the YouTube comments, the trolls instead broke the maxims of quality, by saying what other people no longer believed to be 'true'.

One option for responding to a troll was to laugh at them. In these cases, the statements in support of Pistorius prompted a response that included a laughter acronym in a comment addressed to the commenter. Illustrative examples include the following comment sequences:

Comment 1: Oscar is innocent!!

Response: Lol [name deleted]

Comment 2: Oscar is not guilt only god knows what happened that night

Response: [name deleted] lol no hey

Once again, the laughter acronym functions as a contextualisation cue for a play frame, suggesting that the troll and the troll's comments should not be taken seriously. In this way, the troll's support of Pistorius was reframed as non-serious communication like other forms of mock impoliteness such as baiting (Mitchell, 2015). However, not all commenters detected the potential mismatch in the locutionary and illocutionary force of the troll's support for Pistorius. The commenters who responded to the troll with irritation and thus seemed to interpret the illocutionary force of the troll's pro-Pistorius sentiment seriously (rather than as provocative play) became the target of laughter from others. For example, when one commenter responded,

Gladrap – if I could get my hands on 6 gold medals – I would shove them all up your arse to shut you up

another replied with laughter:

Lol [name deleted].

The laughter directed towards the commenters who took the troll's sentiment seriously (rather than non-seriously) is similar to the interactions within the Twitter-based social television practices that responded to *The X Factor* (see Chapter 8), where the knowing in-group was able to detect parody whilst the mocked out-group did not interpret the interaction correctly.

Other communicative disruptions that prompted a response of *lol* included comments which were off-topic contributions. In terms of Grice's (1975) maxims, these flouted the maxims of relevance. These digressions were often posed repeatedly by the same commenters, who seemed to be using the comment thread as an opportunity to talk about topics that had nothing to do with the content of the trial, often centred in carnivalesque fashion on sexual activity, as in the following example:

Comment: All these months on this chat and I'm still single

Response: lol [name deleted].

Other examples of off-topic posts appeared repeatedly in the AFP comment thread on the day of Pistorius' verdict. These off-topic posts were examples of 'copy pasta' stories, which are stories or anecdotes that are copied and pasted repeatedly with no apparent meaning (Chess and Newsom, 2015). These posts prompted responses of laughter, as in the 'Google Admin' example in the next paragraph. The copy pasta stories illustrate the simultaneously playful, creative and disruptive nature of spam as an unwanted form of 'sharing' (Brunton, 2012). Like its predecessors, the activities that the YouTube commenters described as 'spamming' appear intrusive insofar as they flout Gricean (1975) maxims of quality (they are not relevant) and quantity (in their repeated use, they exacerbate their irrelevance by saying too much). Unlike the spam associated with advertising campaigns, there appears to be little economic benefit to the commenters producing the replicated messages, nor does the content seek to sell some kind of goods or service to the audience. Instead, within the attention economy of social media sites like YouTube, these intrusions seem to 'hijack' the attention of the participants away from the main object of interest, the live trial.

The 'Google Admin' copy pasta story was not found exclusively on this YouTube thread, and occurred widely in a number of forums and online contexts. However, given that Google owned YouTube by the time that the posts appeared in the comment thread, they might be considered particularly humorous as a potentially deceptive message where the commenter was representing 'Google Admin'. Examples of the copy pasta story as it was repeatedly recontextualised and responded to within the YouTube comments include the following:

Hello everyone, this is the Google Admin here to remind you all that while we love the chat experience, please refrain from copy pasting in the chat. This ruins the atmosphere

ello everyone, this is the Google Admin here to remind you all that while we love the chat experience, please refrain from copy pasting in the chat. This leads to some people getting hot legs.

Guys can you please not spam the chat. My mom bought me this new laptop and it gets really hot when the chat is being spamed. Now my leg is starting to hurt because it is getting so hot

lol google

Google Admin lol stfu

Okay, the "hot legs" repost is getting really old now.

The humour of the story relied, in part, on the mismatch between the imperative in the meme ('please refrain from copy pasting in the chat') and the act of repeatedly contravening that command and reproducing the story. The humour also relied on the creativity introduced when the story was modified to introduce innuendo through puns ('getting hot legs') and then reframing the meaning of 'hot' from a metaphorical to a literal interpretation ('starting to hurt it is getting so hot'). As the responses to the copy pasta story show, the playful exploitation of digital replicability was in part humorous, but also short-lived. Even for the commenters within an in-group who shared the joke, there seem to have been limits to how long the repetition of the irrelevant story could last. Like the trolling, the playful engagement with the copy pasta stories became a resource for the commenters to differentiate an in-group and an out-group, dependent on the commenters' ability and willingness to detect humour. In both cases, the laughter acronyms were used to indicate the limits of the play frame (that is, those comments which are judged non-serious versus those which are not). These interpretations of the communicative breaches as non-serious relied heavily on inferential, in-group knowledge rather than specific recontextualisation of available content (as in the responses to the video). They were thus most liable to misinterpretation and the most difficult to pin down as a form of social action.

One way to interpret the copy pasta and the trolling in the comments is to understand them as 'noise'. As Goddard et al. (2012, p. 1) point out, noise is considered as a disturbance within a meaningful sonic system. It is often interpreted as an irritant, a 'glitch' which has disrupted the maximal transfer of a signal within a communicative system. The laughter acronyms in these noises are all the more appropriate as a signifier that communicative 'trouble' has occurred. Goddard et al. (2012) go on to point out that noise is organised socially, and may become a source of transgressive pleasure, or indicate a form of protest. This is an apt interpretation of the trolling and the copy pasta stories, for the presence of the laughter acronyms, as a contextualising cue of a play frame, suggests a similar kind of communicative transgression. The 'noise' created by these comments is truly carnivalesque, as the ultimate inversion of the serious, institutionally organised discourse in the live-streamed trial.

Conclusion

In this chapter, I examined the comments that responded to the videos about Oscar Pistorius in YouTube as a form of citizen journalism commentary. Rather than opening up a civic debate about the trial, the comments were characterised by a particularly ambivalent affective response: laughter. The analysis of laughter as a contextualisation cue in this dataset has implications for a number of fields. First, for media scholars, the analysis of laughter focuses on a hitherto under-scrutinised form of affect that occurs within citizen journalism practices. The linguistic analysis of the laughter acronyms brings empirical substance to the plurality that underpins the carnivalesque nature of affect. Second, within computer-mediated discourse analysis, the analysis of the laughter acronym has expanded the understanding of *lol* and its potential range of meanings, as derived from a new, substantial body of evidence. I argued that the meanings of *lol* are dependent on its context. Where a contextual mismatch occurs, *lol* may signal the potential for an implicature to be interpreted by the recipient of the message. This helps explain why the laughter acronym can retain its earlier referential meaning, 'laughing out loud', in some contexts but does not seem to do so in others. Where contextual mismatches occur, *lol* signals a non-serious interpretation that can be humorous, mocking, insulting or disruptive. Finally, for narrative scholars, *lol* here can be understood as a stance-taking resource that can be combined with intertextuality to recontextualise 'troubling' events and open them up to critique. In this case, the criticism was made of the legal proceedings in *The State* vs *Oscar Pistorius*, but this use of *lol* is transferable to other contexts, both in citizen journalism and beyond.

The meanings of the play frame keyed by the use of *lol* raise important questions about the nature and value of the citizen journalistic commentary enabled in social media contexts. On the one hand, the affective nature of the laughter opened up the possibility of criticising the persons represented in the video content from the news channels (which, in this dataset, included Pistorius and the legal personnel involved in the trial). The co-constructed nature of the playful criticism suggested that this kind of interaction could build rapport between co-tellers who took a shared stance against the outcome of the trial. However, the use of the play frame is inherently ambivalent and, like the carnival as a counter-cultural space, could always be dismissed on the grounds that it is 'play' and therefore not to be taken seriously. The trolling and the copy pasta spam that occurred as disruptions within the comment thread point to the difficulties of interpreting play as provocation. The trolling and the copy pasta stories both disrupted the conversational potential of the comment thread. The trolling was disruptive in that it expressed a sentiment at odds with the dominant affective response in the thread, and as such had the potential to lure commenters into disagreements and disputes that were pointless (Herring, 1994). The 'pointless' nature of the interactions is yet more evident in the copy pasta stories, which in their off-topic content drew on intertextual references outside the context of the video and its comments in a form of 'noise'. The ambivalence of the 'noise' as a form of disruption to the comment thread lies in its resistance to interpretation. As a contribution to the shared story, the analysis of the laughter is an important reminder not to limit the interpretation of 'sharing' to the surface meanings of what is told. Instead, the analysis of the shared story must be contextually sensitive and open to the ways in which its many tellers can creatively disrupt old forms of 'sharing' and come up with new ones.

11 Shared Stories Revisited

Introduction

In this book, I defined the shared story as *a retelling, produced by many tellers, across iterative textual segments, which promotes shared attitudes between its tellers*. I examined the four characteristics of the shared story – its distributed linearity, co-tellership, intertextuality and focus on common ground – as these occur in the four international social media contexts that have dominated the communicative landscape in the early twenty-first century: Wikipedia, Facebook, Twitter and YouTube. Through the empirical investigation of these examples, I showed the value of mediated narrative analysis as an emerging framework that combines multiple methods from applied linguistics to tackle the scale and multimodal scope of stories as they are told in online contexts. In this chapter, I look across the four case studies and sum up what we now know about the powerful form of shared stories, showing that mediated narrative analysis opens up new ways of thinking about stories, their tellers and the contexts in which they are told.

Distributed Linearity

Mediated narrative analysis draws attention to the relationship between stories and the media used to produce, consume and reproduce them. This is particularly important for the distributed linearity of the shared story, which can be told through many different kinds of mediated units, such as multiple versions of a wiki page, successive posts and comments, or episodically unfolding YouTube videos and comments. The shared stories in this book exemplify types of linearity which unfold across different timescales, from the minute-by-minute posts published in Twitter to longitudinal comparisons of narration that can expand across many years, as in the case of Wikipedia and YouTube. Similarly, the retellings found in online contexts can range from extensive expansions on previous tellings or episodes (as seen in the Wikipedia archives analysed in Chapter 3) through to highly compressed allusions that contribute to the shared story, such as a caption that highlights breaking news within a Twitter hashtag (see Chapter 7).

The distributed linearity of the shared story is important for narrative research, as it opens up further exploration of atypical and as yet under-scrutinised patterns of narrative structure. Rather than positioning open-endedness as a single, binary alternative to the 'closed' structures of prototypical narratives, the shared stories in this book included narrative patterns that are more or less like their offline antecedents. As Herring (2013) reminds us, it can be easy to emphasise innovation whilst overlooking the more subtle ways in which online interactions – including narratives – develop. In reviewing the linearity of the shared stories, I follow Herring's (2013) heuristic framework for classifying the open-ended narrative patterns found in the shared story as *familiar* replications of earlier genres, *reconfigured* forms which alter a previous genre in the light of its online environment and *emergent* forms which have no predecessor and are innovative developments found solely in online environments. The examples of shared stories seen in the earlier chapters exemplify a wide range of innovative potential, with familiar, reconfigured and emergent forms of distributed linearity.

Familiar linearity reproduces the kinds of open-endedness that are found in the offline analogues of shared stories. In the case studies I have examined in this book, it is best exemplified by the open-endness found in Wikipedia, which results from the iterative editing of articles, and the addition, alteration and removal of content over time. These serial practices were also possible in print forms of encyclopaedic writing (Dawson, 2012), and the key contribution of Wikipedia is to make this serial open-endedness transparent by documenting every successive change to an article in its page history.

Reconfigured linearity occurs where earlier narrative structures are expanded in new directions when they are transposed into online contexts. A good example of reconfigured linearity is found in the analysis of the nucleus^satellite organisation of television news, where the flexible organisations of satellites that elaborate, contextualise and appraise the news headline observed in earlier forms of the print news can be re-organised within templates such as those offered by YouTube. As I argued in Chapter 9, the models for open-ended narrative news structures needed to be expanded in light of the multimodal forms of television news reporting, especially as these are embedded in YouTube. This narrative model allows us to make comparisons between different mediated forms of journalistic narration: both print and televised, mainstream and citizen journalism.

A second example of reconfigured linearity occurs in the Facebook community pages, where the interactional context created within the comment threads reworks the conversational, turn-by-turn possibilities for co-constructing a shared story across multiple interactions. Like many other comment threads, the responses to Facebook posts on community pages are polylogal, in that commenters can respond to the initial post or to other comments within the thread, addressing themselves to an individual commenter as a reply, or to the wider audience of auditors who are members of the Facebook page. Like many other social networks, the comment threads to the Facebook memorial pages examined in Chapters 5 and 6 were characterised by collapsed contexts, where the audience that might respond to the posts belonged to different groups, not usually brought together in a single interactive context. The possibility for conversational coherence to structure the linearity into open-ended threads of replies and responses is reconfigured in this context to a networked pattern of linearity. This means that the interactive context is multidimensional (connected by 'liking', sharing and commenting) and is unlikely to be coherently integrated into a single thread. A networked model of linearity increases the directions into which open-endedness can extend and weakens the likelihood of a single story emerging from this kind of interactional context. The competing accounts of Margaret Thatcher's leadership juxtaposed in the Facebook comment threads show how this networked linearity could be exploited by tellers who supported or opposed her actions.

Emergent linearity occurs when the narrative patterns do not have an analogue in their offline antecedents. In this book, an example of emergent open-endedness occurs in the hashtag threads that are used to respond to social television practices in Twitter. Like networked open-endedness, the Twitter hashtag threads are characterised by collapsed contexts and polylogal interactions, where the members of Twitter can post content about the topic indicated by the referential hashtag (which, in this case, was a television series), and where the hashtag evolves over time. However, there is little conversational coherence between tweets, or even the replies to tweets. Instead, the primary mechanism by which tweets are connected one to another is the use of a referential hashtag. As a semi-automated resource which brings together disparate content about the same topic, the hashtag creates ambient forms of linearity, where the distribution of the narrative units is generated in part by the design and algorithm of Twitter's architecture, which draws together all tweets with the same hashtag into a chronological sequence of posts about the same topic, where the multiple co-tellers need not interact with one another at all. The narrativity of the hashtag thread is much weaker than any of the other examples of open-ended linearity, and can contain examples where tellers are narrating stories about the same topic, but without a shared stance. As multiple hashtags can be used within the same tweet, this scales up the possibility for a single tweet to be redistributed within many hashtag threads at once, some of which may take different affective stances or emphasise different geographical contexts for their tellers' interests.

Mediated narrative analysis does not conceptualise the different multimodal and technological formats used to tell stories as decontextualised or abstract.

Instead, it seeks to understand the constitutive role that the text and its interactional contexts might have in their various socio-cultural contexts. The analysis of distributed linearity from a mediated perspective has shown how the distribution of the narrative content leads to one version of a story being privileged above another. In this book, the privileged versions of a shared story are based on a principle where the greater the visibility of the story as enabled through its mediated formats, the more value it is assumed to accrue. In each of the social media sites I have considered, visibility is associated with the default view that is presented to the audiences of shared stories. In Wikipedia, this is the front page of an article. In Twitter, visibility is achieved by hashtags, which enhance the searchable status of a tweet. In Facebook, visibility is associated with recency and interaction, where the default view of content published on a reverse-chronological timeline presents the most recent content first, or where a greater number of 'likes' can be interpreted as increasing the value of a post. In YouTube, the searchable nature of videos' titles and Descriptions means that the content published in these sections of the template (which, in this dataset, was typically the 'nucleus' of the news story) occupies a privileged position, and that the comments appended to a video work to boost the visibility of that video, rather than of the comment alone. Together, the patterns in these contexts show clearly that sharing a story is not an equal endeavour in social media contexts. As such, the analysis of shared stories adds to the body of criticism that demonstrates the ongoing hierarchies of interaction which continue to persist in online contexts as much as in their offline counterparts.

Co-tellership

Mediated narrative analysis explores stories as a form of interaction that mediates between the people who produce, consume and reproduce them, and so advances our knowledge about tellership. In Ochs and Capps' (2001) work, they distinguish between narration as the work of one teller and as the work of many tellers. The analysis of shared stories necessarily expands the distinctions available within co-tellership as a narrative dimension, for all shared stories are co-constructed by many participants. The co-tellership analysed in this book allows us now to distinguish between tellers in four respects: their representation, their roles in the processes of narration, their rights to tell or retell a story and the rapport outcomes between them.

Representing Co-tellers: Individual and Collective Identities

In shared stories, co-tellers can represent their identities in different ways. An important distinction that is found in all four of the case studies in this book is the extent to which the co-tellers are individualised or positioned within groups.

In each of the case studies, familiar patterns of representation continue to persist, where the choice to individualise or collectivise the tellers as social actors serves ideological purposes that are shaped by socio-cultural hierarchies. In the Facebook memorial pages, Nelson Mandela as a bonding icon and elite figure was represented visually and verbally as an individual, whilst the commenters used collective identities to unite in a shared national identity. Similarly, in the social television practices, fans represented their shared identities as groups united in support of a particular celebrity figure, whilst the performers from the televised episodes continued to be verbally and visually individuated. In other cases, collective identities used to generate 'us' versus 'them' polarities occur in shared stories as in other offline examples of storytelling. For example, in the Facebook memorial page that marked the death of Margaret Thatcher, the collective identities were used to position the tellers respective to an 'out-group' by invoking negative stereotypes associated with a particular social category (based on age, education and nationality). Far from assuming that shared stories promote an equal representation of tellers, collective identity can be used to promote or devalue the interests of tellers, along lines of either status (elite versus non-elite) or alignment (in-group or out-group), depending on the context of the interaction.

The co-tellership of shared stories is not limited to analysing the representation of the tellers within the reported events. Co-tellership is important as an aspect of the narrative interaction. At the second level of the shared story (the interactional context), a new aspect of co-tellers' identity as collectivised can be analysed based on whether their *interaction* with the story is represented as individual or collective. In the case studies in this book, this is seen most clearly in the analysis of Facebook community pages. The aggregation of the tellers based on their collective interaction with a text as seen through the use of 'liking' and 'sharing' points means that the 'us' versus 'them' polarity between competing groups becomes quantifiable. These numerical outcomes are valued, so that the greater the number of interactions, the greater the 'success' that the collective group is assumed to achieve. However, the aggregation of collective interactions obscures individual identity, ignoring the identity or intention of the tellers in ways that render the superficially objective measures of 'success' open to question. This is particularly the case when the aggregation of collective consumption compares very different kinds of online interaction (clicking a 'like' button as compared with signing a petition, or downloading a protest song).

Co-tellership: Roles in Communication

The interactional context is particularly important for co-tellership within shared stories, where sharing relates not just to the processes of 'telling', but also to the processes of 'distribution'. The mediated forms of shared stories make this distinction clearly, in ways that make it possible to separate the creation of narrative content from its production and reproduction (for example, via a 'share' button). The co-tellership of shared stories thus trains the analytical spotlight on the forms and functions of the co-tellership practices that fall under the heading of 'narrative distribution'. The forms of (re)distribution seen in the shared stories I have examined in this book include specific mediated forms, such as retweets, which may reproduce or modify earlier content, and the editorial practices in Wikipedia, which require editors to cite and synthesise existing source materials as they create the articles within the online encyclopaedia.

The analysis of the co-tellers' communicative roles distinguishes between the extent to which they add to and the extent to which they amend the earlier content. This differentiates the types of co-tellership according to the creative agency of the co-tellers, and the extent to which their contribution is represented as combined with the reproduced content originally created by others. In this book, the redistributive forms of co-tellership were illustrated through the analysis of retweets. Retweeting can involve multiple types of co-tellership roles, such as fans who simply retweet posts from celebrity figures without modification, and those who modify the original tweet, so that they are both animator and author, where the body of the tweet contains words written by both the original author and the retweeter. Beyond the social media sites considered in this book, there are other forms of content redistribution that allow tellers greater scope for adding to and altering the material that they reproduce. For example, Tumblr allows reblogging with notes, and Facebook appends annotations to posts that are 'shared' within the site. As these mediated forms of co-tellership continue to evolve, the distributive forms will require further scrutiny.

Co-tellers' Rights and Responsibilities

Although shared stories draw attention to the collective outcomes of co-tellership, the teller's rights to contribute to the telling, production and reproduction of different shared stories remain related to their individual identity. However, collective and individual aspects of identity are not binary, mutually exclusive characteristics, but, as Hardaker and McGlashan (2016, p. 82) point out, can be mutually constitutive. As with the conversational antecedents of the online shared story, the teller's personal experience of events remains an important criterion by which an entitlement claim is tested. However, the shared stories that are told in the context of large-scale public events suggest that different kinds of personal experience become important as a tellership right. Where personal experience is used as an entitlement claim, the contexts of that personal experience are no longer localised to an event that was co-experienced in the same time and space. Instead, 'shared experience' can become broader in scope. For example, in the disputes between commenters on the Facebook memorial page for Margaret Thatcher, the legitimacy of the tellers' contributions was based on the time at which they had been alive, and on their lived experience within a particular region of the United Kingdom.

In other cases, the tellers' personal experience was at odds with their right to contribute to a shared story. In Wikipedia, the core content policies were developed in line with the generic purpose of the site as an online encyclopaedia. The policy of No Original Research (NOR) precluded certain tellers from contributing to particular articles. Those authors who had created books and reports pertinent to the article's topic (in this case, the 'Murder of Meredith Kercher') could not contribute to the article itself. Of the four social media contexts I explore in this book, Wikipedia appears the most democratic in terms of its ethos towards co-tellership, declaring itself to be the 'free encyclopaedia that anyone can edit'. However, in order to preserve this egalitarian principle, the rights of the co-tellers have to move away from personal experience and to idealise a separation between the offline aspects of the tellers' identities and those that are made relevant in the context of their online interactions within Wikipedia.

Co-tellership and Rapport

The earlier analysis of the shared story's conversational antecedents suggested that for the most part, the co-tellership of shared stories could promote rapport-enhancing relationships between the participants, for example by reiterating a friendship or a family group's shared history. The case studies in this book show that this process is fraught with difficulty and that co-tellership does not necessarily result in harmonious outcomes between tellers at all. The disruptions to rapport between co-tellers can be distinguished in a number of ways, beginning with whether or not the interactional norms for co-tellership within a given context are ratified through stated policies or guidelines.

Some generic contexts for shared stories, like Wikipedia, contain extensive policies that guide the co-tellers' contributions and their conduct with one another. In these cases, the disruptions to the co-tellership can be assessed by other editors relative to these policies as acceptable or unacceptable, and remediating action can be taken to constrain disruption and promote consensus. However, other generic contexts do not contain such extensive guidelines, or do not implement guidelines through the actions of other co-tellers. Although each of the sites considered in this book (Wikipedia, Facebook, Twitter and YouTube) requires its members to agree to terms and conditions, these terms and conditions do not cover the kinds of disruptive behaviour that occurred between the tellers in the case studies in question. In these cases, the interactional norms were implicit, and only became apparent through the responses of other tellers, who gave substance to the otherwise implied 'shared norms' presumed to govern the interaction in question. For example, the forms of face-threatening impoliteness in the Facebook memorial pages were deemed inappropriate under the context-spanning edict to not 'speak ill of the dead'. Other disruptions were treated as more playful, such as the repeated reduplication found in the 'copy pasta' stories in the YouTube comment threads, which at first prompted laughter but later led to criticism from other commenters. Underpinning these responses, the disruptions to the shared story's co-tellership points to the ongoing value of earlier pragmatic research which shows how context-spanning norms, such as Grice's (1975) co-operative principle and its maxims, can be evidenced, albeit in mediated and context-specific ways.

Intertextuality

Mediated narrative analysis takes a multimodal approach to the analysis of a text and its contexts. In this respect, shared stories go beyond traditional accounts of narrativity by considering the ways in which other semiotic resources (such as those used in images, music and video) can be used in narration. The multimodal forms of narration are most important in relation to the shared story's intertextuality. In shared stories, intertextuality takes centre stage as an aspect of the narrative which is both part of the telling (reflecting the meaning of 'sharing as telling') and part of the distributive processes of sharing.

The mediated forms of intertextuality that I analysed in the shared stories include a number of different multimodal and mediated forms. As with distributed linearity, these forms of intertextuality can depart in more or less innovative ways from the intertextuality found in the offline antecedents of the shared story. Once again, using Herring's heuristic of familiar, reconfigured and emergent types of online interaction, I distinguish between the intertextuality in online shared stories as follows. *Familiar* forms of intertextuality include verbal recontextualisations, such as the citations used in Wikipedia articles and the word play found in the YouTube comments that responded to the live-streamed trial of Oscar Pistorius. *Reconfigured* forms of intertextuality include multimodal compositions like image macros, which superimpose captions on to photographs in a format derived from motivational posters, and remixed videos, such as those which circulated following the death of Margaret Thatcher. Remixing musical content has a long history that pre-dates social media, but which is opened up to increasing variation and broadcast via video-sharing sites like YouTube. *Emergent* forms of intertextuality are those which most fully exploit the hyperlink as a mediated means to create networked connections between texts. In this book, examples included the use of hashtags to aggregate Twitter-based responses to a prior text (such as a television programme) and to connect the tweets within a hashtag thread.

The mediated forms of intertextuality are important for their transposable implications, where the multimodal affordances of the intertextuality open up different options for interpreting their narrative content. In this book, the shared stories show the particular importance of images as an intertextual resource. In narrative theory, the potential for images to tell a story has been subject to vexed debate. The traditional argument that scholars have followed claims that visual content tends to be weak in its ability to convey explicit narrative meaning as compared to verbal communication (Forceville and Clark, 2014; Ryan, 2004), which is at odds with the linearity associated with narrative order (Montgomery, 2005). These claims have focused on the narrativity of images in terms of their content, an approach which puts too much stress on the view of narrative as a product. The analysis of shared stories takes a contextual approach, where the intertextual use of images is important as a component within narrative practice. Shifting the perspective from the image as a narrative *product* to the role of the image within narrative *practice* means that the image itself does not need to bear the full communicative burden of conveying events over time. Instead, the image can function as an allusion to another story, and hence evoke narrativity via the knowledge of the events in the story to which it refers. In this respect, the images in the shared story remediate the earlier characteristics of conversational shared stories as a genre documented in small story research, in the same way that selfies remediate the breaking news small story genre (Georgakopoulou, 2016). In conversational shared stories, the intertextuality can include allusive references via the briefest verbal mention recognised by the co-tellers. In mediated shared stories, these compressed allusions can be remediated through images that convey visually a reference point recognised by both teller and audience.

The interpretive value of intertextuality means that it does not just connect one text to another. Rather, intertextuality connects tellers to one another through their more or less shared understanding and evaluation of the intertextual reference. The shared story shows us that intertextuality is interpersonal. This aspect of intertextuality was revealed through its use as a stance object, around which the co-tellers of a story may or may not align. The examples of intertextual stance objects in the shared stories in this book included the reliable sources used by Wikipedia editors, the images posted by the page owner to the Facebook memorial page for Margaret Thatcher and the Twitter images that recirculated in social television practices. It is this interpersonal aspect of the intertextuality which, in part, could bring tellers together or divide them. The more or less shared alignment between co-tellers rested on a number of factors, including the extent to which the intertextual image could generate multiple implicatures (where the greater the number of implicatures, the less likely a shared alignment between co-tellers was to emerge). In addition, the ideological interpretation of the intertextual reference could align tellers more or less successfully. Where intertextual source material conveys a clear ideological position, it may limit how far co-tellers with opposing ideological interests can align with it, and instead give rise to 'in-group' and 'out-group' positioning between the co-tellers. The debates between editors about the use of mainstream news as a reliable source in Wikipedia articles illustrates this kind of interpersonal outcome. Similarly, the use of competing protest songs as a form of stance-taking for the supporters and opponents of Margaret Thatcher in the Facebook comments differentiated between the co-tellers rather than bringing them together.

The highly charged interpretations of intertextuality in the mediated forms of shared stories also rest upon the value of the intertextual resources within their given context of use. The citations in Wikipedia rise to prominence as stance objects not only because of the ideological valence of the cited sources, but also because of their value within Wikipedia as a requirement in support of the policy of Verifiability. Within Twitter, retweets are valued because of their capacity to increase the portability and visibility of a tweet. Like the forms of distributed linearity, it is the mediated contexts in which intertextuality occurs as part of a shared story which increase the story's value, and which render it a site of struggle or open to co-optation by others.

Shared Contexts and 'Common Ground'

Mediated narrative analysis is an explicitly contextual project that understands storytelling as a form of social practice. Shared stories are important within mediated narrative analysis because of their macro-social potential to project common ground between tellers. Precisely because this aspect of the shared story is reliant on factors that lie beyond the text, the 'common ground' of shared stories is more often presumed than explicitly stated. The concepts used in the emerging literature within social semiotics to describe this social connection, such as 'ambient affiliation' and 'bonding', are similarly diffuse and difficult to pin down. Our knowledge about shared stories brings clarity to these important terms, which are intuitively attractive but difficult to operationalise. The analysis of distributed linearity explores how affiliation is achieved through *sharing about* reported events, where the more similar and more explicitly narrated the referential content, the greater the affiliation. The analysis of co-tellership explores how affiliation is achieved through *sharing with* others, where interactions can result in different kinds of rapport outcomes and can position tellers as included within or excluded from particular collective identities. The analysis of intertextuality explores the *shared interpretations* as a resource for aligning co-tellers and content.

The common ground projected between the tellers of a shared story is a contextualised accomplishment. In this book, we have seen that there are multiple levels of mediated contexts which connect tellers and their interaction with, or interpretation of, a shared story (see Chapter 2). The co-text remains important, as seen in the use of the laughter acronym, *lol*, as a contextualisation cue in the YouTube comments that responded to the live-streamed trial of Oscar Pistorius (Chapter 10). The formats for interaction can be used to create common ground, as seen in the use of the 'like' button within Facebook to group tellers into aggregated totals (Chapter 5). The generic context shapes the ways in which common ground is accomplished, as seen through the use of core conduct and content policies to shape the interactions between the editors of Wikipedia articles (Chapters 3 and 4). The situational context is entextualised in hashtags as a means of co-locating the audiences of Twitter-based social television in temporal, geographical and affective proximity to one another (Chapter 7). The interdiscursive context enables tellers to negotiate shared interpretations of macros (Chapter 8) and to join in collective action to commemorate or protest a political figure (Chapter 6). Broader socio-cultural contexts are used as a resource for common ground, as seen in the Facebook comments where tellers referred to the political histories of the different countries in the Margaret Thatcher and Nelson Mandela memorial pages (Chapters 5 and 6), and in how Wikipedia editors chose citations from different news sources to represent events in ways that were in line with their own national context (Chapter 3). The projections of shared contexts from the micro-level co-text to the macro-social cultural factors are rooted in evidence that can be observed in the data, but which requires extra-textual factors for its interpretation. Shared contexts rely on the interpretation of implicatures, on inferred meanings and ideological positioning to bring tellers together. The extra-textual nature of these factors means they are also always at risk of disruption. Shared stories are by no means straightforward, and can result in outcomes that divide tellers rather than creating common ground, as the tellers take different stances, tell different versions of events and disagree with one another about how a story might be told.

Mediated Narrative Analysis as Method

In this book, I have demonstrated the value of mediated narrative analysis as a nexus of interconnected theoretical frameworks. Shared stories told in an online context demand a multifaceted approach, given the large scale of the data (which consist of thousands of posts and interactions) and their multimodal scope (which includes verbal, visual and audio-visual elements). The value of mediated narrative analysis is not limited to the exploration of shared stories; it has wider implications for narrative analysis more generally. If the small stories paradigm marked a shift within discourse analytic research that introduced an analytical shift towards considering the ephemeral, mundane and 'small' examples of storytelling beyond those described by the Labovian paradigm, mediated narrative analysis marks a further turn that allows us to combine the insights of small story research with other kinds of non-canonical storytelling: stories which appear very large by way of comparison, at least in terms of the physical body of data available for scrutiny. The nexus approach of mediated narrative analysis advocates a 'both/and' perspective: narrative analysis need not abandon the 'small story' commitment to micro-analytic detail of the interactional context or to giving voice to marginalised perspectives. Instead, these commitments can be integrated as part of a multidimensional analysis that also considers other aspects of the narrative context and content that may be much larger and so need other tools that extend beyond small-scale qualitative analysis alone.

In this book, the tools and methods of corpus linguistics have enabled me to navigate through large bodies of narrative data. In particular, the use of keywords to identify the overused verbal content in different shared stories has proved an effective and principled way of selecting data for further qualitative analysis. This brought to light aspects of the shared story that would have been very difficult to observe had only small extracts of the data been considered from the outset, such as the use of *lol* as a contextualisation cue that reframed intertextual references in the comment threads within YouTube. Similarly, the importance of evaluative language in the retweets used in social television practices and the references to reliable sources as the centre point for debates between the editors of Wikipedia became apparent through the keyword analysis of each dataset. The use of corpus linguistics within mediated narrative analysis is a mutually beneficial endeavour, where the consideration of the corpora developed to study shared stories increases the potential triangulation that is now emerging in this field (Baker and Egbert, 2016). For example, the repetition generated by the repeated redistribution of shared stories in this dataset led to refinements of the use of keywords as a way into and through the data, for example by establishing additional thresholds beyond keyness alone (Chapter 8). As corpora from social media contexts continue to emerge, researchers will need to make further refinements that take into account how lexical repetition occurs in these kinds of materials.

Corpus linguistics is a useful addition to the mediated narrative analysis I carried out that takes the verbal content of the story as its start point and analyses some types of intertextuality as they are entextualised in verbal forms, such as citations, hyperlinks and hashtags. However, it is by no means the end point. The contextualised emphasis of mediated narrative analysis also requires additional analytic lenses. In this book, social semiotics provided the frameworks for interpreting the multimodal aspects of the shared story, such as the layout and design of the social media sites and the images, music and videos that were integrated within the narration. I have argued throughout that sharing is not just a matter of telling but also a matter of interaction, with socio-pragmatic outcomes for the tellers who produce, reproduce and consume the stories. In this respect, interactional pragmatics provided the vocabulary and methods by which the types of rapport – as evidenced through the interactions between co-tellers – could be identified. The nexus approach of mediated narrative analysis is valuable not only because it brings to light these different aspects of storytelling and the meanings of sharing, but also because it enables us to see the connections between them. Sharing as a form of telling and sharing as a form of distribution are not just textual practices. They are interactional accomplishments with interpersonal outcomes for the tellers who contribute to shared stories. It is the combination of close attention to the verbal patterns (through corpus-assisted discourse analysis), social semiotic analysis of the multimodal content and context, and interactional pragmatics that reveals the connection between the elements and reminds us not to treat an invitation to 'share this story' as a simple action of clicking a button.

Future Directions

One way in which to take forward the analysis of shared stories is to expand the range of examples under consideration. In this book, I have examined shared stories as they were told in four of the international social media contexts that gained significant use in the last decade. I focused on large-scale events that were reported in the mainstream media on an international scale and that attracted substantial response in social media sites. The patterns of sharing that I observed are a result of this focus. There are other sites which rely on sharing resources of different kinds, or which use mediated forms of sharing (such as hashtags) in quite different ways, such as Tumblr (where hashtags need not be searchable). Other sites produce narrative content in ways that rely less heavily on verbal content, and where the scale of sharing is much more modest, such as Snapchat, which is more strongly visual in its use of ten-second video clips and Live Stories that are available for only short periods of time (which, at the time of writing, is 24 hours). Other kinds of stories that are less well covered in the mainstream media might well demonstrate types of sharing that emphasise more clearly the democratic uses of shared stories, and less the interests of the mainstream media.

A cross-cultural comparison of shared stories promises to be particularly important for developing future work on 'sharing'. Given that existing research within interactional pragmatics has suggested that cross-cultural patterns of communication can lead to differing rather than shared interactional norms (Spencer-Oatey, 2008), the ways in which co-tellers from different cultural contexts use and interpret the mediated resources of shared stories needs careful consideration. A second reason to expand shared stories through exploration of cross-cultural comparisons is that in some national contexts, the media is controlled by governmental authorities, and sharing stories outside those mediated channels can be ideologically charged. For example, Wu (2017) showed how Sina Weibo was used by citizens to share stories about the Tianjin explosions in 2015 that provided a critical commentary quite at odds with that promoted by the mainstream media in China. In other contexts, such as Saudi Arabia, the modal affordances of Snapchat open up opportunities, particularly for women, to share stories about their daily experiences in ways that avoid censorship (Albawardi, 2016). The wider cross-cultural expansion of shared stories has a remit to interrogate contexts where digital hierarchies might be sites of struggle that contrast with those in the West, such as in rural areas of Africa (Deumert, 2014). Finally, a more globalised approach to sharing across cultures should also take account of the complexities raised by superdiversity, where the mediated resources for shared stories can interweave linguistic and semiotic resources in forms of translanguaging for diasporic co-tellers (Blackledge et al., 2016).

A second way in which to take forward the analysis of shared stories is to expand the range of methods that are brought together in mediated narrative analysis. The combination of tools and approaches I used in this book is not the only one possible. One trajectory for future research in mediated narrative analysis is made possible through the increasing development of tools that can handle large bodies of data in ways that go beyond corpus approaches to the analysis of the verbal content alone. These possibilities include interdisciplinary expansion; for example, using the network visualisations in tools like gephi (https://gephi.org/). Currently, this kind of network analysis is found in sociological and media studies (see, for example, the work of Highfield et al., 2013 on networked publics). This interactional analysis has quantitative strengths and can model 'big data' effectively, but it is relatively content-less and does not take account of the stories that are embedded within these interactional networks. A second set of tools concerns the annotation of image and video, which can scale up the analysis of multimodal content from mediated sources such as video- and photo-sharing sites. As these tools increase the options for collaborative annotation, possibilities for creating further shared models of interpretation across disciplines and between researchers also develop. As mediated forms of interaction are developing in ways that incorporate embodied interaction (such as the use of touchscreens, voice-recognition software and augmented-reality tools), the possibilities for stories to be shared in ways that can measure human–computer interactions of various kinds may open up as yet untapped options for narrative analysis.

The shared stories in this book have shown the complex ways in which stories produced through mainstream media are retold, reproduced and responded to in different social media contexts. The research from media and communication studies has been a useful means of understanding the critical meanings of sharing, including the socio-economic implications of connectivity (Van Dijck, 2013), social television practices (see Chapters 8 and 9) and affective responses to the news (Papacharissi, 2014). One further way of taking forward the analysis of shared stories, and the project of mediated narrative analysis more broadly, is to extend the connections between media studies and linguistic approaches to narrative. There are areas of journalistic practice yet to be explored where shared meanings take on particular import, such as sports journalism. Other areas of emerging concern, such as the sharing of fake news, would benefit from further analysis of how and why interpretations of authenticity, 'truthiness' and parody in news media occur and the ends to which they are put. More generally, mediated forms of communication that prioritise the dissemination of information in order to harness collective action, such as crisis communication and activism, are areas to which mediated narrative analysis could usefully contribute.

In this book, I have argued that shared stories are a powerful genre which can bring tellers and texts together. However, as the analysis of the stories in social media contexts has shown, sharing is seldom straightforward, neutral or evenly distributed between tellers. Sharing and storytelling are complex, and can serve multiple purposes that simultaneously bring certain ideas and people together whilst excluding others. The differences in sharing are evident in the mediated forms of storytelling observed in this book, and have social, economic and political consequences beyond the social media contexts in which they occur. We clearly need to remain critical about what sharing might mean and how stories selectively represent some versions of events rather than others. However, to paint too bleak a picture would be to ignore the benefits that shared stories might bring. Let me close by returning to the shared story with which I opened this book: the story that reported the death of Jo Cox in June 2016. Amongst the intertextual references that were shared in response to her death were the recordings of her maiden parliamentary speech. In that speech she said, 'While we celebrate our diversity, what surprises me time and time again as I travel around the constituency is that we are far more united and have far more in common with each other than things that divide us'. This is a fitting reminder to us, that whilst shared stories might be a site of struggle, mediated narrative analysis calls us as researchers, as readers and as tellers of stories to find points of commonality across disciplines and national and political contexts. Whilst there will inevitably be points of difference in our perspectives, mediated narrative analysis suggests that we do not need to allow those differences to divide us. Rather, as we discover points of connection through the analysis of the shared story, we might find that we have more in common than it first appears.

References

Agha, A. (2011) 'Meet mediatisation', *Language & Communication* 31 (3), pp. 163–170.

Albawardi, A. (2016) 'Digital literacy practices of Saudi university students'. Conference on Social Media in the Arab World, University of Reading, 3 June.

Androutsopoulos, J. (2010) 'Localising the global on the participatory web', in Coupland, N. (ed.) *Handbook of language and globalization*. Oxford: Blackwell, pp. 203–231.

Androutsopoulos, J. (2011) 'From variation to heteroglossia in the study of computer mediated discourse', in Thurlow, C. and Mroczek, K. (eds) *Digital discourse: Language in the new media*. Oxford: Oxford University Press, pp. 277–298.

Annunziato, S. (2011) 'The Amanda Knox case: The representation of Italy in American media coverage', *Historical Journal of Film, Radio and Television* 31 (1), pp. 61–78.

Anthony, L. (2014) AntConc (3.4.4) [Computer Software]. Tokyo: Waseda University. Available at: www.laurenceanthony.net (accessed 27 March 2017).

Antony, M. G. and Thomas, R. J. (2010) '"This is citizen journalism at its finest": YouTube and the public sphere in the Oscar Grant shooting incident', *New Media & Society* 12 (8), pp. 1280–1296.

Baker, P. (2004) 'Querying keywords: questions of difference, frequency and sense in keywords analysis', *Journal of English Linguistics* 32 (4), pp. 346–359.

Baker, P. and Egbert, J. (eds) (2016) *Triangulating methodological approaches in corpus linguistic research*. London and New York: Routledge.

Baker, P., Gabrielatos, C., Khosravinik, M., Kryzanowski, M., McEnery, A. M. and Wodak, R. (2008) 'A useful methodological synergy? Combining critical discourse analysis and corpus linguistics to examine discourses of refugees and asylum seekers in the UK press', *Discourse and Society* 19 (3), pp. 273–306.

Baker, P., Gabrielatos, C. and McEnery, T. (2013) *Discourse analysis and media attitudes: The representation of Islam in the British press*. Cambridge: Cambridge University Press.

Bakhtin, M. (1984) *Rabelais and his world* [1965]. Translated by Iswolsky, H. Bloomington, IN: Indiana University Press.

Bamberg, M. and Georgakopoulou, A. (2008) 'Small stories as a new perspective in narrative and identity analysis', *Text & Talk* 28 (3), pp. 377–396.

Baron, N. S. and Ling, R. (2011) 'Necessary smileys and useless periods', *Visible Language* 45 (1), pp. 45–67.

Bauman, R. and Briggs, C. (1990) 'Poetics and performances as critical perspectives on language and social life', *Annual Review of Anthropology* 191 (1), pp. 59–88.

Bednarek, M. and Caple, H. (2012) '"Value added": Language, image and news values', *Discourse, Context & Media* 1, pp. 103–113.

Bednarek, M. and Caple, H. (2014) 'Why do news values matter? Towards a new methodological framework for analyzing news discourse in Critical Discourse Analysis and beyond', *Discourse & Society* 25 (2), pp. 135–158.

Bednarek, M. and Caple, H. (2017) *The discourse of news values: How news organizations create 'newsworthiness'.* Oxford: Oxford University Press.

Bell, A. (1991) *The language of news media.* Oxford: Blackwell.

Biber, D., Egbert, J. and Davies. M. (2015) 'Exploring the composition of the searchable Web: A corpus-based taxonomy of web registers', *Corpora* 10 (1), pp. 11–45.

Blackledge, A., Creese, A. and Hu, R. (2016) 'The structure of everyday narrative in a city market: An ethnopoetics approach', *Journal of Sociolinguistics* 20 (5), pp. 654–676.

Blitvich, P. G. C., Bou-Franch, P. and Lorenzo-Dus, N. (2013) 'Identity and impoliteness: The expert in the talent show Idol', *Journal of Politeness Research* 9 (1), pp. 97–121.

Blommaert, J., Arnaut, K., Rampton, B. and Spotti, M. (2016) *Language and superdiversity.* New York and London: Routledge.

Bober, M. (2014) 'Twitter and TV events: An exploration of how to use social media for student-led research', *ASLIB Journal for Information Management* 66 (3), pp. 297–312.

Bogaerts, J. and Carpentier, N. (2012) 'The postmodern challenge to journalism: Strategies for constructing a trustworthy identity', in Peters, C. and Broersma, M. (eds) *Rethinking journalism: trust and participation in a transformed news landscape.* London: Routledge, pp. 60–71.

Bolander, B. (2012) 'Disagreements and agreements in personal/diary blogs: A closer look at responsiveness', *Journal of Pragmatics* 44, pp. 1607–1622.

Bolander, B. and Locher, M. (2014) 'Doing sociolinguistic research on computer-mediated data: A review of four methodological issues', *Discourse, Context & Media* 3, pp. 14–26.

Bondi, M. and Scott, M. (2010) *Keyness in texts.* Amsterdam: John Benjamins.

Bou Franch, P. and Blitvich, P. G. C. (2012) 'Conflict management in massive polylogues: A case study from YouTube', *Journal of Pragmatics* 73, pp. 19–36.

Boyd, D. (2014) *It's complicated: The social lives of networked teens.* New Haven, CT: Yale University Press.

Boyd, D., Golder, S. and Lotan, G. (2010) 'Tweet, tweet, retweet: Conversational aspects of retweeting on Twitter', 43rd Hawaii International Conference on System Sciences (HICSS), 5–8 January. Available at: http://ieeexplore.ieee.org/document/5428313/ (accessed 27 March 2017).

British Association for Applied Linguistics (2016) 'Recommendations on good practice in applied linguistics'. Available at: https://baalweb.files.wordpress.com/2017/08/goodpractice_stud.pdf (accessed 5 September 2017).

Brown, P. and Levinson, S. (1987) *Politeness: Some universals in language use.* Cambridge: Cambridge University Press.

Brubaker, J. and Hayes, G. (2011) '"We will never forget you [online]": An empirical investigation of post-mortem MySpace comments', CSCW 2011, March 19–23, Hangzhou, China.

Bruner, J. (1986) 'Two modes of thought', in *Actual Minds, Possible Worlds*. Cambridge, MA: Harvard University Press, pp. 11–43.

Bruner, J. (1991) 'The narrative construction of reality', *Critical Inquiry* 18, pp. 1–21.

Bruns, A (2008) *Blogs, Wikipedia, Second Life and beyond: From production to produsage*. Berlin: Peter Lang.

Bruns, A. and Highfield, T. (2013) 'Political networks on Twitter', *Information, Communication and Society* 16 (5), pp. 667–91.

Brunton, F. (2012) 'Constitutive interference: Spam and online communities', *Representations* 117 (1), pp. 30–58.

Burgess, J. and Green, J. (2009) *YouTube: Online video and participatory culture*. Cambridge: Polity Press.

Bury, R., Deller, R., Greenwood, A. and Jones, B. (2013) 'From Usenet to Tumblr: The changing role of social media', *Participations* 10 (1), pp. 299–319.

Buschow, C., Schneider, B. and Ueberheide, S. (2014) 'Tweeting television: Exploring communication activities on Twitter while watching TV', *Communications* 39 (2), pp. 129–49.

Caldas-Coulthard, C. (1992) 'Reporting speech in narrative discourse: Stylistic and ideological implications', *Ilha do Desterro* 27, pp. 67–82.

Caple, H. (2010) 'Doubling-up: allusion and bonding in multi-semiotic news stories', in Bednarek, M. and Martin, J. R. (eds) *New discourse on language: Functional perspectives on multimodality, identity, and affiliation*. London and New York: Continuum, pp. 111–133.

Caple, H. (2013) *Photojournalism: A social semiotic approach*. Basingstoke: Palgrave Macmillan.

Caple, H. (2017) 'Results, resolve, reaction: Words, images and the functional structure of online match reports', in Caldwell, D., Walsh, J., Vine, E. W. and Jureidini, J. (eds) *The discourse of sport: Analyses from social linguistics*. London and New York: Routledge, 209–227.

Chess, S. and Newsom, E. (2015) *Folklore, horror stories and The Slender Man: The development of an internet mythology*. New York: Palgrave MacMillan.

Chibba, S. (2014) A media guide to the Oscar Pistorius trial. Available at: www.mediaclubsouthafrica.com/land-and-people/3727-a-multimedia-guide-to-the-oscar-pistorius-trial (accessed 17 March 2017).

Clark, K. (1992) 'The linguistics of blame: Representations of women in The Sun's reporting of crimes of sexual violence', in Toolan, M. (ed.) *Language, text and context*. London: Routledge, pp. 208–224.

Clifford, K. (2014) 'Amanda Knox: A picture of innocence', *Celebrity Studies* 5 (4), pp. 504–507.

Conboy, M. (2006) *Tabloid Britain: Constructing a community through language*. London and New York: Routledge.

Cotter, C. (2010) *News talk: Investigating the language of journalism*. Cambridge: Cambridge University Press.

Coupland, J. (2000) *Small talk*. Harlow: Longman.

Culpeper, J. (2011) *Impoliteness: Using language to cause offence*. Cambridge: Cambridge University Press.

Davies, B. and Harré, R. (1990) 'Positioning: The discursive construction of selves', *Journal for the Theory of Social Behaviour* 20, pp. 43–63.

Dawson, G. (2012) 'Paleontology in parts: Richard Owen, William John Broderip and the serialization of science in early Victorian Britain', *Isis* 103, pp. 637–667.

Dayter, D. (2015) 'Small stories and extended narratives on Twitter', *Discourse, Context & Media* 5, pp. 19–26.

De Beaugrande, R. and Dressler, W. (1981) *Introduction to text linguistics*. London: Longman.

De Fina, A. (2003) *Identity in narrative: A study in immigrant discourse*. Amsterdam and Philadelphia, PA: John Benjamins.

De Fina, A. and Georgakopoulou, A. (2012) *Analyzing narrative: Discourse and sociolinguistic perspectives*. Cambridge: Cambridge University Press.

De Robillard, B. (2014) '"Our Caster" and "The Blade Runner": "Improper" corporealities cripqueering the post/apartheid body politic', *Image & Text* 24, pp. 79–115.

Deery, J. (2014) 'Mapping commercialization in reality television', in Oullette, L. (ed.) *A companion to reality television*. Oxford: Wiley-Blackwell, pp. 11–28.

Deller, R. (2011) 'Twittering on: Audience research and participation using Twitter', *Participations* 8 (1). Available at: www.participations.org/volume%208/issue%201/deller.htm (accessed 27 March 2017).

Deumert, A. (2014) *Sociolinguistics and mobile communication*. Edinburgh: Edinburgh University Press.

Doughty, M., Rowland, D. and Lawson, S. (2012) 'Who is on your Sofa? TV audience communities and second screening social networks', *Proceedings of the 10th European Conference on Interactive TV and Video, Berlin, Germany, 4–6 July, 2012*, pp. 79–86. Available at: http://dl.acm.org/citation.cfm?id=2325635 (accessed 27 March 2017).

Draucker, F. and Collister, L. B. (2015) 'Managing participation through modal affordances on Twitter', *Open Library of Humanities* 1 (1). Available at: https://olh.openlibhums.org/articles/10.16995/olh.21/ (accessed 27 March 2017).

Du Bois, J. W. (2007) 'The stance triangle', in Englebretson, R. (ed.) *Stancetaking in discourse: Subjectivity, evaluation, interaction*. Amsterdam and Philadelphia, PA: John Benjamins, pp. 139–182.

Duranti, A. and Goodwin, C. (1992) *Rethinking context: Language as an interactive phenomenon*. Cambridge: Cambridge University Press.

Duszak, A. (ed.) (2002) *Us and others. Social identities across languages, discourses and cultures*. Amsterdam and Philadelphia, PA: John Benjamins.

Dynel, M. (2009) 'Beyond a joke: Types of conversational humour', *Language and Linguistics Compass* 3 (5), pp. 1284–1299.

Eelen, G. (2001) *A critique of politeness theory*. Manchester: St Jerome Publishing.

Ekström, M. (2000) 'Information, storytelling and attractions: TV journalism in three modes of communication', *Media, Culture and Society* 22, pp. 465–492.

Evans, A. (2016) 'Stance and identity in Twitter hashtags', *Language@Internet* 13 (1). Available at: www.languageatinternet.org/articles/2016/evans (accessed 27 March 2017).

Facebook Helpdesk (2016) What names are allowed on Facebook. Available at: www.facebook.com/help/112146705538576 (accessed 27 March 2017).

Fairclough, N. (1989) *Language and power*. London and New York: Routledge.

Firer-Blaess, S. and Fuchs, C. (2014) 'Wikipedia: An info-communist manifesto', *Television and New Media* 15 (2), pp. 87–103.

Fiske, J. (1987) *Television culture*. London: Methuen.

Fiske, J. (1992) 'Audiencing: A cultural studies approach to watching television', *Poetics* 21 (4), pp. 345–359.

Fitzgerald, R. and Rintel, S. (2013) 'From lifeguard to bitch: How a story character becomes a promiscuous category in a couple's video call', *Australian Journal of Communication* 40 (2), pp. 101–118.

Forceville, C. and Clark, B. (2014) 'Can pictures have explicatures?', *Linguagem Em Discurso* 14 (3), pp. 1–21.

Forman, A., Kern, R. and Gil-Egui, G. (2012) 'Death and mourning as sources of community participation in online social networks: RIP pages in Facebook', *First Monday* 17 (9). Available at: http://firstmonday.org/ojs/index.php/fm/article/view/3935/3288 (accessed 27 March 2017).

Fowler, R. (1991) *Language in the news*. New York: Routledge.

Gee, J. (2004) *Situated language and learning: A critique of traditional schooling*. New York: Routledge.

Genette, G. (1980) *Narrative discourse: An essay in method*. Translated by Lewin, J. E. Ithaca, NY: Cornell University Press.

Georgakopoulou, A. (2005) '"Same old story?" On the interactional dynamics of shared narratives', in Quasthoff, U. and Becker, T. (eds) *Narrative interaction*. Amsterdam and Philadelphia, PA: John Benjamins, pp. 223–241.

Georgakopoulou, A. (2007) *Small stories, interaction and identities*. Amsterdam and Philadelphia, PA: John Benjamins.

Georgakopoulou, A. (2008) '"On MSN with buff boys": Self- and other- identity claims in the context of small stories', *Journal of Sociolinguistics* 15, pp. 597–626.

Georgakopoulou, A. (2013a) 'Small stories research and social media: The role of narrative stance-taking in the circulation of a Greek news story'. *Working Papers in Urban Language and Literacies*, Paper 100.

Georgakopoulou, A. (2013b) 'Small stories and identities analysis as a framework for the study of im/politeness-in-interaction', *Journal of Politeness Research* 9 (1), pp. 55–74.

Georgakopoulou, A. (2014) 'Small stories, transposition and social media: A micro-perspective on the Greek crisis', *Discourse & Society* 25 (4), pp. 519–539.

Georgakopoulou, A. (2015) 'Sharing as rescripting: Place manipulations on YouTube, between narrative and social media affordances', *Discourse, Context & Media* 9, pp. 64–72.

Georgakopoulou, A. (2016) 'From narrating the self to posting self(ies): A small stories approach to selfies', *Open Linguistics* 2(1), pp. 300–317.

Giaxoglou, K. (2015a) 'Entextualising mourning on Facebook: stories of grief as acts of sharing', *New Review of Hypermedia and Multimedia* 21(1–2) pp. 87–105.

Giaxoglou, K. (2015b) '#JesuisCharlie: Narrative stance-taking in shared stories of global mourning'. *The 6th International Language in the Media Conference, Hamburg, 7–9 September 2015*.

Gibson, J. (1977) 'The theory of affordances', in Shaw, R. and Bransford J. (eds) *Perceiving, acting, and knowing*. Hillsdale, NJ: Lawrence Erlbaum, pp. 67–82.

Goddard, M., Halligan, B. and Hegarty, P. (2012) *Reverberations: The philosophy, aesthetics and politics of noise*. London and New York: Continuum.

Goffman, E. (1974) *Frame analysis: An essay on the organization of experience*. Boston, MA: Northeastern University Press.

Goffman, E. (1981) *Forms of talk*. Philadelphia, PA: University of Pennsylvania Press.

Goode, L. (2009) 'Social news, citizen journalism and democracy', *New Media & Society* 11 (8), pp. 1287–1305.

Goode, L., McCollough, A. and O'Hare, G. (2011) 'Unruly publics and the fourth estate on YouTube', *Participations* 8 (2), pp. 594–615.

Goodson, M. and Kwasny, R. (2016) 'Apparently false news attracts widespread coverage in UK newspapers'. Available at: https://evolution.ai/jo-cox-twitter (accessed 14 December 2016).

Gray, J. (2005) 'Antifandom and the moral text: Television without pity and textual dislike', *American Behavioral Scientist* 48 (7), pp. 840–858.

Grice, H. P. (1975) 'Logic and conversation', in Cole, P. and Morgan, J. L. (eds) *Syntax and semantics, Volume 3: Speech Acts*. New York: Academic Press, pp. 41–58.

Grishakova, M. and Ryan, M. L. (eds) (2010) *Intermediality and storytelling*. Berlin: De Gruyter.

Gumperz, J. (1982) *Discourse strategies*. Cambridge: Cambridge University Press.

Günther, S. (2005) 'Narrative reconstructions of past experiences: Adjustments and modifications in the process of recontextualizing a past experience', in Quasthoff, U. and Becker, T. (eds) *Narrative interaction*. Amsterdam and Philadelphia, PA: John Benjamins, pp. 285–302.

Halliday, M. A. K. (1994) *An introduction to functional grammar*, 2nd edition. London and New York: Edward Arnold.

Hardaker, C. (2013) '"Uh.....not to be nitpicky,,,,,but...the past tense of drag is dragged, not drug.": An overview of trolling strategies', *Journal of Language Aggression and Conflict* 1 (1), pp. 57–86.

Hardaker, C. (2015) '"I refuse to respond to this obvious troll": An overview of responses to (perceived) trolling', *Corpora* 10 (2), pp. 201–229.

Hardaker, C. and McGlashan, M. (2016) '"Real men don't hate women": Twitter rape threats and group identity', *Journal of Pragmatics* 91, pp. 80–93.

Harman, S. and Jones, B. (2013) 'Fifty shades of ghey: Snark fandom and the figure of the anti-fan', *Sexualities* 16 (8), pp. 951–968.

Harrington, S. (2013) 'Tweeting about the telly: Live TV, audiences and social media', in Weller, K., Bruns, A., Mahrt, M., Puschmann, C. and Jean Burgess, J. (eds) *Twitter and society*. Berlin: Peter Lang, pp. 276 248.

Harvey, C. (2015) 'What's disability got to do with it? Changing constructions of Oscar Pistorius before and after the Death of Reeva Steenkamp', *Disability & Society* 30 (2), pp. 299–304.

Haugh, M. (2015) *Im/politeness implicatures*. Berlin and New York: Mouton de Gruyter.

Herman, D. (1997) 'Scripts, sequences and stories: Elements of a postclassical narratology', *Publications of the Modern Language Association* 112 (5), pp. 1046–1059.

Herman, D. (2002) *Story logic: Problems and possibilities of narrative*. Lincoln, NE and London: University of Nebraska Press.

Herman, D. (2004) 'Toward a transmedial narratology', in Ryan, M. L. (ed.) *Narrative across media: The languages of storytelling*. Lincoln, NE and London: University of Nebraska Press, pp. 47–75.

Herman, L. and Vervaeck, B. (2005) *Handbook of narrative analysis*. Lincoln, NE and London: University of Nebraska Press.

Herring, S. (1994) 'Politeness in computer culture: Why women thank and men flame', in Bucholtz, M. (ed.) *Cultural performances: Proceedings of the Third Berkeley Women and Language Conference*. Berkeley, CA: Women and Language Group, pp. 278–294.

Herring, S. (2007) 'A faceted classification scheme for computer-mediated discourse', *Language@Internet* 4. Available at: www.languageatInternet.org/articles/2007/761 (accessed 27 March 2017).

Herring, S. (2013) 'Discourse in web 2.0: Familiar, reconfigured, and emergent'. In Tannen, D. (ed.) *Georgetown University Round Table on Language and Linguistics 2011: discourse 2.0: language and new media*. Washington, DC: Georgetown University Press, pp. 1–25.

Herring, S. and Dainas, A. R. (2017) '"Nice picture comment!" Graphicons in Facebook comment threads'. Proceedings of the Fiftieth Hawai'I International Conference on System Sciences (HICSS-50). *Los Alamitos, CA: IEEE*. Available at: http://ella.slis.indiana.edu/~herring/hicss.graphicons.pdf (accessed 10 March 2017).

Hicks, M. (2010) 'Connecting to everything you care about'. Notes by Facebook, 19 April 2010. Available at: www.facebook.com/notes/facebook/connecting-to-everything-you-care-about/382978412130 (accessed 30 January 2017).

Highfield, T., Harrington, S. and Bruns, A. (2013) 'Twitter as a technology of audiencing and fandom', *Information, Communication and Society* 16 (3), pp. 315–339.

Hoey, M. (2001) *Textual interaction: An introduction to written discourse*. London: Routledge.

Hoffmann, C. R. (ed.) (2010) *Telling a story in the age of new media*. Amsterdam and Philadelphia, PA: John Benjamins.

Hogan, P. (2014) 'Intertextuality and allusion', in Stockwell, P. and Whiteley, S. (eds) *The Cambridge handbook of stylistics*. Cambridge: Cambridge University Press, pp. 117–131.

Huddleston, J. T. (2016) 'Nielsen is adding Facebook to its social TV ratings'. Available at: http://fortune.com/2016/01/20/nielsen-facebook-social-tv (accessed 8 September 2015).

Hutchby, I. (1996) *Confrontation talk: Arguments, asymmetries and power on talk radio*. Mahwah, NJ: Lawrence Erlbaum.

Hutcheon, L. (2006) *A theory of adaptation*. London and New York: Routledge.

Jefferson, G. (2004) 'A note on laughter in "male-female" interaction', *Discourse Studies* 6 (1), pp. 117–133.

Jenkins, H. (2006) *Convergence culture: Where old and new media collide*. New York: New York University Press.

John, N. (2013) 'Sharing and Web 2.0: The emergence of a keyword', *New Media & Society* 15 (2), pp. 167–182.

Jones, R. (2005) 'Sites of engagement as sites of attention: Time, space and culture in electronic discourse', in Norris, S. and Jones, R. (eds) *Discourses in action: Introducing mediated discourse analysis*. New York: Routledge, pp. 141–154.

Jones, R. (2012) *Discourse and creativity*. London and New York: Taylor and Francis.

Jones, R. and Hafner, C. (2012) *Understanding digital literacies: A practical introduction*. London and New York: Routledge.

Keating, P. (2013) 'Narrative dynamics in the competitive reality show', *Storyworlds: A Journal of Narrative Studies* 5, pp. 55–75.

Kellner, D. (2009) 'Media spectacle and the 2008 Presidential election', *Cultural Studies – Critical Methodologies* 9 (6), pp. 707–716.

Kern, R., Forman, A. E. and Gil-Egui, G. (2013) 'R.I.P.: Remain in perpetuity: Facebook memorial pages', *Telematics and Informatics* 30 (1), pp. 2–10.

Klink, M. (2010) *Laugh out loud in real life: Women's humor and fan identity*. Unpublished Master of Science in Comparative Media Studies Dissertation, Massachusetts Institute of Technology.

Koller, V. (2012) 'How to analyse collective identity in discourse: Textual and contextual parameters', *Critical approaches to discourse analysis across disciplines* 5 (2), pp. 19–38.

Kress, G. and van Leeuwen, T. (1996) *Reading images*. London and New York: Routledge.

Labov, W. (1972) *Language in the inner city: Studies in the Black English Vernacular*. Philadelphia, PA: University of Pennsylvania Press.

Labov, W. (2013) *The language of life and death: The transformation of experience in oral narrative*. Cambridge: Cambridge University Press.

Labov, W. and Waletzky, J. (1967) 'Narrative analysis: oral versions of personal experience', in Helm, J. (ed.) *Essays on the verbal and visual arts: Proceedings of the 1966 annual spring meeting of the American Ethnological Society*. Seattle, WA: University of Washington Press, pp. 12–44.

Lambrou, M. (2014) 'Narrative, text and time: Telling the same story twice in the oral narrative reporting of 7/7', *Language and Literature* 23 (1), pp. 32–48.

Langlotz, A. and Locher, M. (2012) 'Ways of communicating stance in online disagreements', *Journal of Pragmatics* 44 (12), pp. 1591–1606.

Larsson, A. O. and Moe, H. (2011) 'Studying political microblogging: Twitter users in the 2010 Swedish election campaign', *New Media & Society* 14 (5), pp. 729–47.

Lee, C. K. (2007) 'Affordances and text-making practices in online instant messaging', *Written Communication* 24 (3), pp. 223–249.

Leitch, T. (2008) 'Adaptation studies at a crossroads', *Adaptation* 1 (1), pp. 63–77.

Liddle, R. (2011) 'What does it take to save a she-devil? Good PR', *Spectator* 8. Available at: www.spectator.co.uk/2011/10/what-does-it-take-to-save-a-shedevil-good-pr/ (accessed 13 March 2017).

Linde, C. (1993) *Life stories: The creation of coherence*. Oxford: Oxford University Press.

Lindgren, S. (2012) '"It took me about half an hour, but I did it!": Media circuits and affinity spaces around how-to videos on YouTube', *European Journal of Communication* 27(2), pp. 152–170.

Locher, M. and Watts, R. (2005) 'Politeness theory and relational work', *Journal of Politeness Research* 1 (1): 9–33.

Locher, M. and Watts, R. (2008) 'Relational work and impoliteness: Negotiating norms of linguistic behaviour', in Bousfield, D. and Locher, M. (eds) *Impoliteness in language: Studies on its interplay with power in theory and practice*. Berlin and New York: Mouton de Gruyter, pp. 77–99.

Loveland, J. and Reagle, J. (2013) 'Wikipedia and encyclopedic production', *New Media & Society* 15 (8), pp. 1294–1311.

Lyotard, J. F. (1984) *The postmodern condition: A report on knowledge* [1979]. Translated by Bennington, G. and Massumi, B. Manchester: Manchester University Press.

Maagaard, C. (2014) 'Employee testimonials: Animating corporate messages through employees' stories', *Discourse, Context & Media* 6, pp. 22–32.

Machin, D. (2004) 'Building the world's visual language: the increasing global importance of image banks in corporate media', *Visual Communication* 3 (3), pp. 316–336.

Machin, D. and Mayr, A. (2012) *How to do Critical Discourse Analysis: A multimodal introduction*. London: Sage.

Machin, D. and Mayr, A. (2013) 'Personalising crime and crime-fighting in factual television: an analysis of social actors and transitivity in language and images', *Critical Discourse Studies* 10 (4), pp. 356–372.

Mahlberg, M. (2016) 'Corpus stylistics', in Sotirova, V. (ed.) *The Bloomsbury companion to stylistics*. London and New York: Bloomsbury, pp. 139–156.

Mahrt, M., Weller, K. and Peters, I. (2013) 'Twitter in scholarly communication', in Weller, K., Bruns, A., Burgess, J., Mahrt, M., Puschmann, C. (eds) *Twitter and society*. Peter Lang, New York, pp. 399–410.

Markham, A. (2013) 'Remix cultures, remix methods: Reframing qualitative inquiry for social media contexts', in Denzin, N. K. and Giardina, M. D. (eds) *Global dimensions of qualitative inquiry*. Walnut Creek, CA: Left Coast Press, pp. 63–81.

Markham, A. and Buchanen, E. (2012) 'Ethical decision-making and Internet research: Recommendations from the AoIR Ethics Working Committee (Version 2.0)'. Available at: https://aoir.org/reports/ethics2.pdf (accessed 10 March 2017).

Martinec, R. and Salway, A. (2005) 'A system for image-text relations in new (and old) media', *Visual Communication* 4 (3), pp. 339–374.

Marwick, A. (2013) *Status update. Celebrity, publicity and branding in the social media age*. New Haven, CT and London: Yale University Press.

Marwick, A. and Boyd, D. (2011) 'To see and be seen: Celebrity practice on Twitter', *Convergence* 17 (2), pp. 139–158.

Marwick, A. and Ellison, N. (2012) '"There isn't Wifi in heaven!" Negotiating visibility on Facebook memorial pages', *Journal of Broadcasting and Electronic Media* 56 (3), pp. 378–400.

McCloud, S. (1993) *Understanding comics*. New York: Harper Perennial.

McCosker, A. (2014) 'Trolling as provocation: YouTube's agonistic publics', *Convergence* 20 (2), pp. 201–217.

McCosker, A. (2015) 'Social media activism at the Margins: Managing visibility, voice and vitality affects', *Social Media and Society* 1 (2).

McEnery, T. and Baker, P. (2015) *Corpora and discourse studies: Integrating discourse and corpora*. London: Palgrave MacMillan.

McKerrell, S. (2015) 'Social distance and the multimodal construction of the Other in sectarian song', *Social Semiotics* 25 (5), pp. 614–632.

McSweeney, M. (2016) *Literacies of bilingual youth: A profile of bilingual, academic, social, and txt literacies*. Unpublished PhD thesis, The Graduate Center at CUNY, New York.

Mildorf, J. and Thomas, B (2017) *Dialogue across media*. Amsterdam: John Benjamins.

Mitchell, N. (2015) 'Goading as social action: non-polite evaluations in targeted banter', in Terkourafi, M. (ed.) *Interdisciplinary perspectives on impoliteness*. Amsterdam and Philadelphia, PA: John Benjamins, pp. 121–148.

Montgomery, M. (2005) 'Television news and narrative: How relevant are narrative models for explaining the coherence of television news?' in Thornborrow, J. and Coates, J. (eds) *Sociolinguistics of narrative*. Amsterdam and Philadelphia, PA: John Benjamins, pp. 239–260.

Montgomery, M. (2007) *The discourse of broadcast news: A linguistic approach*. London: Routledge.

Moreau, E. (2016) 'Snapchat stories explained. Share snaps in a narrative style'. Available at: www.lifewire.com/what-is-a-snapchat-story-3486000 (accessed 28 March 2017).

Myers, G. (2010) *The discourse of blogs and wikis*. London and New York: Continuum.

Newton, C. (2016) 'Instagram's new stories are a near-perfect copy of Snapchat stories'. Available at: www.theverge.com/2016/8/2/12348354/instagram-stories-announced-snapchat-kevin-systrom-interview (accessed 28 March 2017).

Norrick, N. (2000) *Conversational narrative: Storytelling in everyday talk*. Amsterdam and Philadelphia, PA: John Benjamins.

Norrick, N. (2005) 'Contextualizing and recontextualizing interlaced stories in conversation', in Thornborrow, J. and Coates, J. (eds) *The sociolinguistics of narrative*. Amsterdam and Philadelphia, PA: John Benjamins, pp. 107–128.

Norrick, N. (2007) 'Conversational storytelling', in Herman, D. (ed.) *The Cambridge companion to narrative*. Cambridge: Cambridge University Press, pp. 127–141.

Norrick, N. (2008) 'Using large corpora of conversation to investigate narrative: the case of interjections in conversational storytelling performance', *International Journal of Corpus Linguistics* 13, pp. 438–464.

Norris, S. and Jones, R. (2005) *Discourse in action: Introducing mediated discourse analysis*. London and New York: Routledge.

Ochs, E. and Capps, L. (2001) *Living narrative: Creating lives in everyday storytelling*. Cambridge, MA and London: Harvard University Press.

Onega, S. and Landa, J. A. G. (1996) *Narratology: An introduction*. London and New York: Longman.

Page, R. (2003) '"Cherie: lawyer, wife, mum": Contradictory patterns of representation in media reports of Cherie Booth/Blair', *Discourse and Society* 14 (5): 559–579.

Page, R. (ed.) (2010) *New perspectives on narrative and multimodality*. London: Routledge.

Page, R. (2012a) *Stories and social media: Identities and interaction*. London and New York: Routledge.

Page, R. (2012b) 'The linguistics of self-branding and micro-celebrity: The role of hashtags', *Discourse and Communication* 6 (2), pp. 181–201.

Page, R. (2013) 'Seriality and storytelling in social media', *Storyworlds* 5, pp. 31–53.

Page, R. and Thomas, B. (eds) (2011) *New narratives: Stories and storytelling in the digital age*. Lincoln, NE and London: University of Nebraska Press.

Page, R., Harper, R. and Frobenius, M. (2013) 'From small stories to networked narrative', *Narrative Inquiry* 23 (1), pp. 192–213.

Papacharissi, Z. (2014) *Affective publics: Sentiment, technology and politics*. Oxford: Oxford University Press.

Papacharissi, Z. and de Fatima Oliveira, M. (2012) 'Affective news and networked publics: The rhythms of news storytelling on #Egypt', *Journal of Communication* 62 (2), pp. 266–282.

Partington, A. (2006) *The linguistics of laughter: A corpus assisted study of laughter talk*. London and New York: Routledge.

Peters, C. (2011) 'Emotion aside or emotional side? Crafting an "experience of involvement" in the news', *Journalism* 12 (3), pp. 297–316.

Phillips, W. (2011) 'LOLing at tragedy: Facebook trolls, memorial pages and resistance to grief online', *First Monday* 16 (12). Available at: http://firstmonday.org/ojs/index.php/fm/article/view/3168/3115 (accessed 28 March 2017).

Polanyi, L. (1985) *Telling the American story: A structural and cultural analysis of conversational storytelling*. Norwood, NJ: Ablex.

Porter Abbott, H. (2002) *The Cambridge introduction to narrative*. Cambridge: Cambridge University Press.

Potts, A., Simm, W., Whittle, J. and Unger, J. (2014) 'Exploring "success" in digitally augmented activism: A triangulated approach to analysing UK activist Twitter use', *Discourse, Context & Media* 2 (1), pp. 65–76.

Puschmann, C. (2015) 'The form and function of quoting in digital media: The case of retweets', *Discourse, Context & Media* 7, pp. 28–36.

Reilly, P. (2015) 'Every little helps? YouTube, sousveillance and the "anti-Tesco" riot in Bristol', *New Media & Society* 17 (5), pp. 755–771.

Reisigl, M. and Wodak, R. (2001) *Discourse and discrimination: Rhetorics of racism and antisemitism*. London: Routledge.

Richardson, B. and Langford, R. (2015) 'A shifting collective identity: A critical discourse analysis of child care advocacy association of Canada's public messaging in 2005 and 2008', *Critical Discourse Studies* 1, pp. 78–96.

Richardson, J. (2006) *Analysing newspapers: An approach from Critical Discourse Analysis*. Basingstoke: Palgrave MacMillan.

Rieder, B. (2013) 'Studying Facebook via data extraction: the Netvizz application'. *WebSci '13 Proceedings of the 5th Annual ACM Web Science Conference, May 2–4, Paris*. Available at: http://dl.acm.org/citation.cfm?id=2464475 (accessed 11 September 2017).

Ryan, M. L. (2004) *Narrative across media: The languages of storytelling*. Lincoln, NE and London: University of Nebraska Press.

Ryan, M. L. (2007) 'Toward a definition of narrative', in Herman, D. (ed.) *The Cambridge companion to narrative*. Cambridge: Cambridge University Press, pp. 22–38.

Salway, A. and Herman, D. (2011) 'Digitized corpora as theory-building resource: New methods for narrative inquiry', in Page, R. and Thomas, B. (ed.) *New narratives: Stories and storytelling in the digital age*. Lincoln, NE and London: University of Nebraska Press, pp. 120–137.

Sanderson, J. and Cheong, P. H. (2010) 'Tweeting prayers and communicating grief over Michael Jackson online', *Bulletin of Science, Technology & Society* 30 (5), pp. 328–340.

Scollon, R. (2002) *Mediated discourse: The nexus of practice*. London: Routledge.

Scollon, R. (2008) *Discourse itineraries: Nine processes of resemioticization*. London: Routledge.

Scott, K. (2015) 'The pragmatics of hashtags: inference and conversational style on Twitter', *Journal of Pragmatics* 81, pp. 8–20.

Shah, C. (2009) 'ContextMiner: Supporting the mining of contextual information for ephemeral digital video preservation', *International Journal of Digital Curation* 4 (2), pp. 171–183.

Shuman, A. (2005) *Other people's stories: Entitlement claims and the critique of empathy*. Urbana, IL: University of Illinois Press.

Sinclair, J. (2004) *Trust the text. Language, corpus and discourse*. London: Routledge.

Smith, C. (2017) '160 Amazing YouTube Statistics (February 2017)'. Available at: http://expandedramblings.com/index.php/youtube-statistics/ (accessed 28 March 2017).

Soukup, P. (2014) 'Looking at, with, and through YouTube', *Communication Research Trends* 33 (3), pp. 1–32.

Spencer-Oatey, H. (2002) 'Managing rapport in talk: Using rapport-sensitive incidents to explore the motivational concerns underlying the management of relations', *Journal of Pragmatics* 34 (5), pp. 529–545.

Spencer-Oatey, H. (2005) '(Im)Politeness, face and perceptions of rapport: Unpacking their bases and interrelationships', *Journal of Politeness Research* 1 (1), pp. 95–119.

Spencer-Oatey, H. (2007) 'Theories of identity and the analysis of face', *Journal of Pragmatics* 39 (4), pp. 639–656.

Spencer-Oatey, H. (2008) *Culturally speaking: Culture, communication and politeness theory*, 2nd edition. London and New York: Continuum.

Stefanone, M., Lackaff, D. and Rosen, D. (2010) 'The relationship between traditional mass media and "social media": Reality television as a model for social network site behaviour', *Journal of Broadcasting & Electronic Media* 54 (3) pp. 508–525.

Stein, L. (2013) 'Policy and participation on social media: The cases of YouTube, Facebook and Wikipedia', *Communication, Culture and Critique* 6, pp. 353–371.

Stenglin, M. (2004) *Packaging curiosities: Towards a grammar of three-dimensional space*. Unpublished PhD thesis, University of Sydney.

Stever, G. S. and Lawson, K. (2013) 'Twitter as a way for celebrities to communicate with fans: Implications for the study of parasocial interaction', *North American Journal of Psychology* 15 (2), pp. 339–354.

Stivers, T., Mondada, L. and Steensig, J. (2011) 'Knowledge, morality and affiliation in social interaction', in Stivers, T., Mondada, L. and Steensig, J. (eds) *The morality of knowledge in conversation*. Cambridge: Cambridge University Press, pp. 3–24.

Stokoe, E. and Edwards, D. (2007) '"Black this, black that": Racial insults and reported speech in neighbour complaints and police interrogations', *Discourse & Society* 18 (3), pp. 337–372.

Suh, B., Hong, L., Pirolli, P. and Chi, E. H. (2010) 'Want to be retweeted? Large scale analytics on factors impacting retweet in Twitter network'. *Social Computing IEEE Second International Conference, 2010*, pp. 177–184. Available at: http://www.parc.com/content/attachments/want-to-be-retweeted.pdf (accessed 27 March 2017).

Tagliamonte, S. A. and Denis, D. (2008) 'Linguistic ruin? LOL! Instant Messaging and teen language', *American Speech* 83 (1), pp. 3–34.

Tann, K. (2010) *Semogenesis of a nation: An iconography of Japanese identity*. Unpublished PhD thesis, University of Sydney.

Tashakkori, A. and Creswell, J. (2007) 'The new era of mixed methods', *Journal of Mixed Methods Research* 1 (1), pp. 3–8.

Thompson, R. (2012) 'Screwed up, but working on it: Disordering the self through e-stories', *Narrative Inquiry* 22 (1), pp. 86–104.

Tognini-Bonelli, E. (2001) *Corpus linguistics at work*. Amsterdam and Philadelphia, PA: John Benjamins.

Toolan, M. (2009) *Narrative progression in the short story*. Amsterdam and Philadelphia, PA: John Benjamins.

Toolan, M. (2016) *Making sense of narrative text: Situation, repetition and picturing in the reading of short stories*. London and New York: Routledge.

Turner, G. (2010) *Ordinary people and the media: The demotic turn*. London: Sage.

Uygur-Distexhe, D. (2014) 'Lol, mdr and ptdr: An inclusive and gradual approach to discourse markers', in Cougnon, L., Fairon, C. and Crystal, D. (eds) *SMS communication: A linguistic approach*. Amsterdam and Philadelphia, PA: John Benjamins, pp. 239–263.

Van Dijck, J. (2013) *The culture of connectivity: A critical history of social media*. Oxford: Oxford University Press.

Van Dijck, J. and Nieborg, D. (2009) 'Wikinomics and its discontents: A critical analysis of Web 2.0 business manifestos', *New Media & Society* 11 (5), pp. 855–874.

Van Dijk, T. (1991) *Racism and the press*. London: Routledge.

Van Dijk, T. (2009) *Society and discourse: How social contexts influence text and talk*. Cambridge: Cambridge University Press.

Van Leeuwen, T. (1991) 'Conjunctive structure in documentary film and television', *Continuum* 5 (1), pp. 76–114.

Van Leeuwen, T. (1996) 'The representation of social actors', in Caldas Coulthard, C. R. and Coulthard, M. (eds) *Texts and practices: Readings in Critical Discourse Analysis*. London: Routledge, pp. 32–70.

Van Leeuwen, T. (2008) *Discourse and practice: New tools for Critical Discourse Analysis*. Oxford: Oxford University Press.

Van Leeuwen, T. (2012) 'The critical analysis of musical discourse', *Critical Discourse Studies* 9 (4), pp. 319–328.

Van Zoonen L., Vis F. and Mihelj S. (2010) 'Performing citizenship on YouTube: Activism, satire and online debate around the anti-Islam video Fitna', *Critical Discourse Studies* 7, pp. 249–262.

Vasquez, C. (2014) *The discourse of online consumer reviews*. London and New York: Bloomsbury.

Viégas, F. (2007) 'The visual side of Wikipedia'. *HICSS '07 Proceedings of the 40th Annual Hawaii Conference on System Sciences. 3–6 January 2007*. Available at: http://dl.acm.org/citation.cfm?id=1255492 (accessed 27 March 2017).

Walker Rettberg, J. (2014) *Seeing ourselves through technology: How we use selfies, blogs and wearable devices to see ourselves*. Basingstoke: Palgrave MacMillan.

Wall, M. and El Zahed, S. (2011) 'The Arab Spring: "I'll be waiting for you guys": A YouTube call to action in the Egyptian revolution', *International Journal of Communication* 5, pp. 1333–1343.

Wall, T. (2013) 'The X Factor', in Bennett, P. and McDougall, J. (eds) *Mythologies today: Barthes reimagined*. New York: Routledge, pp. 19–23.

Way, L. C. S. (2016) 'Protest music, populism, politics and authenticity', *Journal of Language and Politics* 15 (4), pp. 422–445.

West, L. (2013) 'Facebook sharing: A sociolinguistic analysis of computer-mediated storytelling', *Discourse, Context & Media* 2, pp. 1–13.

West, L. (2015) *Responding (or not) on Facebook: A sociolinguistic study of Liking, Commenting, and other reactions to posts*. Unpublished PhD thesis, Georgetown University.

West, L. and Trester, A. (2013) 'Facework on Facebook: Conversations on social media', in Tannen, D. and Trester, A. (eds) *Discourse 2.0: Language and new media*. Washington, DC: Georgetown University Press, pp. 133–153.

White, P. (1997) 'Death, disruption and the moral order: The narrative impulse in mass-media hard news reporting', in Christie, F. and Martin, J. R. (eds) *Genres and institutions: Social processes in the workplace and school*. London: Cassell, pp. 101–133.

Wikipedia Contributors (2014a) 'Wikipedia'. *Wikipedia, The Free Encyclopedia*. Available at: https://en.wikipedia.org/w/index.php?title=Wikipedia&oldid=637722569 (accessed 13 March 2017).

Wikipedia Contributors (2014b) 'Identifying reliable sources'. *Wikipedia, The Free Encyclopedia*. Available at: https://en.wikipedia.org/w/index.php?title=Wikipedia:Identifying_reliable_sources&oldid=635915178 (accessed 13 March 2017).

Wikipedia Contributors (2014c) 'Quotations'. *Wikipedia, The Free Encyclopedia*. Available at: https://en.wikipedia.org/w/index.php?title=Wikipedia:Quotations&oldid=638008390 (accessed 13 March 2017).

Wikipedia Contributors (2015a) 'Neutral point of view'. *Wikipedia, The Free Encyclopedia*. Available at: https://en.wikipedia.org/w/index.php?title=Wikipedia:Neutral_point_of_view&oldid=714753741 (accessed 13 March 2017).

Wikipedia Contributors (2015b) 'Wikipedia conduct policies'. *Wikipedia, The Free Encyclopedia*. Available at: https://en.wikipedia.org/w/index.php?title=Category:Wikipedia_conduct_policies&oldid=676241977 (accessed 13 March 2017).

Wikipedia Contributors (2017a) 'Talk: Murder of Meredith Kercher'. *Wikipedia, The Free Encyclopedia*. Available at: https://en.wikipedia.org/w/index.php?title=Talk:Murder_of_Meredith_Kercher&oldid=751912364 (accessed 13 March 2017).

Wikipedia Contributors (2017b) 'Verifiability'. *Wikipedia, The Free Encyclopedia*. Available at: https://en.wikipedia.org/w/index.php?title=Wikipedia:Verifiability&oldid=798245920 (accessed 15 September 2017).

Wodak, R. (2007) 'Pragmatics and Critical Discourse Analysis: A cross-disciplinary inquiry', *Pragmatics & Cognition* 15 (1), pp. 203–225.

Wood, M. and Baughman, L. (2012) 'Glee fandom and Twitter: Something new, or more of the same old thing?' *Communication Studies* 63 (3), pp. 328–344.

Wu, X. (2017) 'Discursive strategies of resistance in Weibo – A case study of Tianjin explosions in Sina Weibo in China'. *The Ross Priory Broadcast Talk Seminar Group. University of Strathclyde*, 3–6 July 2017.

Yasseri, T., Sumi, R., Rung, A., Kornai, A. and Kertesz, J. (2012) 'Dynamics of conflicts in Wikipedia', *PLoS ONE* 7 (6). Available at: http://journals.plos.org/plosone/article?id=10.1371/journal.pone.0038869 (accessed 27 March 2017).

Zappavigna, M. (2011) 'Ambient affiliation: A linguistic perspective on Twitter', *New Media & Society* 13 (5), pp. 788–806.

Zappavigna M. (2014a) 'Coffeetweets: Bonding around the bean on Twitter', in Seargeant, P. and Tagg, C. (eds) *The language of social media: Communication and community on the Internet*. London: Palgrave, pp. 139–160.

Zappavigna M. (2014b) 'Enacting identity in microblogging through ambient affiliation', *Discourse and Communication* 8 (2), pp. 209–228.

Zappavigna M. (2015) 'Searchable talk: The linguistic functions of hashtags', *Social Semiotics* 25, pp. 274–291.

Zappavigna, M. (2016) 'Social media photography: Construing subjectivity in Instagram images', *Visual Communication* 15 (3), pp. 271–292.

Zappavigna, M. and Zhao, S. (2017) 'The selfie as a genre of visual self-representation', *Discourse, Context & Media*. In production.

Index